D A L I
AND POSTMODERNISM

SUNY Series in Postmodern Culture
Joseph Natoli, editor

D A L I
AND POSTMODERNISM

This Is Not an Essence

MARC J. LAFOUNTAIN

STATE UNIVERSITY OF NEW YORK PRESS

Cover: Salvador Dali, *Endless Enigma*
© 1997 Demart Pro Arte, Geneva / Artists Rights Society (ARS), New York

Pages viii and ix: Six preparatory drawings by Dali for *Endless Enigma*
© photo Descharnes & Descharnes

Published by
State University of New York Press, Albany

© 1997 State University of New York

For information, address State University of New York Press
State University Plaza, Albany, NY 12246

Production by Dana Foote
Marketing by Nancy Farrell

Library of Congress Cataloging-in-Publication Data

LaFountain, Marc J.
    Dali and postmodernism : this is not an essence / Marc J.
LaFountain.
        p.   cm. — (SUNY series in postmodern culture)
    Includes bibliographical references and index.
    ISBN 0–7914–3325–0 (hc : alk. paper). — ISBN 0–7914–3326–9 (pbk.
: alk. paper)
    1. Dali, Salvador, 1904–   —Criticism and interpretation.
2. Surrealism. 3. Postmodernism. I. Title. II. Series.
N7113.D3L24 1997
709'.2—dc21
                                                                  96–48415
                                                                  CIP

10 9 8 7 6 5 4 3 2 1

For my mother, (t)here now
For my father, here now
For Sheila, mad love

CONTENTS

Beach at Cape Creus with seated woman seen from the back mending a sail, and boat.

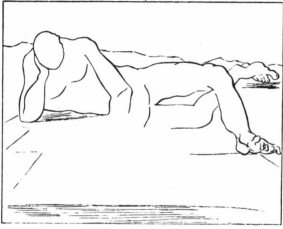

Philosopher lying stretched out.

Visage of the great cyclopean cretin.

Greyhound.

Mandolin, fruit dish with pears, two figs on a table.

Mythological beast.

PREFACE:
NOTES FOR "NEW DALI STUDIES"

... we would like to establish a strict demarcation line between *what is* surrealist in *essence* and what attempts to pass as such, for reasons of publicity or whatever ... [and thereby define] *the true* human condition.

—André Breton[1]

It has to be said once and for all art critics, artists, &c., that they need expect nothing from the *new* surrealist images but disappointment, distaste, and repulsion ... the *new* images of surrealism must come more and more to take the forms and colours of demoralization and confusion ... the desperate activity of these *new* images ... will come to follow the free bent of desire at the same time as they are vigorously repressed.

—Salvador Dali[2]

Already from an initial encounter what appeared to be the visible face was only the dissimulative condition of efface-ment and disappearance, of *con-fusion* and phantom mean-ing.

—Unknown

The artifice of *Dali and Postmodernism* is to take Dali seriously and to deploy the delirium of interpretation advocated by his "para-noiac-critical method," certainly one of the most notorious and pow-erful of all Surrealist devices. In the essay "The Stinking Ass," and elsewhere, Dali advanced his view that such delirium is limitless, depending only upon the "paranoiac capacity" of each individual.

To take Dali seriously is to engage in a performative text that is at once experimental but not necessarily antitheoretical. Dali's "theory" of *surreality* and liberatory praxis is an extravagant performance, and only occasionally does it reveal the qualities of "academic" theory. Read against Breton's "theory" of Surrealism, which also has intense performance features and many more academic qualities, Dali's images and writings betray in Breton's discourse a profound interest in establishing dogma, edict, and canon. *Dali and Postmodernism* disjunctively positions performance and academic texts, plays upon elements of the styles of both Breton and Dali, and grafts onto them aspects of those maneuvers now known as "postmodern," "poststructural," and "posthistorical."

Such a rereading and rewriting of Dali's relation to Surrealism is dangerous on at least two counts. First, it celebrates Dali's dangerousness to Surrealism by affirming his extraordinary difference from Surrealism, a difference that irrupted just when it had appeared he was ever so compatible with its ends. The latter point has been sorely underestimated and has resulted in dismissals of Dali that do not fully appreciate his eccentricity's alterity and exorbitance. Second, this rereading invigorates the claim that the *post modo* was (is) always already in motion as a becoming-other irreducible to identifiable being. The perilousness of such an enigmatic, performative event is that it unsettles philosophical, aesthetic, political, and other projects that aim to establish knowledge by corrupting their foundations. Dali's surrealism, in addition to contesting the Royal Canon of Surrealism, intervenes also as a deterritorializing desire that interminably pushes intertextuality toward hypertextuality. Neither an automatic message nor collage or *pastiche*, the text *Dali and Postmodernism*, like the painting *Endless Enigma*, is an encounter with phantom meaning. Advanced as both provocation and evocation, its "toward which," "for," and "from whence" linger on as *con-fusion*.

When Dali's theoretical and painterly productions are revealed to have anticipated and instantiated such outcomes, it is obvious they could have been little more than a scandalous rending of Breton's official Surrealism. For Breton aspired to do away with any moral and physical obstructions that kept individuals from being free to see what truly IS. Against Breton's claim that there is "something hidden"[3] whose recognition is emancipatory, there "are only, everywhere, differences and traces of traces."[4] The subversive brilliance of Dali, I suggest, was his ability to dissimulate difference, trace, and multiplicity for the sake of a happy understanding of an ostensibly smooth, though convulsive, transcendence from miasmic immanence. *Dali and Postmodernism* is the story of this dissimulation, whose deployment supports an affirmation of desire both as becoming without being or lack and as a proactive resistance to subjectifying forces. The latter strategies, which would seem at odds with each other, are conjoined in the strangely magnetic spaces of *Endless Enigma*, the most diabolical and ingenious of these stories, told first by Dali circa 1938—and again, now.

Vis-à-vis Surrealism's imperative that subjectivity must take a creative and critical role in the transformation of reality, and in keeping with *Endless Enigma's* lack of a particular identity or meaning, it is crucial to underscore that there is no one voice or style operative in *Dali and Postmodernism*. *Endless Enigma* itself is a mélange of voices and styles that are not one, and so too is this text—not because it mirrors *Endless Enigma*, but because it is quickened by any number of points of departure and paths that are juxtaposed and cross each other without end.

Dali and Postmodernism is equivocal as performance and academic "theory." There is no one academic or philosophical voice; there is no particular appeal to any one writer or thinker. Likewise, the text has no particular performative style. At times it is passive, exuberant, celebratory, bombastic, playful, and outrageous, perhaps even self-indulgent and precious, as were both Dali and Breton, as well as many of the other figures who appear here. At other moments it is intensely determined, serious, obsessive, scholastic, and deliriously studious. Such a profusion of styles and voices (designated here as *con-fusion*) must be read against the guiles of *Endless Enigma*.

A variety of philosophical and critical thinkers, texts, and tactics thus perform in *Dali and Postmodernism*. Their strange juxtapositions might at first appear to be an indiscriminate lumping together of heroic figures under some unrecognized or hoped-for illusion that they all are, or can be made to appear as, one. That in some way they might go together, or that there is a phantasy or fiction that could make sense of them together, is precisely the point—only a fiction or paranoia could achieve that identity or unity. For just as the phantoms and figures that play in the space of *Endless Enigma* do not together make anything in particular, even though they appear to do so (e.g., a "face"), the figures and schemes working here do not of necessity coalesce either. That they do not, though they appear to, is disastrous and catastrophic for a position such as that of Breton, whose operative faith rested on the emergence of an alchemically, dialectically convulsive identity. I suggest that Dali's *Endless Enigma* was the extreme limit of such faith, and that his paranoiac-critical method was as subversively ironic and dissimulatively surrealistic as it was dialectical and meaning-endowing.

I contend that Dali anticipated the theoretical and critical practices that have emerged in the past twenty-five years that are known as "postmodern." Formulating the latter will be the basis of my claim that another reading of Dali yields a heretofore unacknowledged reason for the tension between him and Breton and for his final, irrevocable exclusion from the anointed few of Surrealism. While my intent here is to explore the tensions and politics of Dali's critique of Surrealism and Breton, I emphatically do not aim to make of Breton an ogre, nor do I intend to denigrate his magnificent work.

There is also a parallel of sorts between the multitude of perspectives in *Endless Enigma* and the diversity of solutions posed to the political questions of the 1930s—such as materialism, positivism, rationalism, romanticism, and idealism—and their sedimentation in humanism, Catholicism, Judaism, Fascism, capitalism, Marxism, and the like. The 1930s were indeed terribly tormenting times for artists and intellectuals. It is well known, for instance, that Bataille struggled, in his novels as well as in his more overtly philosophical works, to arrive at positions from which to address the troubles of the day. Recently, Suleiman has questioned the "virility" around which much of Bataille's writing formed.[5] She wonders if at all he was virile. Breton likewise questioned Dali's virility. Here "virility" is associated with taking a specific and tolerable philosophical stance where subjectivity is endowed with an agency capable of certain theoretical critiques and syntheses leading to knowledge as well as to resistance and emancipatory practices.

Traditional versions of the various reasons Breton and Dali differed are well known. The version offered here aims to go to the very heart of their "debate" about subjectivity, identity, agency, knowledge, autonomy, transformation, and liberation. In the same sense that Sartre considered Bataille impotent and useless, Breton also came to consider Dali a menace to the utility of Surrealist praxis. *Dali and Postmodernism* reveals how Dali's insidiousness led to his dismissal by Breton. Perhaps what is offered here will be consistent with what other histories of Dali (during the 1930s) have proposed. That, however, will be for others to figure.

In her discussion of Bataille, Suleiman notes that Hollier has articulated Bataille's political stance(s) by arguing that his movements between Hegel and Nietzsche, "inner" and "outer" experience, political activism and inaction, and so on, were a form of "equivocation" against which fascism and totalitarianism cannot operate.[6] Agreeing with Hollier, I suggest that *Endless Enigma* is a space of equivocation and intransitivity where no singular position is clear, obvious, or stable, where strange alliances fleetingly form but are not championed, where paranoiac coherence, order, and enigma are *con-fused*, and where meaning is phantom. It marks a step out of politics—as were, according to Hollier, Bataille's "meditations" on inner experience and Blanchot's "dissidence." That these steps— Bataille's and Blanchot's written, Dali's painted—transpired around the late 1930s is not an uncanny coincidence. Yet neither is it col- lusion, either interpersonal or with some particular secret. Although there might be intransitivity, Dali's work in the 1930s should *not* be misconstrued as an absence of difference or resistance, or as com- plicity with an enemy.

Whether or not the latter framing of Dali's actions clarifies or absolves his "politics," or lack thereof, is certainly disputable, espe- cially now when "we" so desperately desire salutary ways to address what currently menaces us. That, however, is not the debate that *Dali and Postmodernism* seeks to engage. Does Dali deserve to be counted in the company of Bataille and Blanchot (particularly in the context of the 1930s)? The issue, I suggest, is infinitely more nuanced[7] than can be drawn from Bataille's several essays against Dali and/or the Surrealists, including *The Absence of Myth*, largely written in the 1940s. A complication worth noting is that Bataille considered Dali, especially during the 1930s, to be one of the Surrealists and did not entertain the view presented here, which places Dali closer to Bataille than to Breton.

It is thus crucial that Dali be reread and rewritten again now, for "Dali" has receded into repetitious psychobiographies and bland, redundant histories—the discursive enunciations of rarified archival indentions—what Foucault called "commentaries": tried and tired recitations of the Same, rehearsals of the Interior.[8] Indeed, most of what exists about Dali now is but commentary.

Dali and Postmodernism does not ignore the weight of the lan- guid histories of the latter commentaries. Questioning both those histories and Dali's works circa 1927–38, it refuses to prefigure or posit particular outcomes. The obstinacy of this querying is not sim- ply written from the "site" of postmodernism. It is instead read and written from posts that flow from other contextualizations of "Dali" that are not dependent on certain versions of archival coherence or succor. Drained of essence obsession, contexts are refigured, not in ignorance of or in spite of certain historical renditions, but despite them.

Dali and Postmodernism reads Dali's surrealism in the 1930s more in the light of the politics of philosophy and canonicity than in

the context of cultural politics, though this distinction is very difficult to achieve given their incestuous relationship. Nonetheless,
Dali is presented as one who *anticipated* postmodernist tactics. I
will not, however, endeavor to apply to Dali, or assess him in light
of, the very latest advances of postmodernist art/critical theory. I
specifically do not concern myself here with current interests that
raise questions about his relationships to Fascism, gender, pornog-
raphy, misogyny, Marxism, or commodification. The primary focus
of *Dali and Postmodernism* is on Dali's politics with regard to the
totalitarian nature of essentializing thought.

Dali and Postmodernism is about a delirious blooming. Its
frenzy does not trace the same trajectory as did Breton's blooming
sunflower, whose arborescence climaxed in a burst of teleological
magnificence, embodied as a marvelous flower facing the sun.
Instead Dali's enigmatic blooming arose and persisted as an endless
enigma. *Endless Enigma* is also the name of an extraordinary painting, completed circa 1938, that animates and haunts this book. *Dali
and Postmodernism* is an unlikely story—a heterology—of a leaking,
burgeoning multiplicity rather than a likely story about a blossoming
arborescent structure whose radicle can be identified and represented.

To write a preface presumes upon a face. *Dali and Postmodernism* places "face," which here is synonymous with the essence given
surreality in Breton's discourse, under erasure. Effacing the face does
not invoke nihilism. It cannot. Plentitude and endlessly repeating
becoming without being are affirmed. A face? A preface? They prevail only where consciousness is privileged and linked with projects
of knowledge, comfort, predictability, and control. Abounding in
the vicinity of *Endless Enigma*, they are sentenced to a life of fiction
where their borders and margins only simulate an ability to stem the
flow(er) of the enigmatic for at least one sublime moment.

ACKNOWLEDGMENTS

Many have supported and made possible this work. A grant from the State University of West Georgia Learning Resources Committee enabled my travel to the Salvador Dali Museum in St. Petersburg, Florida, where I graciously was granted permission by Mr. and Mrs. A. Reynolds Morse to use their archives. While there I was kindly assisted by the museum's curator, Joan Kropf. I am deeply obliged to Ted Simons, Chair of the Sociology and Anthropology Department at the State University of West Georgia, for release from teaching duties, and for his strong encouragement of this project in all phases of my research and teaching.

I am grateful to the National Endowment for the Humanities for enabling me to participate in 1988 in the seminar "Dada and Surrealism Revisited," conducted by Anna Balakian and assisted by Barbara Lekatsas, Curator of the Weingrow Collection of Avant-Garde Art and Literature at Hofstra University. Portions of the writing were also developed while I participated in a National Endowment for the Humanities Summer Institute, "The Linguistic Turn in Recent Continental Thought," conducted by Calvin O. Schrag at Purdue University in 1986. Portions of the text were presented at the International Human Science Research Conference in 1985 at the University of California at Berkeley, the International Conference on Surrealism and the Oneiric Process in Atlanta, Georgia, in 1990, and the International Conference on the Hideous and the Sublime in Atlanta, 1994.

I wish to thank Daniel Cottom, Robert Merrill, Barbara Lekatsas, and Ross Glover for their critiques of earlier drafts of the text. In particular, I thank my mentor and teacher, Anna Balakian, for her concern for this project, aspects of which she supported even though philosophically she found herself at odds with them. Most especially, I thank Sheila LaFountain for her undying patience, dedication, encouragement, technical and creative assistance, and love and passion.

Introduction

CON-FUSION AND R(H)UMORS OF MEANING

In *Camera Lucida*, Roland Barthes struggled to define the reality of the photograph, finding its Referent in the intractable "that has been."[1] His phenomenologically grounded position is that the referent of photography is not the same as that of other systems of representation. Unlike painting, or discourse, for instance, which can rely on "optionally" real things to which images or signs refer, photography relies only on the "necessarily" real thing without which there would be no photograph.[2] Painting can feign a reality unseen, and discourse combines referents that most usually are chimeras. For Barthes, photography stands alone among schemes of representation in that only it possesses the "evidential force"[3] capable of generating a realism grounded in a certainty: that of which the photograph is evidence was present, in fact, was there.

That the referent upon which the photograph leans might now be absent does not detract from the existential absoluteness of its prior existence. It is important to note, however, that Barthes was powerfully moved by the death of his mother and by a desire to have a "just image" of her, an image that would utopically deliver her "unique being" or "essence."[4] This could quell his grief, and this motivated his assertion of photographic realism. In *The Burden of Representation*, John Tagg takes issue with Barthes's realism and suggests that Barthes's Desire was grounded in a sense of crisis, loss, and nostalgia that gave way to a compelling need for certainty and unity. It was this need, Tagg assumes, that set in motion a particular phantasy on which Barthes founded his certainty and identity-securing realism. In moments of weakness, terror, or nostalgia, I too often find myself drawn to Barthes's position. Nonetheless, I find myself in deep agreement with Tagg, who goes on to articulate the meaning(s) of photographs in Foucauldian terms.

I have opened with this very abbreviated sketch of two impressive works to anticipate the approach taken here to the work of Dali and his relation to André Breton and the Canon of Surrealism. Dali's practice, I suggest, amounts to an insistence upon what is taken these days as "poststructural" or "postmodern" criticism. If Tagg is correct about photographs—that there is something that exceeds representation (with which Barthes would agree) and that this something is an "effect of the production of the subject in and through representation to give rise to the phantasy of this something more"[5]— then it is necessary to approach *what else* is also operating that makes a print more than paper, a painting more than colored paint, a text more than a flock of words. The focus of such an inquiry is on the conscious and masked processes, practices, institutional and historical relations, and strategies that incite particular phantasies and signifying schemes. Such an inquiry shies away from existential approaches in favor of power/knowledge/truth relations and focuses attention on another set of factors that "lie" "behind" what appears as "real." What is to be taken as "evidential force" is not, however, something that resides under or behind or beyond or hidden within some existent reality, as phenomenology, abstract painting, psychoanalysis, or symbolism, for instance, would have it. The latter observation, indeed, is the outcome of such an approach: a critique of representation, identity, and essences behind appearances that gives them their features and foretells of their future. And more disturbing for approaches subjected to such a critique is the exposure of the fictive nature of their assertions and productions by an ensemble of discursive and non-discursive formations.

What I argue here is that the theoretical and pictorial work of Salvador Dali, particularly that of the late 1920s until 1938, constitutes an assault on the evidential structure of the realism and modernism of Surrealism. I maintain that his critique of representational and identity thinking, which appeared at one point to be so consistent with Surrealism's critique of reality and culture, was instead a devastating deconstruction of Surrealism that ultimately spelled the demise of Dali as a Surrealist. In particular, I suggest that his great contribution to Surrealist tactics—the paranoiac-critical method— became a technique that undercut Surrealist Desire by instigating multiple readings and realities that could not be recuperated in the coherently convulsive and liberating identity articulated by Surrealism. His very critiques of identity thinking and clear and certain knowledge of essences and foundations insited a crisis in *surreality* by substituting laterality and *con-fusion* for depth and latency, and deferral and dissemination for identity and totality.

Because *con-fusion* is a crucial notion in this rereading of Dali, I provisionally sketch it now as a scene where conjunction, disjunction, and sublation coincide without convergence, destiny, or end. It names a conjunction of accidental and intentional juxtapositions where the entire event inscribes itself in such a way that only artifice, vis-à-vis truth, is likely. Such a scene, complicated by the incursion of simulation and dissimulation, can exist only when a "con" is at work. That Dali was a con-artist extraordinaire is well known, but the extent of his con-artistry, I suggest, has not been fully appreciated.

With such con-artistry, ironies arise with Dali's celebrations of individualism and particularism. Worked out as a Nietzschean embrace of life (though Nietzsche was not necessarily his inspiration), a Foucauldian *techne tou biou*, of sorts, his exultation of creativity, imagination, and difference was, by 1938, already being relegated to the rubbish piles of kitsch, zany eccentricity, and weird selfishness. His histrionics and exotic aesthetics installed an irony in Surrealism in that his surrealism also reveled in surprise, coincidence, metamorphosis, chance, and the like, but did not espouse the sublative, collectivist tendencies underwriting Breton's sense of fervent life (*la vie à perdre halience*). In this sense, Dali exposed the degree to which Breton, ever the revolutionary, was a modernist who took it as his duty to impose certain standards on aesthetic production. Here Dali's work becomes deeply political, for it reveals an essentializing moment in Breton's Surrealism that, for Dali, worked itself out as a neoconservative *garde*. In the language of *Camera Lucida*, this essentializing tendency of official Surrealism was, for Dali, a most delectably succulent "punctum." That Dali's work after the 1939 excommunication is little more than self-aggrandizement is perhaps debatable. Whatever conclusions can be drawn from such discussions, however, can attenuate neither the powerful challenge he registered nor the ruptures he anticipated that "posthumanist" discourses address.

To present such an argument, however, is not to privilege Dali's approach. Dali's interpretation, as is this of his, is but another reading and is not exempt from the claim that it too is fictive. The issue of who is correct or who has the truth is not the point, for that only props up the view that there is something present behind appearances that can ground appeals to settle such matters. Rather, the issue is the liberation of a suppressed text or texts in Dali's work—a text or texts repressed by the ontotheology of Surrealism and modernism. The resistances to Dali's work in the 1930s serve to highlight the arbitrary nature of discourses. What I shall reveal about Dali's work is that, contrary to criticism that persistently locates it within the orbit of psychoanalysis, Hegelianism, alchemy, and the hermetic and occult traditions, it anticipates what is now advanced in "poststructural" and "postmodern" thought and their concerns with literary, aesthetic, and cultural politics. The latter, I advance, were at the heart of Dali's encounter with Surrealism, and this deconstructive radicalism led to his expulsion.

Following Nadeau's *The History of Surrealism*, especially his accounts of Breton's "excommunication mania" and his purging of the ranks of the Surrealists,[6] recent essays by Kuspit and Cottom[7] suggest that various designations Breton has garnered over the years (e.g., "magus," "Pope," "cop") were not undeserved. That such tags reveal a juridical and quasi-positivistic approach to *surreality* corroborates the sense that Breton intended to carefully cultivate what Surrealism would and would not be. For instance, as early as 1920, according to Soupault's memoirs, Breton insisted on numerically grading various writers, artists, or politicians or various feelings, attitudes, or sensibilities.[8] Though played by Breton as a game, this empirical approach is significant in that the averages computed for each thing graded formed the basis for a collectivist or communal approach to particular persons, objects, and issues. In 1924, the short-lived *Bureau de recherches surréalistes* opened to continue the collection of data, the intent being to identify the essential "substance common to all men" that would form "the disturbing machine at the center of the world,"[9] a "dialectical machine,"[10] which would revolutionize the world. The parallel of such a scientific approach bears an uncanny resemblance to Husserl's view of phenomenology as a rigorous science that aims to establish knowledge of essences via learning to see things again with the uncontaminated innocence of a child's vision. This coincidence is all the more remarkable given Breton's claim that

Perception and representation are to be taken only as products of the dissociation of a unique original faculty, to which the eidetic image bears witness, and of which one finds some trace in the primitive and the child . . . All those who care about defining *the real human condition* aspire more or less clearly to rediscover this state.[11]

Breton never delegated or abdicated his position as collator and protector of the essence and purity of Surrealism. Against this purity *Endless Enigma* arises, taking the shape of the nomadic, guerilla writing of a minor science against the Royal Science and Law of Surrealism. As minor writing seeks to inc(s)ite different rhetorical and pictorial possibilities, for Dali such work was an endless enigma that assumed the contours of phantom meaning and its catastrophic and disastrous slippage and acephalic breathlessness.

Breton's basic interest was the link between psychic automatism and artistic production. Out of this linkage he constructed an elaborate rhetorical edifice grounded in the textual flesh of poetry. Gradually, however, he opened Surrealism to the possibility that this constitutive flesh could also be pictorial. This was the opportunity Dali seized, and at the levels of written and painted texts he promoted an alternative rhetoric. Its aim was a countercanonical minor writing[12] that would simulate the legitimacy of a restricted economy until the general economy it both exploited and excluded burst open, with a smile, in 1938, on the canvas of *Endless Enigma*. The rereading of Dali offered here is thus not simply a Derridean deconstructive reading, but simultaneously a situating of that reading within a Foucauldian grid of differences. Dali's guerilla writing might then be taken as a deflagration of what Kittler referred to as the "discourse network of 1900."[13]

When Stoekl, examining the writings of Bataille, Blanchot, Roussel, Leiris, and Ponge, declared that the "phenomenon of inner sacrifice" is one of the most crucial issues readers of literature face today,[14] he could have included Dali and his written and painted texts as well. For much has been made of Dali's asexuality and/or perverse sexuality and the autoeroticism and automutilation that traveled with it. Without consulting psychology, however, such matters can be approached via contemporary interpretations of writing and its proclivities toward autoeroticism and inner sacrifice. Dali's eroticism must be liberated from the tyranny of psychoanalysis so as to catch at work the voluptuousness of desire where *eros* is a relation between the I and the alterity of the other. In the proximate juxtapositions of the I and the alterity of the other, voluptuousness gives way to responsibility, as Levinas has suggested.[15] This migration profoundly disturbs the creativity and spontaneity of the I and unsettles reigning moral codes and ideologies.

Dali and Postmodernism renders these very rendings. In doing so, it also concerns itself with what senses of the sacred and the ethical there could be in acts that otherwise would be taken by convention as repugnant, devolved, nihilistic degradations of self, society, and beauty. Such a rereading also forces a rethinking of Dali's destitution (cf. Levinas) and how it ironically generated a deliverance that contested Breton's moral claims about what it means to be whole (i.e., what it means to be a Surrealist).

This rewriting of "Dali" thus does not turn on the strategies of psychobiography or psychoanalysis for a retrieval of the artist's intentions. Nor does it rely on any hermeneutic model to establish authorial or textual intent. Rather, Dali is here positioned as a localized site of resistance, a genealogical apparatus or micropractice of difference, a capillary of deterritorialization of the space of Surrealism. A nomad war machine, "Dali" insited the endlessly enigmatic desire of another disturbing machine in the "disturbing dialectical machine" of Breton's Surrealism. This war machine's catastrophic dessication of the past and the future effaced the canvas as a vessel or tissue for conducting the shock that would revolutionize the world.

The *mise-en-scène* of the perpetual deferral of this transformative shock prevented the convulsive identity of the self/universe from arriving at an identity. Instead, the increasing entropy of high-quality meaning (supposedly retained in the eidetic image) fragmented into greater and greater degrees of vulnerable and deranged meaning. The *noesis* of interiority Breton so valiantly promoted was never able to overcome the noises of the war machine, *Endless Enigma*.

Indeed, in some cases, Dali must be read against himself so as to contest some of his own claims against the provocative and evocative unruliness of his own aleatory subterfuge. For instance, in the essay "The Stinking Ass," Dali suggests that the double image may be extended to create a third image, or even a limitless multiple image. It would be a mistake, though, to think that the very multiplicity of a multiple image could be reducible to a binary that would permit an "idealism with no ideal," which he had earlier supported in *The Immaculate Conception*, where he "despised genealogy" in favor of "dialectially reconcilable" entities within the system of an image.[16] Nonetheless, beyond any evanescence Breton could ever have hoped automatism could channel, *Endless Enigma*, grafted onto the discourse of Surrealism, eventually exceeded Breton's proclamation that the surrealist object is "oneiric, symbolic, real and virtual, mobile and mute, phantom, found, etc."[17]

The sovereignty of Dali's own claims that he was the only true surrealist must be read against Breton's claim that anyone can be a

surrealist. Such a reading highlights the individuality of the particular who stands out to say that being the only true surrealist is tantamount to saying that all "lowercase" renderings (*surrealism*) are
more significant than the capitalized, homogenized version. That
is, to be a Surrealist one must be a surrealist, for to be a Surrealist is
to be a fiction that denies heterogeneity. For "Dali," to be a Surrealist
is to seek what Nietzsche might have named the "reactionary"
energy of essence rather than the fecundity of diversity. As will be
evident as *Dali and Postmodernism* moves on, the celebration of
the lowercase over the capitalized case (surrealism instead of Surrealism) amounts to a decapitation, the sacrificial remains of which face
us on the canvas of *Endless Enigma*.

   After the *Second Manifesto's* purging of dissidents who cor-
rupted the Surrealist principles Breton demanded, Desnos published
"The Third Surrealist Manifesto" (1930). Echoing Prévert and
Ribemont-Dessaignes, who, in *Un Cadavre* (a response to the politics
of the *Second Manifesto*), referred to Breton as a "bishop," "priest,"
"Pope," and "cop," Desnos attacked Breton's religiosity. He argued
that Breton's clerical moralizing and idealizing amounted to tossing a
lifeline across abysses toward God. The "Third Manifesto" declared
that the "the surreal exists only for non-surrealists."[18] While Dali
had sworn allegiance to the *Second Manifesto's* principles, Desnos's
"Third Manifesto" became a phantom object of sorts, haunting the
borders of Dali's ostensible fidelity to Breton. Transubstantiated,
however, in its encounters with alterity, this phantom object arrived
later in the lambent incandescence of *Endless Enigma* as phantom
meaning. *Endless Enigma* and phantom meaning: an affirmative,
fecund, laughing, silent, ethical gesture after the death of God—a
Fourth Surrealist Manifesto(?).

   Returning to Barthes's and Tagg's characterizations of referents
for a moment, what if we were to combine and intertextualize the
"feigned, optional" referents of painting with the "chimeras" of discourse and the arbitrary referents of photography—what would we
have? In Dalinian discourse, we would have the "delirio-critical synthetic"[19] products that arise when painting, titles for those paintings, manifestoes, and treatises intermingle. An extraordinarily tech-
nically gifted painter, Dali created "instantaneous and hand-done
color photography,"[20] as he referred to his paintings, that approached
and exceeded phenomenal and virtual reality by secreting "extravagant . . . deceptive . . . hypernormal and sickly images of concrete
irrationality . . . authentically unknown images . . . [that] makes the

world of delirium pass tangibly onto the plane of reality . . . carried
out with scrupulous realism."[21]

Dali's "realism" deliberately aimed to destablize and discredit
prevailing interpretations of reality, but his approach, while flying
under the banner of Surrealism (which he later in his life confessed
was the only vehicle available at the time for his machinations),
also deeply disturbed the Surrealist's reality. So profound was this
disturbance that it not only cretinized conventional culture, it even
shocked and ridiculed Surrealism itself. It accomplished this by
inscribing *r(h)umors of meaning* into the domain of immediate and
practical experiences of life and into the very philosophical and aesthetic systems that sought either to interpret those domains (e.g.,
exoteric philosophy running from Descartes to Hegel, esoteric philosophy running from Heraclitus through Paracelsus, Hermes Tris-
megistus, Swedenborg, and Novalis, and psychoanalysis running
from Charcot and Janet to Freud and the early Lacan) or to critique
them (e.g., Surrealism).

The Dalinian apparatus is a discourse of *r(h)umors of meaning*.
Subversive in its dissociative lateral juxtaposition (i.e., *con-fusion*) of
horizons and texts of literal and possible meaning, this discourse
stood outside Surrealist realities in that it deployed multiple readings
whose tumescent and overdetermined delirium exceeded the poten-
tial for Surrealist recuperation. For *r(h)umors* deride and elide at the
very moment they solicit and avow. In Dalinian discourse, rumor
and humor are consubstantial. Only a deconstruction of their conjoined spaces can reveal the contrivance Dali deployed.

Rumor suggests. It insinuates and intimates something uncon-
firmed, something insubstantial. As insinuation, rumor operates to
detract and scandalize by inserting into the possibility of both presence and identity the specters of hoax, fable, fiction, phantasy. Deftly
supplementing clarity and certainty with a pall of undecidability,
rumor is a powerful and slippery substitute for truth that easily
seduces the most competent and resistant.

Humor, on the other hand, suggests something capricious,
laughable, amusing, even ludicrous. Humor insinuates comedy and
joke, something droll or funny or whimsical. It operates by invoking
and playing upon surprise, the unexpected, the odd, and it possesses
the capacity to disorder and unsettle. Humor also suggests, however, within the context of the arcane, certain fluids that influence
and determine the character and disposition of a body's integrity
and coherence (e.g., to be sanguine [blood], phlegmatic [phlegm],
choleric [yellow bile], melancholic [black bile]). Humor is thus inher-
ently related to presence and identity. That humors rumor that liq-

uidation and determination travel together is potentially humorous. So too is it humorous that presence and identity can be capricious. And that there can be clear knowledge of the essence of things in all this play is not only humorous, and rumorous, but ironic.

The ins(c)itation of *r(h)umors of meaning* was Dali's foil against the bourgeois philosophical, aesthetic, and moral ideologies of his day. Strategically unleashing these r(h)umors, he intensified the crisis of the subject and the object instigated by the Surrealists. According to Surrealist Hope, this crisis would bring about an emancipating metamorphosis of human existence. For his part, Dali was especially contemptuous of rationalism, identity thinking, and essentialization. To discover the philosopher's stone, his goal was to derail such fancies. For instance, in *The Conquest of the Irrational*, he denounced the "abject misery" of modern art.[22] He accused "abstract art, abstraction-creation, and non-figurative art" of being a disgraceful model of "mental debility" that contributed to the "intellectual and modern desolation of our epoch." He singled out in particular "sticky and retarded Kantians" and "sordid neo-Thomists." Within their orbit he also located traditional mathematics and physics, gestalt and related "structural" theories, idealism, and other approaches that seek "localized and comfortable objects of consciousness with their lazy atoms." Against these despicable tendencies Dali proposed (and, I argue, accomplished fully with *Endless Enigma*) the "coming philosophy of paranoiac-critical activity."[23]

It is important to note that from Aquinas through Descartes, Kant, and later Fichte, Hegel, and Brentano, we find an emphasis on a philosophy of consciousness that leans heavily on the intentionality of consciousness to identify essences upon which knowledge of reality can be grounded. Through acts of reflection and abstractive appropriation, "obscure and turbulent passions" are transformed into "clear, analytical, and carnal anatomy."[24] Untiringly loathing such thought, Dali's assault on representational thinking was epitomized by his scrutiny of abstract art. Much as Foucault and Deleuze, echoing Nietzsche, railed against lazy assumptions about the ability of consciousness to locate the origins and self-evident necessity of meaning, so too did Dali suggest that history and meaning are not an unbroken continuity sited upon identifiable foundations. Rather, any meanings that can or do accrue are transitory, accidental, and constituted of a proliferation of episodic singularities that exist within fragmented fields as autonomous vectors and trajectories contesting systematization.

R(h)umors of meaning, then, are an alternative formulation of the event of meaning that strips away the twin figures of a sovereign, essence-identifying consciousness and its secure humanism. As a means of articulating Dali's stance, the work of Husserl is presented as an instance of the philosophy he abhorred. Although Dali did not read or critique Husserl per se, Husserl, nonetheless, is one of the twentieth century's greatest spokespersons for the ability of consciousness to extract essences and establish groundings. Further, Husserl's philosophy of presence is carried over into the sphere of art via its familial relationship to the methods (and, in some cases, goals) of such painters as the Synchromists and Kandinsky. Is it not uncanny that the period 1912–13 is common to Husserl, the Synchromists, and Kandinsky? The last decades of the 1800s and the first of the 1900s were the scenes of important and violent confrontations between those who championed and those who detracted from subjectivity as a source of indubitable meaning. Phenomenology and abstract painting, as well as occult/mystical abstraction, were significant arenas of contestation. Thus, I suggest that Husserl, Kandinsky, and the Synchromists signify for Dali the tendencies of sordid neo-Thomism and retarded Kantianism. Like Adorno, Dali railed against the rage of idealism and its "hatred of reality."[25] Breton alleged that he himself did, too, but Dali took issue.

With Husserl, Kandinsky, and the Synchromists there are distinct proclivities toward essentialization, replete with notions of presence, origins, coherence, totality, self-evident necessity, foundations, and continuity (despite the disclaimers of infinitely transitional profiles whose character is always unfinished). For instance, the process or urge behind Kandinsky's work, like that of other members of *der Blaue Reiter*, Mondrian and *de Stijl*, and Malevich's Suprematism, was figured as early as 1908 in Wilhelm Worringer's *Abstraction and Empathy: A Contribution to the Psychology of Style*. Worringer noted parallels between abstract and transcendental thinking, and suggested that both sprang from an "inner unrest inspired . . . by the phenomenon of the outside world . . . [by] an immense spiritual dread in relation to the extended, disconnected, bewildering world of phenomena . . . [by] a feeling of being lost in the universe."[26] The urge of abstraction stemmed from the vertiginous experience of being "tormented by the entangled inter-relationship and flux of phenomena in the outer world . . . [by their] obscurity and caprice."[27] Abstraction, by wresting things from "arbitrariness . . . and fortuitousness," locates meaning in a tranquil space that is a refuge from the swarm of appearances. This activity purifies the object and meaning so as "to render it necessary and irrefragable."[28] Because abstraction is concerned with a realm of knowing far removed from materialistic worldviews, Worringer took abstraction to be concerned with the same issues he saw German expressionism seeking: "elementary possibilities" that could overcome "the rationalistic optics of European upbringing."[29]

For Kandinsky, of course, who was inspired by symbolist, theosophist, and other occult and mystical traditions, abstraction was an idealism with messianic and utopian overtones. When properly and sensitively realized, abstraction was considered capable of penetrating the obscure, tormenting veil the mundane had draped over the truths and realities of the cosmos. The heightened consciousness derived from such practice was held to possess extraordinary transformative power.

The Kantian quality of Worringer's spiritual stance, annunciated in his praise of Simmel in the foreword to *Abstraction and Empathy* and reiterated in the appendix on transcendance and immanence, was directly opposed to the aesthetic subjectivism of Schopenhauer and especially to Theodore Lipps's empathic approach. Against the "happy pantheistic relationship of confidence between man and the phenomena of the external world"[30] that grounded Lipps's argument, Worringer counterposed the strain *toward* the pure, the abstract, the absolute, and its notions of law and necessity. Leaning heavily on the spirit of Alois Riegl and Novalis, and thus invoking both the exoteric and the esoteric traditions, Worringer promoted a view of abstract art that has since been abandoned by modern art critics and historians. Since the 1940s it has been common practice to equate abstraction and abstract art with non-representational expression. Non-representational abstraction operates with its own sensibilities, which tend to forget other meanings. It was these meanings Worringer espoused, and Dali reviled.

In the very same sense that Kandinsky sought to violate the world of everyday appearances in the name of a simpler, purer, clearer comprehension of the nature and meaning of things, so too did Husserl. Husserl's work, while suspicious of the materialistic tendencies dominating knowledge, was, of course, devoid of the occult and noumenal features that colored Kandinsky's thought and canvases. *The Crisis of the European Sciences and Transcendental Phenomenology*, for example, was, like Kandinsky's work, written against a sense of inner turmoil and loss, against the same legacy of rational optics and objectivism that concerned Worringer. While both Kandinsky's and Husserl's transcendental tendencies were nostalgic and utopian (i.e., Kandinsky's laws of the Spirit and cosmos and Husserl's "perfectly irreal essences"), what distinguishes Husserl from Kandinsky is Husserl's stripping away of the mystical, esoteric aura of essences by locating inquiries into meaning within the practicalities (and security) of epistemology. Doing this made it possible to lend a certainty and clarity to meaning by shielding findings from the noumenal. By focusing on phenomena, Husserl was able to avoid contending with the problem of the sublime and the rhapsodic. Sidestepping the latter, for Husserl, was tantamount to surmounting the problem of the inexpressible while at the same time retaining the desire for and possibility of totality and unity.

What Husserl averted, Kandinsky embraced. It is significant that abstraction and the very spirit or consciousness that animates it display a resemblance despite the disparities in their respective projects. For both Kandinsky and Husserl, certainty, unity, and origin functioned against a backdrop of reminiscence and forfeiture. Each (abstraction and consciousness/spirit) lays down a realism and representation that make the hidden (absent) real, or makes the passed-over retroflectively real as that-which-was, or is. Herein, phantasy and fiction become decisive; they are crucial to the very production of reference and the possibility of meaning as an experience of coherence.

Dali despised the duplicity of simplicity and coherence.[31] Not only did he attack it in art and philosophy, but he also identified in Surrealism a similar essentializing drift. The site where this became obvious is Surrealism's emphasis on the evolution of consciousness and identity. While indeed Husserl and Kandinsky are vastly different from Surrealism, there is a point where they touch. That is their abiding concern with the metamorphosis, transcendence, and evolution of consciousness and knowing as manifested in a progressive alteration of consciousness that inclined it to be more sensitive, more pure, and more aware of its grounding, its own inner necessity and relation to the objective necessity of the "world," and its very self-evident presence. The moment of coherence, marked in Kandinsky by a revelation of cosmic totality and in Husserl by the grasp of essence, was for the Surrealist a *point suprême*—a marvelous moment where all negation and difference are relieved in a synthetic spark of harmony and reconciliation.

Perhaps then it is more than coincidental that 1913, a crucial year concerning its proximity to the publication of Husserl's *Ideas* and Kandinsky's *Concerning the Spiritual in Art*, was the year of intellectual awakening for Breton. (In addition, 1913 also saw Apollinaire's labyrinthine *Alcools*, Gide's *Les Caves du vatican*, Stravinsky's *The Rite of Spring*, as well as the appearance of Proust's first works.)[32] That there is an essentializing moment *and* the apparition of a release from essentialization in the work of Breton and Surrealism was a tantalizing and luscious notion for Dali, one he did not at all hesitate to exploit. That Breton held essentialization in tension with the wiles of objective chance was, for Dali, an untenable binary ripe for deflation. Perhaps it was the affinity Breton showed in *Nadja* for the tarot and the occult, or perhaps it was Breton's undying interest in Romantic and Symbolist works that positioned the artist as a "seer" (a root metaphor in the visually weighed philosophies of Husserl and Kandinsky), that alerted Dali, ever the voyeur himself, to Surrealism's longing for healing and wholeness. In "Crise de l'objet" (1936), Breton indicated such healing overcoming was most profoundly embodied in "the marvelous" (*merveilleux quotidien*), and in subsequent writings he referred to "le signe ascendant."

Or perhaps it might have been Breton's continual adoration of Rimbaud and Lautréamont. While they were inspirations for Breton, Dali did not permit their wildness to be completely coopted by Surrealism. The appeal of Rimbaud and Lautréamont was their tandem capacity to undermine the activity of the ego or consciousness and the toil of rationality. Modern thought, Breton noted in "Crise de l'objet," is characterized by a will to objectify and a tendency to see the real in what is given (*le donné*). Rimbaud and Lautréamont were able to upset this penchant for circumscribing reality by confusing and deranging the cogito by inserting the irrational, the ambiguous, and the unknown into processes forming meaning. Rimbaud's *alchimie du verbe* and *dédoublement* of the ego, and Lautréamont's humorous cretinization of subjectivity and objects, deformed and made insecure the hubris of both ego and world to be what they appeared to be. Yet against the obliquely derealizing activity of Rimbaud and Lautréamont, Breton constantly sought the marvelous and the ascendant, the point where contradiction is surmounted and *l'objet insolite* effects emancipatory transformation versus reckless careening. The abrogation of difference was crucial to Breton because however long and strange the route of the marvelous, it was the hope that the interior separation of desire and spirit could be overcome. That in turn would eclipse the separation of humans and the world.

This much is evident in two of Breton's most exemplary narratives—*Nadja* and *Mad Love*. *Nadja* is filled with descriptions of disorienting and hauntingly mysterious experiences, places, and objects, which are magnified by Breton's inclusion of enigmatic photographs, but the text nonetheless is a dialectic of order and disorder, rationality and irrationality, that ultimately comes down on the side of an instinctually self-preserving, though convulsive, representation of reality. Seeking "the beyond" in this present life, *Nadja* unfolds in such fashion that Breton casts aside as an unproductive distraction the dizzying madness so crucial to Surrealism. The very possibility of a deranging answer to the query "Who am I?"—central to the task *Nadja* was to accomplish—was too threatening to Breton to leave open, for such an opening could surely have undercut the very nature of hope, which, after all, supposedly was incarnate in the name "Nadja." Ending *Nadja* with the proclamation "Beauty will be CONVULSIVE, or will not be at all," Breton saved himself, the budding sunflower of Surrealism, and the chance of a *point suprême* for another time.

Mad Love is about just that time. Because love, for Breton, was a peerless transformative agent, and because *Nadja* left such love unrealized, as did "X" in *Communicating Vessels*, *Mad Love* sanctifies love found. What is momentous about *Mad Love* is that Breton promotes an inductive, aleatory arrival at that singular state of awareness where the essence of love appears.[33] Indeed, "mad love" is love situated in the unification of the subjective and objective and the spiritual and the physical. With the twin necessities of chance and coincidence celebrating the place of the irrational and the arational in arriving at this site of identity, *Mad Love* announces the revelation that true love is the marvelous coherence in which all disparities vanish. Mad love is the simulacrum of essence: that elusive, synchronous coherence, that "beyond," that is present in life. Essence, incarnate in love and the marvelous, is the philosopher's stone for which the Surrealists searched, Breton their beacon.

But in *Mad Love* Breton clarified his earlier notion of convulsive beauty such that it "will be veiled-erotic, fixed-explosive, magic-circumstantial, or it will not be."[34] That hyphens separate and connect binary poles in his formula is testimony to his undying faith in the dialectical notion that presence is immanent in or constituted by binaries. In his letter to Aube, his infant daughter, at the end of *Mad Love*, Breton tells her she is the unique love that is the culmination of his search to triumph over objective chance. He reveals to her that the supreme point, to which he has aspired through all hyphenated, truncated realities, was not a place he aimed to make his abode. "It was never a question of establishing my dwelling on this point. It would, moreover, from then on, have ceased to be sublime and I should, myself, have ceased to be a person."[35]

While this in some ways would appear to be a deferral of essence in deference to its forever becoming, I suggest rather that it is an affirmation of the possibility of essence knowledge. After all, Aube was this very possibility incarnate. Love is the simulacrum of essence. That one cannot dwell in this essential space is a crucial observation consistent with Breton's own incessant assaults on idealism (to retrieve "the pearl from the dung heap of idealism").[36] His critique of idealism and his claim that one cannot posit oneself in an essence, however, should not be confused with his assertion of the very reality and representability of essences. For without representable essences, Surrealism could not have "produced" its "objects," and Breton's notion of "phantom objects" would have been utterly non-sensical. While transformation itself is not the critical issue for Surrealism (a point central to this book), what is critical is that it be represented and identified as a healing of all openings, traumas, and degradations foisted on the human psyche, soul, and passions by the machinations of sociohistorical existence. In that Breton was a positive, affirmative voice in the 1930s, a time when Heideggerian "nothingness" and Sartrean "nausea" were showing their force, locates him, despite his differences from Kandinsky and Husserl, in the orbit of abstraction-creation phantasies as defined by Dali. That is, Breton's essentializing proclivities continuously recognized that what is e(a)(i)lusive yet present—what is beyond and transcendent yet is capable of representation and identification—is luminously coherent meaning and form-giving stuff possessing emancipatory vigor. It is this feature of Surrealism, I suggest, that Dali correctly recognized and aimed to undo. Into the deformation of meaning and sense emanating from Rimbaud's *dédoublement* of the seeing ego and Lautréamont's hallucinatory metamorphoses so evident in Dali's discourse are also inscribed the shenanigans of Alfred Jarry. Ever the irreverent, clowning renegade, his repertoire of perversions and caricatures gave substance to a blasphemous "pataphysical" field of knowledge—a space "beyond" where confusion reigns, where exceptions, not the rule, prevail. For instance, in "The Passion Considered as an Uphill Bicycle Race,"[37] Jarry parodies Jesus as a stumbling racer who, when the course became "thick with thieves," continued the race "airborne." Invoking tradition by declaring in the last words of this sketch "but that is another story," Jarry had nonetheless already implanted the notion of Jesus as flighty, wandering passion, an instability among mortals. Desecrating Jesus as the essence of the beyond, Jarry installs his aberration as a puncture in the occult-Hegelian-Christian trinity of transformation.

In much the same fashion, Dali, with Peret giggling in the foreground, assailed the possibility of a central organizing design, introducing instead an exceptional, excessive passion not at all conducive to ascension. Jesus' essence—*je suis essence*—becomes *jouissance*—an incorrigible, pleasant otherness that escapes. After all, Dali informed us many times that "Dali" is Catalonian for desire! Dali's "essences," if such a term can be used in his discourse, are airborne essences—eternally bleeding, absconding, peregrinating—more like snowflakes in a blizzard than the becoming of something ascendant. With such movement, however, Bataille's "jesuve"[38] is also evoked, a specter sure to invert vision and blind the I/eye that would pretend to see and know.

In his own inimitable manner, Dali took to heart Jarry's notion of the pataphysical field as a space—a "beyond" that is also here in this life—where everything is equal. In this space, essences are desultory, for things are always other than they appear to appear. The notion of presence itself is radicalized. Self-presence, necessary for essence knowledge, is undermined always by an anomaly, an exorbitance. The sense of the beyond Dali evokes, then, is not that of the Symbolists or Breton, but instead that of eversion and ecstasy.

The coincidence of Dali's appropriation of Rimbaud, Lautréamont, and Jarry into Surrealism came as a mixed blessing in the 1930s. Breton, affirming marvelous somethingness against absence and despair, was a rising star in a sky shared with Nietzsche and Godot. Against Breton, however, Dali reasserted absence, but without a sense of despair, in the masque of overdetermined *con-fusion*. Flavored by Jarry's pataphysical dictum that "all things are equal" and that all solutions are fictive, Dali progressively recommended that anything can mean anything, anything can mean nothing, and nothing necessarily means anything. Paralleling Bataille's decapitation of Hegel's architecture of synthesis and sublation, Dali rethought Baudelaire's "forest of symbols" as a convulsive an-archetexture. But Dali's is no forest of ineffable symbols that capture and confound the imagination, as Baudelaire had suggested, nor is it a "forest of indices," as Balakian offered, that, like pebbles in a labyrinth, beckon the lost toward revelation.[39]

Displacing this forest with his own rhizomatic tangle of signs, Dali deconstructed the very notion of what a "symbol" is or could be. As the term *symbol* is derived from *symballein*—"to throw together"—Dali's thicket is a profusion of entities, experiences, phantoms, and spaces thrown together without prophecy or oracle. Or, his revelation is not a re-veiling that gives the labyrinth of symbols an exit, but an un-veiling that shows the labyrinth to have myriad exits and to be inhabited by slippery cyborgs. Again, though, this is not necessarily a cause for melancholy or desperation. Dali, like the Surrealists who searched for and even figured they had discovered the philosopher's stone, also arranged his discourse around a stone. However, like Mentor in Aragon's *The Adventures of Telemachus*, he repeatedly lost it, through no fault of his own, and without it he found many other stones and never found a marvelous home.

Finkelstein, a modernist Dali critic, offers that "Dali's tantalizing sense of humor and his efforts to 'cretinize' his readers very often results in an ambiguity of sense for everyone but himself."[40] Such a stance, imbued with a faith in the possibility of seeing (Kandinsky, Husserl, and Breton's *donner à voir*), would characterize Dali as an excessive subjectivist and relativist. But, I would argue, to do this is to consent to a modernist desire to occlude the terror and freedom of alterity and exorbitance by making them *prima facie* anarchistic or nihilistic. Such a preference for depth over surface and interiority over exteriority excludes heterotopic space. For heterotopic spaces, like those of *Endless Enigma*, confound the consolation of the fantastic, untroubled region of the fable of utopia where things "hang together." Instead, they displace, they "dessicate speech, stop words in their tracks, contest the very possibility of grammar at its source; they dissolve our myths and sterilize the lyricism of our sentences."[41]

Though different in their tactics and goals, Kandinsky, Husserl, and Breton were "seers." So was Dali. Kandinsky, Husserl, and Breton were also architects, each reacting to his own interpretations of materialism, rationalism, nihilism, and other crises. Breton, for instance, as Balakian noted, represented the "essential modernism" of the Surrealists with his concept of art as a "building process, not as an expression or statement of existence as it is, but as a modification or an addition to it."[42] To be able to modify or add to something, however, is to first grasp its nature in some way as a condition for its alteration. Balakian glosses Breton's gloss of this activity, even though Breton seemed acutely aware of the way his assumptions worked in his discourse, as evidenced in the way he took his poetics to double as a moral code. In his effort to counter the nihilism and destruction of Dada, Breton's project was, for Dali, too closely aligned with the humanism and phenomenology of modernism's abstract-creation.

In opposition to this scornful tendency, Dali offered his own version of the heterotopic spectacle of seeing and building, one that would "end" in *Endless Enigma* as a metastatic perversion of discerning and founding. Reminiscent of Duchamp's *Large Glass*, it refracts a visage from which no sense can be made, one that only simulates the face of the ascendant reflected in the convulsive mirror of some beyond. Rather there is only a being-thrown into commotion and play. The seventh face of the die was no longer conceived of by Dali as chance, but as deferral. In *Endless Enigma* the seventh face surfaces as no face, or as a displaced face—the face of the pagan baring dissemination and supplementation—a talking head making too much sense. Indeed, the event of the endless was Dali's *l'amour fou*. For Breton it was an insidious derision of the Surrealist aesthetic and ethic.

The perfidious temper of Dali's production during the 1930s is also heavily marked by the work of de Chirico. It is well known that de Chirico's hauntingly melancholic, nostalgic dreamscapes were a watershed for Surrealist visions and creations. First celebrated by Apollinaire, their metaphysical, hermetic enigmatics, their power to dislocate, their ghostly emptiness, were ever so instrumental in articulating the Surrealist notions of the crisis of the object, *l'objet insolite*, and *la connaissance irrationelle de l'objet*. Among others painted between 1910 and 1919, when de Chirico's (and Carra's) metaphysical theories assumed other regions of the mind could be stirred and transformed by the counterrealities contained in his images, *The Enigma of the Oracle* (1910), *The Lassitude of the Infinite* (1913), *The Mystery and Melancholy of a Street* (1914), *The Anguish of Departure* (1914), and *The Disquieting Muses* (1917) are indicative of de Chirico's grid. Reverie, nostalgia, suspense, meditative contemplation, anguish, melancholy, and enigma conspire in gratuitous combinations to produce unforeseen meanings and *non-savoir*. *The Destiny of the Poet* (1914) and *The Uncertainty of the Poet* (1914) suggest that each of us is on an endless voyage (*Endless Voyage*, 1914). Hidden in us is a seer and a metaphysician infused with melancholy (*Hermetic Melancholy*, 1919) who can be liberated. But from what? and whence?

For Breton the provocative atmosphere of anticipation, the possibility of chance encounters and of the revelation of the marvelous, ultimately became a boring, closed circuit, a sterile castle too much akin, Balakian suggests, to a stage setting for *Waiting for Godot*— "when nothing comes out of them . . . Breton's criticism . . . becomes harsh . . . indicative of his deep disappointment in Chirico's lack of progress in the labyrinth and his own belief that the darkness is fascinating only as a prerequisite to illumination."[43] Thus, while the Surrealists were compelled by the moods and visions induced by de Chirico's images and titles, and while they recognized the similarity of the *Scuola Metafisica* to their own Freudian roused symbolic strategies, ultimately they felt claustrophobic, lost in the very corridors and caverns of an uninhabitable dream. Dali, however, with no malice toward de Chirico, revisited these corridors, intensified them, and slipped them into the circuitry of Surrealism. He recognized in the seer the voyeur of allusive spectacles, and in the grand metaphysician a great masturbator, much to Bataille's delight. Liberation now doubled as expenditure. For Dali, though, the expenditure of seeds is not waste or degradation (as Breton earlier and Rojas[44] recently interpreted such acts) but the incandescence of fecundity.

As Dali's paintings and theoretical apparati moved through the 1930s toward *Endless Enigma*, nothing was seen coming out of the labyrinth, and the labyrinth itself began to take on the features of a sieve. Not only does nothing emerge, but the seeing and building discussed above continue to accelerate. De Chirico's *Hebdomeros*, published in 1929 and grossly underestimated then (as now), portends what happens in the discontinuous spaces of the sieve from which things do not progress. Whereas his *Enigma of a Day* (1914) stimulated considerable experimentation by the Surrealists, *Hebdomeros*, well received for a very brief time, was only a further index to the verdict that de Chirico had failed. That it was a "failure" put Dali in a peculiar relationship to de Chirico's *oeuvre*.

On the one hand, Dali was apparently heavily influenced by de Chirico's iconography (e.g., silhouettes, mannequins, shadows, towers, vanishing perspective, empty space), moods (e.g, melancholy, nostalgia, desire, languishment, contemplation, anguish), and by his ability to dislocate and disorient via surprising juxtapositions of images and words. On the other, there was somewhat of a tendency manifest in de Chirico that was also apparent in Kandinsky and Breton and the Surrealists. Evident in them was a desire for awakening and illumination, for an experience of the infinite and absolute that in its own astonishing fashion would heal the psyche and soul. These same yearnings are what Dali so strongly reacted to as the "abject misery of abstraction-creation." Of course, Dali did not locate de Chirico precisely on this trajectory, for had he, de Chirico would not have been as important in Dali's work as *Endless Enigma* intimates.

Perhaps the subtle twist in Dali's imbibing of de Chirico is displayed in their respective approaches to Nietzsche. Nietzsche moved de Chirico deeply, particularly the "symbolical dream-pictures" advocated in *The Birth of Tragedy*. According to Nietzsche, these dream-pictures facilitate the artist's oneness with the primal source of the cosmos. Further, they forebode

> that underneath this reality in which we live and have our being, another and altogether different reality lies concealed, and that therefore it is also an appearance; and Schopenhauer actually designates the gift of occasionally regarding men and things as mere phantoms and dream-pictures as the criterion of philosophic ability.[45]

For de Chirico this statement presumably revolved around the "underneath" and its attendant sense of depth, which in turn lent a special hermetic or transcendent sense to "hiddenness." Surprise, then, would be the mechanism by which the incantations and revelations of phantoms would come alive in dream-pictures to awaken those who walked asleep in the fields of the absolute. The capacity of these surprising "objects" was to cut through the mundane and communicate with the subconscious and unconscious mind (for Husserl the prereflective, for Kandinsky the uninitiated) and permit a primal understanding already long at work and constitutive of being and meaning.

For Dali, too, especially in the early 1930s in the heyday of the Surrealists' fascination with Freud, this stance was quite obvious. But as he moved toward *Endless Enigma*, his accent shifted away from the "underneath" and toward another altogether different reality. This predisposed his discourse to focus more heavily on the alterity and exteriority of "phantoms." In the dark blush of the sun of excess, surprise assumes another figure, one more subversive and liberating than that at work in the "conventional" Surrealist object. More insurgent because Dali inverted surprise such that not only is there no meaning "underneath," there is no ascendant meaning at all.

Surprise is not the savior of the problem of enigma, but rather the occasion of *non-savoir*. The enigma is that there is no essential meaning. The journey is endless, leading nowhere and everywhere. Hebdomeros is still wandering, and Telemachus has yet to reach home, even in death. What Dali discerned in de Chirico was not the possibility of liberation from ignorance and unfulfillment, but a liberation from the myth that unity and wholeness are in fact a solution—that coherence is phantasy and the "laws" of Surrealism are fibs. Hebdomeros thus becomes the story of the deferral of identity and meaning. Ariadne becomes threadbare. Phantoms trace about randomly. Incandescence displaces incantation, revelation defers to re-veil-ation, itineration erases (re)iteration. What remains hidden for de Chirico's Hebdomeros is so because appearances occlude what is underneath. What remains hidden for Dali's Hebdomeros is so because of its overabundant surplus and slipperiness. Whereas de Chirico's dream-pictures gave the Surrealists empty surfaces *in which* they found latencies, Dali pushed those symbols and signals beyond their potentiality toward their demise as a tangle of signs impotent and sterile in their ability to refer to anything beyond themselves, condemning them to endless circulation and meaninglessness, as well as to complicitous interruptions of each other. In this Baudrillardian scene, implosion is substituted for eruption and identity collapses. *Endless Enigma* is not an *innovation* Breton could bless, but an *invention* of which Lyotard might say, "Sublime!" Perhaps Dali knew well what he meant when he named "Dali" "sublime"?

Within the grid of Surrealist elasticity Dali thus introduced slippery Hebdomerian crutches. In Hebdomerian space Breton's notion of convulsive beauty is delayed by the very undulatory avenues on which it must arrive. In this space symbols become hysterical. The heterology Dali inc(s)ites postpones representability. Image and meaning, and their possibility as "text," become terribly problematic, for *Endless Enigma* is countermemory. While maddening, this is not madness. Schopenhauer told us the mad are those who lose memory—Dali has told us many times that the difference between himself and a madman is that he is not mad. Spouts Dali in the catalogue for his exhibition at the Julien Levy Gallery in New York in March, 1939, "Of a cubist picture one asks: 'What does that represent?'—Of a surrealist picture, one sees what it represents and asks: 'What does it mean?'—Of a paranoiac picture one asks abundantly: 'What do I see?' 'What does that represent?' 'What does that mean?'"

In Dalinian space, Surrealism's project of enlightenment is both debilitated and intensified by its becoming the exorbitant, undecidable wandering of a pagan. Dalinian space is a site of entangled, immortal nonsequiturs, where the recuperation of meaning, like de Chirico's verbs, "declines."[46] Unlike Odysseus or Ulysses, Hebdomeros does not find home. But unlike Horkheimer's and Adorno's Odysseus, Dali does not suppress or exclude plentitude and desire in the blissful singularity of the moment in favor of a myth of enlightenment. Enlightenment is henceforth other and elsewhere. Unlike Abraham, Dali's wandering does not issue from a divine source, and unlike de Chirico's Hebdomeros, Dali is not nostalgic. Nor is Dali Maldoror, a sublime ape, tortured and in horror, caught in a battle with God and man. And most of all, unlike Breton, who, like Husserl and Kandinsky, sought to "draw up the scale of vision" of the "wild eye" that exists in a "savage state,"[47] there is no return to the lost colors of the time of ancient suns[48] that can be retained in eidetic images or mimetically brought forth. Herein is Dali's resistance and heresy to Surrealism: There is nothing latent or hidden in the face of the surface or the appearance. Countenance is counterness, incontinence: a gala where the distant realities of Breton's one-dimensional *surreality* and the expanding entropy of fecund immanence are juxtaposed.

Endless Enigma is another story of the I, one complicated by the stealthy and surprising arrival of **phantom meaning** and its displacement of the climax of Breton's phantom object.

This is not an essence: rather, just little stories.

BEAUTY WILL BE PHANTOM, OR NOT AT ALL.

OPENINGS, SCENES:
IRREALITY, SURREALITY,
ALTEREALITY

Transformation of the everyday world of consciousness and experience are the beginning sites of the projects of Edmund Husserl and Salvador Dali. From here, though, the lines each takes move in different directions: for Husserl toward irreality, for Dali toward surreality. Because both projects contend with essence and phantasy, the intention here is to explore, through words and painted images, the paths and desires of Husserl and Dali. A consideration of their differences contextualizes what I claim is the phenomenologically grounded essentializing nature of Breton's discourse and Dali's transgressive stance toward it.

Robert Sokolowski argues that phenomenology requires a theory of description to justify the notion that unperceived complexions of things do in fact exist along with what is naively experienced.[1] The same can be argued of the work of the artist. Husserl's project falls squarely within the realm of a description of phenomena of the world and those features of consciousness that make possible knowledge of that world. It would be a violation of Dali's project, however, to describe it as description, for it is deliriously more. Yet as statements about world and nature, both assume a critical posture toward the notion that what is seen is in fact what is. Through a consideration of the relation of essence and phantasy, we shall wonder about what it is we do when we assert, with any degree of certainty, what something "is" or "means." Because essence and phantasy are pivotal to knowledge, reflections on their relations raise questions about us who look at the world and about the world that allows our stance (similar concerns were, of course, crucial to the Surrealist project of transforming both the subject and the object).

We will proceed by an examination of essence and phantasy as they appear in both Husserl and Dali. Not only will the ideas of each be explored in terms of philosophical and methodological thought, they also will be read through paintings. Dali's paintings are manifestations of and comments on his own thought. Husserl, not a painter, will be read through the works of the Synchromy painters (Morgan Russell and Stanton Macdonald-Wright) and through Kandinsky. Such a comparative reading is designed to explore the intertextuality of written and painted texts. Such a task involves specific referential movements, but it also generates an intermezzo text that asserts its own particularity. The concern then is to open the spaces of that evocative intertext that is always the promise and deferral of what is "present."

HUSSERL AND IRREALITY

Phenomenology begins in silence.[2] Phenomenology's task, for Husserl, is to grasp what is indubitably given as consciousness and in consciousness as the possibility of concrete experience and knowledge in the natural attitude. Husserl's contention is that consciousness is epistemologically antecedent (transcendental) to the world in the sense that things in the world gain meaning and "existential status" for us through the intentionality of pure consciousness.[3] This intentionality, however, is typically hidden from view and undetected:

> We must rise above the self-forgetfulness of the theorizer who, in his theoretical producing, devotes himself to the subject-matter, the theories, and the methods, and accordingly knows nothing of the inwardness of that producing—who lives in producing, but does not have this productive living itself as a theme within his field of vision.[4]

Husserl's Desire is to "stand . . . at the gate of the entrance to the realm, never before entered, of the 'mothers of knowledge.'"[5]

The means by which we can pass through the gates and expand our vision is the phenomenological *epoché* (or reduction). Phenomenological reflection "directs" our attention to the acts that accomplish the "natural reflection" of everyday life.[6] Phenomenological reflection "liberates"[7] and "delivers"[8] us from the naiveté of the natural attitude. While in the natural attitude the flesh of the world naively appears as given, Husserl's Desire is to recover the Flesh of that flesh. That Flesh dwells in the space of Essential Being[9] and is open to transcendental reflection.

The phenomenological *epoché* allows one to "stand above" the world, and thus to know it as a "phenomenon."[10] As Husserl notes, "eidetic intuition," along with the phenomenological reduction, constitutes transcendental reflection.[11] In particular, it is through a consideration of eidetic intuition that the essence (*eidos*) of a phenomenon is grasped. It is also here that phantasy becomes visible and crucial.

Eidetic intuition (*Wesensschau*) is a privileged species of intuition (*Anschuung*), which itself is a central feature of the intentionality of consciousness. The intentionality of consciousness, of course, is the fundamental insight of Husserl's analysis of consciousness and its constitution of meaning. Intentionality unifies, objectifies, constitutes, and synthesizes materials experienced in the world and, by so doing, gives them meaning. Intentionality, and thus eidetic intuition, are indispensable in Husserl's epistemology, whose commitment is to certainty and indubitability.

Eidetic intuition, or ideation, transforms individual, empirical experiences and reveals hidden in them their possibility, i.e., their essence. Essence is that which a number of distinct entities have in common. It refers to the structure of the object without which it cannot be:[12] the intimate self-being of a thing that tells what-it-is.[13] The description of an essence, and its presentation as a concept, identifies not only what a thing is, but also its necessary inability to be anything else (which Husserl takes up in his complex discussions of evidence and apodicticity).

Essences are the objects of ideation. Nonempirical via their apprehension in eidetic reduction, they are grasped through examples. It is only through examples that the phenomenologist is able to accomplish eidetic insight. Examples are crucial and are treated neither as facts nor as essences; they may stem from actual concrete experience or from imagination.[14] In fact, Husserl argued that "free fancies assume a privileged position over against perceptions." He further adds that "*fiction . . . makes up the life* of phenomenology as of all eidetic science" and is "*the source whence the knowledge* of 'eternal truths' draws sustenance."[15] As Sokolowski suggests, the effort to isolate a viable instance is a

somewhat plodding procedure...In fact what usually happens
is that . . . (one) . . . will project a single imaginative variant, but
one that is strategic, crucial, and usually colorful, one that
brings out a certain necessity in the thing we wish to examine.
It is not easy to capture the right imaginative variant, to pick
out the dramatic, vivid example that shows a *necessity*. We
need *fantasy* to do so . . . We have to be able to think of things
being very different than the way they are, and it is by no
means everyone's power to do so. We have to be able to imagine
the impossible and to see it as impossible.[16]

The relationship of eidetic intuition and imagined examples
marks the first crucial place of phantasy (fancy, imagination) in
phenomenology. A more profound moment of its appearance, however, is realized in "free imaginative variation." In Husserl's terms,
in fancy he has perfect freedom in the *arbitrary* recasting of the figures he has imagined, in running over continuous series of possible
shapes, in the production therefore of an infinite number of new
creations; a freedom that opens up to him for the first time an
entry into the spacious realms of essential possibility with their
infinite horizons of essential knowledge.[17] Imaginative variation
enables us

to vary the form of a material object without limits; we can
also imagine it in different places at different times. In this
case our imagination is absolutely free, nothing stops it, the
object remains concrete, that is to say, it can exist "in itself."[18]

Essences or essential structures are thus grasped and clarified
by virtue of imagination. What is revealed is a coherence or necessity, a thematic core that persists as a "felt resistance to the negating
force of imagination."[19] In the *Logical Investigations*, which Husserl
considered his first truly phenomenological work, he referred to a
"law" that characterizes the essence's necessity,[20] a theme that persists through *Ideas*. This legal space is classified and fulfilled by
imagination. Via its clarifying capacity, we encounter imagination's
crucial role in phenomenological inquiry. Phantasy makes essence-
knowledge possible, and it is from here also that the "irreality" of
essences arises. For essences possess the feature of not being indi-
vidualized or localized in time and space. They neither perish nor
come into being.[21] Irreal things are "everywhere and nowhere," they
are "non-real."[22] As phenomenology is an investigation of essential
being, of the transcendental, its objects (essences) are always irreal. In

the play of fancy it is a matter of indifference in this connexion whether such things (melodies, social happenings) have ever been given in actual experience or not . . . we can through 'ideation' secure . . . primordial . . . and adequate insight into essences."[23]

Although Husserl thought himself a "beginner" even at a stage where his work could be considered mature, he envisioned the "promised land"[24] and lamented that he would never set foot on it.[25] Yet he had, for he had immersed himself in the irreality of Essential Being ("qua Being as it is in itself").[26] By treating essences (Essential Being) in such a fashion, Husserl was later able to claim for his investigations an "authentic metaphysics" of experience that was to be taken as superior to and more certain than the "speculative excesses" of perverse and "historically degenerate metaphysics."[27] Not only did Husserl restrict the speculative "beyond" of any metaphysics to the here and now, he goes even further to posit *only one Objective world*, only one Objective time, only one Objective space, only one Objective nature," which is known by a "single community of co-existing monads."[28] The emphasis on essences, essential knowledge, and "only one Objective world" whose "beyond" is here in this world is precisely the same essential, apodictic claim Breton made for the essence of *surreality* when he took it to be the "pearl" of a nonidealistic idealism that could be retrieved from the "dung heap of absolute idealism."[29]

It is important to note that Husserl recognized that the apprehension of essences is marked by "grades of clearness," and that there are "grades of intuitability" of givenness.[30] The task of eidetic reflection is to make clear what is intuitable, and we can

> always bring the data nearer to us even in the zone of obscure apprehension. What is obscurely presented comes closer to us in its own peculiar way, eventually knocking at the door of intuition . . . possessing its own way of effecting the transition through a process of "unfolding" . . . until the object referred to (*das intendierte*) passes into the brightly lit circle of perfect presentation.[31]

The recognition of gradations of clarity led Husserl to an inevitable and controversial distinction between types of essences. This distinction is between essence (*eide*) and pure essence, between what is apprehended in "ideation" and what is rarefied in "idealization." Idealization pushes essences grasped in eidetic intuition (and the concepts that embody them) toward perfection, toward fixity, giving them a "second existence."[32] The legal character of essences is thus problematic. Levinas notes, however, there is a certain primacy of the *eidos* over the "idea."[33]

Essences intuited by acts of direct ideation, which express the essence of the concrete world, are inexact essences. These "generic" or "morphological"[34] essences and concepts, however, are descriptive of their world. They do possess a certain distinct legal nature despite the fact it is not the higher gradation of purity and exactness embodied by pure essences achieved in idealization. Inexact morphological essences are irreal, but not perfectly irreal, and "the constancy and clear-cut distinguishability of generic concepts or generic essences . . . should not be confused with the exactness of the ideal concepts."[35] For as Husserl notes:

> The geometer is not interested in actual forms intuitable through sense, as is the descriptive student of nature. He does not, like the latter, construct *morphological concepts* of vague types of configuration, which on the basis of sensory intuition are directly apprehended, and, vague as they are, conceptually or terminologically fixed, the *vagueness* of the concepts, the circumstances that they have mobile spheres of application, is no defect attaching to them; for they are flatly indispensable to the sphere of knowledge they serve, or, as we may also say, they are within this sphere the only concepts justified. If it behooves us to bring to suitable conceptual expression the intuitable corporeal data in their intuitively given essential characters, we must indeed take them as we find them. And we do not find them otherwise than in flux, and typical essences can in such case be apprehended only in that essential intuition which can be immediately analyzed.[36]

For Husserl, then, imagination discloses essences. They and their meanings become evident through its work. In more rarefied gradations, essences point toward exactness, clarity, and purity, toward irreality and toward an other existence. In phantasy is clarity. Certainty is achieved in fancy. Is a fiction. What an extraordinary admission! A wonderful idea, and lovely. And to imagine it is not ironic? Husserl's Desire!

PAINTED IRREALITY: INEXACT MORPHOLOGICAL ESSENCES

Visual displays of irreality are available in the painting of modern abstract artists, many of whose advances were contemporaneous with the works of Husserl. One of the most striking kinds of these, "Synchromy" painting, appeared almost precisely at the same time as Husserl's *Ideas*. In Synchromist painting, particularly prior to its turn toward pure, nonobjective painting, one finds insights into essences that are presented as the possibility and coherence of concrete experience. While Synchromy indeed has a nonfigurative, nonobjective moment, early Synchromist works present a visual grasp of morphological essences, which, while not purely irreal, are, nonetheless, irreal.

Synchromism (meaning "with color") plays on the notion of a symphony of color rhythms, and represents the first American, and one of the earliest efforts, at painting based on color and abstract form. It was initiated by Morgan Russell and Stanton Macdonald-Wright and articulated in their paintings, notebooks, and essays between 1912 and 1914.[37]

Synchromist painting asserts that color is generative of form and space, the idea being to "make the form and space with waves of color" by realizing and using the naively undetected "rhythmic basis to color."[38] These "color rhythms" infuse a painting with the notion of time: they create the illusion that the picture develops, like a piece of music, within a span of time. This is contrasted with the old view that paintings exist strictly in space, their very expression grasped by the spectator simultaneously and at a glance.[39] Russell's *Synchromist Poster* (1913) illustrates this principle in an advertisement for the first Synchromist exhibit in Munich. Reflecting on Russell's approach over forty years later, Macdonald-Wright noted:

> on rotund objects illuminated from the viewer's direction, he made his highlights yellow and graded them toward shadow through greens and blues on one side, on the other through oranges, reds and purples. For him local color, as such, did not exist, and this left him free to play with the use of a pure color gradation . . . He called this method the "orchestration of tonalities" and, as we are cognizant of solidity only by means of light, this process produced intense form.[40]

Several entries in Russell's notebook, dated 1912, and one from his personal introduction for the Paris exhibition of 1913, are remarkably akin to Husserl's *epoché*. For instance:

> Place in mind or vision clearly the subject as form—the points nearest you in projection—those furthest and side projections and seize the order of this . . . the sentiments of the whole as

color and as line. And in working ignore, forget the linear out-
lines of objects—never will you arrive at complete expression
until this habit is lost.[41]

And further:

One often hears painters say that they work on the form first,
in the hope of arriving at the color afterwards. It seems to me
that the opposite procedure should be adopted . . . I have
worked solely with color, its rhythms, its contrasts, and certain
directions motivated by the color masses. There is no subject to
be found there in the ordinary sense of the word.[42]

In September 1912, he exhorted, "makes lines color . . . never
paint "the Thing" or the subject."[43] And in October 1913, he
reflected, "I am not concerned, so to speak, with the local color of
objects."[44]

Such statements took Synchromist painting out of the realm of
naive taken-for-granted representational/figurative reality and
pushed them toward abstraction, toward the realization of what it
was that constituted and made possible that reality. In *Still Life
Synchromy* (1912–13) and *Still Life with Bananas* (1912–13) Russell
demonstrated his point. The painting is indeed figurative, but one is
first immersed in color, out of which are generated recognizable
forms.

In a September 1912 entry to his notebook, Russell looked
beyond local, concrete, "factual" reality toward more essential features of its presence:

to forget the object entirely, yes to forget it-to put it out of our
mind entirely and think only of planes, lines, colors, rhythms,
etc. emotional visual quality . . . Some artists sacrifice or ignore
these qualities and accent the fact—but one must do the contrary, accent the rhythm, the rapport, and let the object suffer.
Keep the "music" at all costs—the palpitation or undulation—
sacrifice the fact.[45]

As Levin notes, Russell was perhaps anticipating the future of
Synchromy painting in particular, and modern painting in general.[46]

It is important to note, however, that the early formative years
of Synchromist work were primarily abstract and not simply nonobjective. There is a distinct "legal space" referenced by "abstract"
and by "nonobjective." In some cases the delineation is very thin,

but in the work of the Synchromists, "abstract" refers to non-localized, nonfactual, or we might say derealized, objects that nevertheless retain a certain essential figurativeness due to their embeddedness in nature and world. "Nonobjective," on the other hand, refers to completely derealized objects—objects constituted by color and form or motion, as if color, form, and motion were the purified realm from which objects arise. In the words of Macdonald-Wright:

> We are incapable of imagining a form that is not the result of some contact of our senses with nature. Or at least the forms that issue from this contact are infinitely more expressive and varied than those born of the inventive labor of the intellect . . . In opposition to purely logical theories, we mean to stay true to reality. In it is the foundation of every pictorial work . . . It would not displease me if my art were down to earth; the essential is that it should not be abstract.[47]

("Abstract," in Macdonald-Wright's lexicon, is what is referred to here as "nonobjective"). The distinguishing factor between "natural" and "purely logical" here is the same factor that for Husserl distinguishes between objects revealed by ideation and objects revealed by idealization, respectively.

A natural form that heavily influenced Russell and Macdonald-Wright was the human form. In particular, Michelangelo's *Pieta* and *Dying Slave* were inspirational. *Sketch after Michelangelo's "Pieta"* (1912) makes visible in the larger watercolor *Sketch after Michelangelo's "Pieta"* (1912) the abstraction of the essence of the human form and its generation by color rhythm. Likewise, *Sketch after Michelangelo's "Dying Slave"* (1910–12) and *Study after Michelangelo's "Dying Slave"* (1910–12), whose essence is constituted by an imagined spiral, formed the basis for the famous *Synchromy in Deep Blue-Violet* (1913). The notions developed in these latter sketches and painting also were central to another of Russell's major works, *Synchromy in Orange: To Form* (1913–14). Other paintings that also exhibit a decidedly morphological concern are Macdonald-Wright's *Self-Portrait* (1915), *Synchromy in Blue* (1916), *Oriental Synchromy in Blue-Green* (1918), and *Aeroplane: Synchromy in Yellow-Orange* (1920). (Also illustrative are Sheeler's *Abstraction: True Form* [1914], Sayen's *Scheherazade* [1915], and Yarrow's *Flowers* [c. 1920].) Macdonald-Wright's *Abstraction on Spectrum (Organization No. 5)*(1914) and *Conception Synchromy* (1914) appear to be moving toward nonobjectivity, but nevertheless still turn on the spiral extracted from the earlier interest in the essence of the human form. When Levin observed that the essential figurativeness of *Synchromy in Deep Blue-Violet* and *Synchromy in Orange: To Form* has been consistently overlooked and misinterpreted, she called attention to the Synchromists' interest in the empirical, natural world prior to their departure toward a more purified realm of nonobjective foundations.[48]

Precipitated by his "spiralic plunge into space, excited and quickened by appropriate color contrasts,"[49] Russell's *Cosmic Synchromy* (1913–14) and *Conception Synchromy* (1915) move even closer toward nonobjectivism and are works that perhaps blur the line between abstract and nonobjective moments of early Synchromist aesthetics. These works, too, play upon the rhythmic undulation of color in a spiral that unfolds in time. It can be argued though not only that the painting itself unfolds in time like music, but also that the level of abstraction itself spirals toward nonobjectivity and progressively more pure realizations of what were previously cruder morphological essences, i.e., that the idealized or purer essential form of the morphological essence is made visible in a dramatically more irreal gradation of clarity.

Russell's *Archaic Composition No. 1* and *Archaic Composition No. 2*, both of 1915–16, are illustrative of the closest early Synchromy came to a statement of pure irreality. In fact, Russell noted of these works that he "sought a 'form' which, though necessarily archaic, would be fundamental and permit of steady evolution."[50] The gradations of clarity and the level of eidetic purity (irreality) are most profound in these works. Yet Levin points out that these two paintings were based on the artist's self-portraits.[51] As such the morphological is purified as much as possible without actually obliterating its grounding in the concrete, which would have had the effect of idealizing the prior ideation and moving it toward the more purely fictive, a level of intellectualism to which the Synchromists were deeply opposed.

Macdonald-Wright remained within the framework of Synchromy theory after 1915, even through his works in the 1950s. Russell, on the other hand, in a series of works in the early 1920s known as the *Eidos* paintings, explored synchromy in its most nonobjective possibility. Nonetheless, it can be said that Synchromist painting remained faithful to nature and to the heroic figure, pursuing the "the happy risk of falling on some of the correspondences that exist between reality and our sensations of color."[52] Its conception and display of essences thus remained within the orbit of the morphological, with intimations of the possibility of imagining purer essences.

PAINTED IRREALITY: PERFECTLY IRREAL ESSENCES

In the painting and philosophy of Vasilii Kandinsky the notion of the irreal is given a sense that resonates with and is more profound than Husserl's renderings. For Kandinsky art is a vehicle of transcendence, a means by which noumenal and cosmic ideas can be evoked and expressed. Art for Kandinsky possessed a spiritual, messianic character, evident in the apocalyptic and eschatological themes and motifs embedded in his works. It could be no other way, for operative in the artist, as in the cosmos itself, is the undeniable "inner necessity" of the Spirit unfolding. A conception of transcendence resides in the works of both Husserl and Kandinsky, yet they are dramatically different in their philosophical commitments (though similar in their therapeutic desire). Nonetheless, Kandinsky's expression of essence, imagination, and irreality addresses a realm not completely unfamiliar to that of Husserl, particularly Husserl's notion of pure essences.

Kandinsky developed his thought in the light of a pervasive antimaterialist philosophy that swept through Europe and Russia at the end of the century. Voices of this *zeitgeist* included the French symbolists, theosophy, anthroposophy, gnosticism, mysticism, and related sciences of the "occult." The force of this chorus rippled through philosophy, music, painting, architecture, science, and the literary arts. As Kandinsky observed:

Our epoch is a time of tragic collision between matter and spirit and of the downfall of the purely material world view; for many, many people it is a time of terrible, inescapable vacuum, a time of enormous questions; but for a few people it is a time of presentiment or of precognition of the path to Truth.[53]

It was Kandinsky's belief that abstract painting, like music and other contemporary abstract arts, could induce a new vision for humanity. He envisioned the artist as one capable of revealing the indubitable foundations of truth. He saw the artist as an "invisible Moses,"[54] a prophet who brings to the blind the "inner vibrations" that were "lied about or passed over in silence" by positivists and materialists.[55] As Volboult noted, for Kandinsky "naturalism with its monotonous repetitions hovered on the surface of things. Form loses its vitality in repetition."[56]

To overcome this mundane taken-for-grantedness and its loss, the artist is required to hold this reality in abeyance or to fathom it and look toward its possibility. In Husserl's phenomenology, this is the *epoché*. In a line from Kandinsky's autobiography, published in the same year as Husserl's *Ideas* (1913), he remembered the passage into the world of form and color:

> I first learnt to look at a picture not only from the outside but to enter into it, to move around in it and to take part in its life . . . I had noticed this sensation before . . . but unconsciously and confusedly. Now only for the first time I received it in its fullness.[57]

To enter and move around inside the thing, thus seeing and knowing its genesis as well as essential structure, was crucial for Kandinsky. This grounded his interest in abstraction. Abstraction was a means of bypassing the world of appearances that masks the soul of things. He sought to dissolve or dematerialize objects in order to know the "inner sounds" or "inner vibrations" constitutive of their presence.[58] He aimed to "make the invisible visible."[59] This invisible is "the spirit," the "origin," and "true author" of all works and things.[60] It is here that Kandinsky's supreme principle becomes visible: the principle of "inner necessity."[61]

Inner necessity is the interiority or essential inner meaning that lends things their presence and form, which in turn is constitutive of their objectivity. Inner necessity is the metaphysical or cosmic principle of the spirit manifesting itself, knowable with greatest clarity in the intuitions of the soul. While Kandinsky implied a mystical and occult rather than intellectual sense in his use of the word *spiritual*,[62] nonetheless, the intellect and imagination of the artist are important in selecting and translating intuitions into forms capable of generating a transformative radiance. Inner necessity is the realm of Essential Being—that which is irreal and gives things their coherence and meaning, that without which they would not be. The harmony of each form is not only a resonance of truth and beauty, but also an indication of that which, if violated or omitted, would destroy the fundamental essentiality of the thing. Inner necessity is the legal space of all that is, and it

> arises from the colour and rhythm of movement, from forms in space, as an extremely sensitive demand from a categorical imperative and an *élan vital* of the creative conscience aspiring to express the 'eidetic presences' which are *purer than phenomenological perception*, in the more mysterious and fascinating reality which is the essence of the spirit in its infinite variety.[63]

As Kandinsky noted, "every phenomenon passes man, leaving behind its trace brushing against his soul."[64] Volboult suggests of inner necessity that it is a

> radiance spreading within the artist's consciousness, becoming part of the very movement of his actions. It is a presence, as it were, which affects and determines his deepest being. It introduces events, images, and impulses in the artist's mind and forces him to express them.[65]

It is thus unavoidably necessary that the artist "eliminate" the world of mundane reality. Again Volboult: "to reach the concrete, the 'real' in Kandinsky's terminology, one must aim for the extreme limits of reality until its very existence is abolished."[66] Kandinsky's world of the "real" is Husserl's world of the irreal. This inner or reduced "invisible" world of essences is a world of objects. Husserl considered them so, noting they possess their own objectivity; so did Kandinsky. In fact, Kandinsky progressively preferred the term *concrete* as a description of his painting, indicating that the "objects" he presented (color, form) indeed possess an objectivity or reality.[67]

The objects created by the artist have their genesis in the inner necessity of the transcendent spirit manifesting itself in the soul of the artist. It surfaces in the intuition of the soul and resonates with the mind, generating

> strange illuminations. Images and signs are born, allusions to an inexpressible world, a universe of *virtualities* which the creator discovers like a disconcerting and familiar reality that would be at one and the same time intimate and unknown. The artist is the mediator of this '*elsewhere*' whose laws and conventions he has established.[68]

Indeed the artist helps establish this "elsewhere," this irreal "everywhere and nowhere." For although a work of art is born of the artist in a mysterious and secret way,[69] it becomes flesh only through the artist. It is here that intellect and imagination fulfill the "will" of inner necessity. Kandinsky observed in his autobiography, dated June 1913, that forms come almost exclusively "from within the artist." This echoes his positions elaborated earlier in *Concerning the Spiritual in Art* (1912) and in "The Problem of Form" (an essay in the <u>Blaue Reiter Almanach</u>, 1912). In *Point and Line to Plane* (1926) Kandinsky further clarified his revelations, effecting a full reduction of natural forms to point and line and their relations to space, form, and color: "in the last analysis, all have originated as points, and it is to the point in its geometrical essence that everything returns."[70] Earlier, in *Concerning the Spiritual in Art*, he had anticipated that "the final abstract expression of every art is number."[71]

It is clear that Kandinsky was very much concerned with the grasp of essential possibility. Kandinsky's Desire, like Husserl's, was to move in the space of the irreal. Volboult notes the intention of Kandinsky's Desire:

> The imagination moves freely in a labyrinth of possibilities. Kandinsky wished to penetrate these "spiritual" sites and, in this way, break away from this side of the visible and travel to infinity . . . to find oneself at the center of a reality that has been freed of all accidents, where one can discover the simplest and at the same time most intense structures of sensibility.[72]

Kandinsky's work is concerned with the genetic and with the irreal. From intuition supplied by inner necessity, form begins to appear, and its voyage toward the natural, mundane object is traceable. For Kandinsky, as for Husserl, spirit begins where conventional materialism ends. While separated by their respective metaphysical and epistemological commitments, the focus on the possibility and creation of meaning and the coming-to-be-of-form of objects is of profound interest to each. A journey through Kandinsky's paintings illuminates the stripping away and transcendence of the mundane, the recovery of possibility in abstraction, the statement of that possibility as eidetic object, and the progressive movement from ideation to idealization, thus purifying the object so its very constitution becomes evident.

Visible in Kandinsky's work is a continually evolving meditation on the purer forms of irreality, those closer to and more profoundly evocative of the "unknown voice," the title of a painting done in 1916. As this painting would suggest, by 1916 Kandinsky had effected his *epoché* in full—his vision had recovered the source of meaning and plentitude, though it did not by any means exhaust its infinity. In phenomenological terms, the period between 1900 and 1916 is particularly interesting, for it reveals Kandinsky's continual overcoming of the mundane via a presentation of morphological essences, and a progressive overcoming of the morphological in favor of the more rarefied irreality of nonobjective constructions.[73] As he noted in the magazine *XXme Siècle* in 1938, "this art creates alongside the real world a new world which has nothing to do externally with reality. It is subordinate internally to cosmic laws."[74]

In the time between 1900 and about 1906–7, Kandinsky experimented with postimpressionism (e.g., *Beach Chairs in Holland*, 1904; *Santa Margherita*, 1906) and with Fauvism (e.g., *Couple on Horseback*, 1903; *Landscape at Murnau*, 1907). These appealed to him more than cubism or futurism because of their intense penchant for color and feeling and for their de-emphasis of rationalism. The dematerialization of naturalistic forms is obvious in a series of paintings done after this time. For instance, in such works as *Landscape with Tower* (1908), *Village Church* (1908), *Picture with Archer* (1909), *Train in Murnau* (1909), *Mountain* (1909), *Murnau with Church I* (1910), *Study for Composition II* (1910), *Improvisation XII* (1910), *Lyrically* (1911), *Romantic Landscape* (1911), and *Arabs II* (1911), Kandinsky began to reduce the representational aspects of objects. Yet a commitment to naturalistic morphology still reigned. As he became more and more concerned with his procedure of "hidden construction," accomplished by "stripping and veiling,"[75] as a means of developing the spirit-evoking nature of color and form, morphological essences were progressively reduced. Yet he wrote, "however diminished in importance organic forms may be, their internal sound will always be heard, for this reason the choice of natural objects in painting is an important one."[76]

Stripping and veiling led to more abstract and purified renderings of the irreality of morphological essences. This is evident in the two panels of 1911, *St. Georg I* and *St. Georg II*. It is also exemplified in *Impression 3* (1911), *Improvisations V, VII, XIV, 19, XXVI*, and *Arabs III (with Pitcher)* (1911). As Kandinsky noted, an improvisation is a "largely unconscious, spontaneous expression of inner character, non-material nature."[77] He further stated, "the hidden construction may be composed of seemingly fortuitous shapes, without apparent connection. But the outer absence of such a connection is proof of its inner presence. Outward loosening points toward an internal merging."[78] The movement from intuition as felt, sensuous apprehension toward ideation and on toward idealization continued to accelerate.

The movement toward a purer revealing of essence and spirit lead to a sustained stripping away of representation. The interest in abstract morphology gave way to more rarefied, nonobjective works. In an entry in his autobiography dated June 1913, he noted his paintings now were derived from *within the artist* rather than from nature, referring to them as "objectless."[79] What he meant by this can be seen in works such as *Composition IV* (1911), *Improvisation 30* (1913), *Painting with White Form* (1913), *Composition VII* (1913),

Improvisation Deluge (1913), *Improvisation Gorge* (1914), and *Untitled Improvisation* (1914). Indeed, he had plunged fully into the irreal, where the "outward loosening" and "outer absence" of connections surrendered the full presence of inner necessity.

In the 1920s, and up to 1944, when he died, Kandinsky's work became vigorously more nonobjective and precise. The essential relations of color, form, and space were presented with greater exactness and clarity. His works took on the character he described in 1912 as "compositions": an expression of a slowly formed inner feeling, tested and worked over repeatedly . . . Reason, consciousness, purpose play an overwhelming part."[80] Ideation gave way to idealization, and his paintings became statements of pure essence—"perfectly irreal" manifestations of the imagination of inner necessity. That his works had nothing to do externally with reality, as he had proclaimed in _Xxme Siècle,_ is made abundantly obvious in works such as *Red Oval* (1920), *On White* (1923), *Composition VIII* (1923), *Calm Tension* (1924), *Yellow, Red, Blue* (1925), and *Circles* (1926). *Hard and Soft*, 1927 is particularly interesting, pictorially as well as thematically, for it suggests the coalescence of the essential, the innerly necessary, in the miasma of the accidental and inessential. It is this that defines essence, whether inexact morphological or perfectly irreal: that which makes things form, that form which makes things—that which is the very possibility of their meaning. Works such as *Quiet Assertion* (1929), *Moving Veils* (1930), *Soft Pressure* (1931), *Movement I* (1935), *Dominant Curve* (1936), *Animated Stability* (1937), and *Yellow Canvas* (1938) can be considered instances of further elaborations of essential insight into perfect irreality—imaginative variations of the infinite transcendental spirit peering as far as possible into the inner necessity of itself and of things.

The year 1913 was a pivotal year for many artists searching for an abstract style.[81] Kandinsky did not refer to his own works as abstract (i.e., "objectless") until then. The year 1913 was also a critical turning point in Husserl's phenomenology. Breton similarly locates 1913 as the year of his true awakening.[82] Though Kandinsky noted that by "spiritual" he did not necessarily mean "intellectual,"[83] he also did not exclude it as a dimension of artistic creativity. With the assistance of reason and imagination, the artist "chooses" and "constructs" objects that fulfill the presence of inner desire. Husserl, on the other hand, confined himself to the intellectual aspects of "spiritual," particularly those aspects relative to epistemology, leaving issues of noumena, Spirit/Being, and soul out of his discourse. Yet despite these profound differences and the uncanny coincidence of their appearance, in Kandinsky's meditations on pure irreality,[84] Husserl's thought comes to light in color and form. One witnesses the utter beauty and allure of pure essentiality. And its necessity!

FROM IRREALITY TO SURREALITY, TOWARD ALTEREALITY

The critiques of positivism, rationalism, and materialism that so moved Husserl, the Synchromists, and Kandinsky also moved Dali. More frenzied and radical than theirs, however, his derealizing practices included an intransigent desire to scandalize and cretinize subjectivity and objects of knowing. To the Surrealists, and to Dali, the complacency of bourgeois philosophy and aesthetics was despicable. Dali was especially contemptuous of their obsession with abstraction, logical intuition, and logocentric discourses that constituted the means by which knowing and perceiving, and thus reality, were grasped and understood. The accompanying assumptions of the decipherability of consciousness and objects, and a discerning of their immanent, essential structures, i.e., their "real" nature, were, for Dali, a disgraceful and miserable feature of modernity. Referring to the wretchedness of abstract art, abstract creation, and nonfigurative art, Dali exclaimed:

> Sticky and retarded Kantians of scatological *sections d'or*, they continue to want to offer us upon the fresh optimism of their shiny paper the soup of the abstract aesthetic, which really and truly is even worse that the cold and colossally sordid vermicelli soups of neo-thomism, which even the most convulsively hungry cats would not go near.[85]

While not specifically singling out Husserl, the Synchromists, or Kandinsky, Dali was outraged by any rhetoric of purity[86] that would presume the certainty and clarity of essential meaning. He "hated simplicity in all its forms,"[87] for the character of consciousness (i.e., the noetic) and objects (i.e., the noematic) is that they are exorbitantly fecund and deliriously *con-fused*.

Dali's dithyrambic discourse, in the form of the productions of the paranoiac-critical method, gave Surrealism one of its most potent and controversial strategies. The paranoiac-critical method shared with the phenomenologies of Husserl, the Synchromists, and Kandinsky the recognition that things are other than they appear and that consciousness has access to and desires this other. This parallel interest in what exceeds the mundane nature of reality, however, is where Dali separated himself from logical intuitionists and abstractionists generally, and from Husserl specifically. For Husserl's epistemological approach was one given to apodictic foundations whose clarity and necessity were made evident via the apparatus of the "rigorous science" of phenomenological reflection and the "return to things themselves." Dali delighted in observing that the aseptic intellectualism and sterile cleanliness of such approaches were inevitably cuckolded by the ecstasy of realities whose shameless exhibitionism enticed only the slaves and fools of rational clarity.

The phenomenological *epoché* of Husserl, as well as the abstraction of the Synchromists and the dematerialization of Kandinsky, shared with Surrealist derealization the notion of rupture. Such rupture is desirable and permits a grasp of what is "really" real, as distinguished from the "false" reality of the natural attitude whose tendency is to unquestioningly take things for granted. Yet there is a distinct difference between the Surrealist notion of derealization and that of Husserlian phenomenology. Like Husserl, Surrealism eschewed Cartesian and Kantian metaphysics that posited a duality between the knowable and the unknowable. Unlike the Surrealists, however, Husserl ignored metaphysical questions in favor of epistemological issues. The Surrealists, on the other hand, collapsed epistemological questions into the metaphysical problem of locating within the world (vs. otherworldliness, e.g., spiritualism, Kandinsky) and within the relation of consciousness and world, the possibility of encountering the Other that would open and transform consciousness and world. Surreality thus was promoted over irreality. Rather than stripping and reducing features of the world to their transcendental and immanent possibilities and then gathering them together in the embrace of discrete, universal (though non-Platonic) essential structures, whose coherence was guaranteed by a certain necessity, Surrealism celebrated a consciousness that synthesized, convulsively and ambivalently, and supposedly without unity,[88] any number of disparate realities: dreams, hallucinations, libidinous callings, logic, delirium, madness, illusion, objective chance, phantasy, and the like. All such realities were considered to hold equal validity and credibility on the same plane of the real, i.e., the *surreal*. Together they would overcome the conflict generated by the unfortunate, arbitrary sociohistorical separation of inner consciousness and external reality. It was Breton's hope that such surrealist activity would "bring about the state where the distinction between the subjective and the objective loses its necessity and value."[89]

The Surrealist project aimed at reconciling knowledge and world, desiring to set the record straight as to what is real and what is necessary to make humans whole. As such it shared phenomenology's therapeutic and revolutionary ambitions. For Dali, though, the issue was much more serious. Although he did align himself early on with Surrealist aesthetics and with the desire to discredit ordinary consciousness and its sensibilities, he quite often was ideologically farthest from Surrealism when he appeared closest. His diatribes against science, rationalism, logic, idealism, and the clarity of essential knowing went far beyond the kind of reconcilable tensions the Surrealists aimed to deploy.

What Dali shared with Surrealism, initially, was the tendency to derealize conventional (and mediocre) mundane consciousness. He too sought to surprise, bewilder, and disrupt the rational crutches that the coherence and discourse of such consciousness so heavily leaned upon. He drew upon the fluidity of reality, celebrated in Breton's *Poisson soluble* and in Gaudi's undulatory architecture, as well as upon the deranging possibilities of humor, love, and poetry. Installing them as liquidation, colliquation, and digestion, he generated in them the simulacra of breakdown and excess that were inevitably to grow beyond and transgress the Surrealist desire to expose the wholeness of humans as they "really are." Liquescence was to tell of more than just the motility and flux of things fluid and their evocation of metamorphosis. It was also to call out anamorphosis, desecration, and *aneconomimesis*:[90] liquidation, eradication. This much was further supported by his paranoiac cannibalism, which made of reality a delectable object and event of digestion.[91] Transgressive and violent, cosmic and aesthetic, the edibility of anything and everything was more than simply a gastronomic indulgence. Succulence ravished and devoured was a simulacrum of chymic flow, dissolution, and efflux.

At the core of Dali's problem with logic, idealism, rationalism, logical intuition, and the like, and thus with Husserl, was the issue of certitude and foundationalism. Husserl's Desire was to establish knowledge on an unquestionable foundation of certainty. The search for certainty was for him synonymous with the development of European culture (what Dali termed, *L'age d'or*) and he feared the threat of skepticism and relativism. The very notions of contingency, temporality, and existential situatedness were contaminants that could be overcome by establishing unshakable foundations. What Husserl sought was a primordial insight where things are revealed directly and undistortedly to consciousness. This insight would yield apodictically necessary knowledge that would constitute a certainty not dependent on actual experience. Such transcendental knowledge would be pure, secure, and undubitable.

Husserl's Desire was moved by a will to presence. It took as evident that presence is the *telos* of consciousness. The "miracle of miracles" was the immediate self-givenness of subjectivity to itself. According to Husserl, certitude inhabits meaning due to the absolute immediacy of subjectivity to itself, its ability to intuit its own presence. The assumption that consciousness is transparent or immanent to itself assures there is no mediation capable of distorting or deferring certitude. The ability to immediately intuit its own presence situated consciousness as a foundation beyond any reference to a psychological or historically constituted subject or any of its emanations. Indeed the transcendental nature of consciousness displaced existential identity in favor of an ideal identity.

The ideality or irreality of identity is arrived at not by any perceptual process, but by imagination, and it is here that imagination is elevated over perception (and history). Husserl described an imaginary conversation subjectivity has with itself concerning its presence to itself. This soliloquy or monologue is, however, fictive, and even Husserl noted that fiction makes up the life of phenomenology as well as all the eidetic sciences. In his scheme the fictive and the ideal were complicit and parasitic, and without them certainty would vanish into the vicissitudes of temporality. Meaning then, as an apodictic necessity, as certainty, exists only as it is constituted in and by transcendental consciousness. Meaning did not exist independently but was supplied by creative acts of, or as an accomplishment of, consciousness. To say that this meaning is transcendental, then, is to say that its validity is independent of actual experience. Husserl's Desire to capture this knowledge was deployed so that the possibility of meaning could be established. Establishing this idea fictively is what yields certainty.

It is not enough that Husserl complicated knowledge of meaning with the assumption of intuitive self-presence. Intuition, as the grasp of what is given, was further complicated by Husserl's insistence that consciousness constituted the object of knowing. This can be seen clearly through the process of eidetic intuition, i.e., the process by which what is interior to an object is separated from what is not essentially given in it. The essential structure of an object is a correlate of the intentional acts of transcendental consciousness that constitute it; thus, the facility of imagination is operative here too. The process of free imaginative variation illustrates how imagination clarifies and fulfills what is intuited, thus real-izing the teleological destiny of meaning. The necessity that provides the initial coherence is, of course, never completed in phenomenological description of essences, but a necessity is established as a means of distinguishing one thing from another. In Husserl's scheme, intuition is the primordial act; imagination establishes the full sense of what a thing is. Imagination provides clarity and certainty and delineates interiority and alterity.

What is curious about this is not just the admission that fiction, as a constitutive act, provides the meaning of things, but that the idealistic requirement of such thought carries with it an arbitrariness. That this arbitrariness protrudes so ostensibly is something that cannot be ignored. The effort to establish certainty inevitably structures and makes static what is oblique and fugitive. Precisely this is what so disturbed Dali—not just that "reality" was thwarted by being held captive by arbitrary essentializing, but that phantasy was being enslaved and prostituted for the sake of purity and security. Even though Husserl's views on the properties of essences shifted during his career from a concern with the intuition of essences (*Wessenchau*) to the constitution of essences (*Leistung*) to the considerations demanded by a return to the lifeworld taken up in his final works, there is nonetheless the notion throughout Husserl's work that essences can be known with coherence and certainty by a consciousness that generates determinate fictive understandings.[92] That essential knowledge and clarity are fiction or phantasy is a delicious and digestible notion Dali could not resist submitting to the machinations of paranoiac-critical activity.

The strategy Dali deployed played on the notion of self-evident givenness and its ability to explicate its own sense. To a degree this anticipates Derrida's critiques of Husserl in *Speech and Phenomena* and *Edmund Husserl's Origin of Geometry: An Introduction*. What makes such reference possible is Dali's siting of an abiding and enigmatic crevice in the mythology of "the present"— an absence that is more and other than simply the opposite of presence in the logic of the dialectical binary of presence/absence. Such a siting is akin to Derrida's sense that Husserl generated a logocentric discourse by granting a primacy to cognition, reason, and science, and a simultaneous autonomy to the latter to explore and thereby establish themselves as a font of certain knowing. This opened an enormous space of unrecuperable difference, one that even set Dali at odds with Surrealism itself. For this space made it

possible for multiple and disparate phantoms to meander in unbecoming ways.

Dali promoted a delirious *epoché* that asserted the power of
surreality over irreality. The "irreal" for Husserl were those features
of transcendentally reduced pure phenomena that were other than
the real, physical, everyday world. These "ideal realities" were available mediately, via logical intuition, to a transcendental subject (ideally) primordially present to itself. Husserl's irreality belongs to or
inhabits the eidetic or essential character of things in the world.
Yet, due to their ideality, the irreal and the essential persist as an
alterity within the real, physical world. They are not, however,
divorced from meaning. In fact they are the possibility and indubitable ground of any possible meaning of a thing. What is presup-
posed is that in intuition there is intended or grasped an ideal, objective noematic sense that is capable of being fulfilled as a logical and
general concept. It is presumed that there is a necessity here that
operates as a "truth" that in principle is repeatable *ad infinitum*.
Meaning, then, as a noematic structure, emerges as atemporal,
invariant, and ideal. Particular worldly meanings either belong to
(i.e., refer to and adumbrate) a particular noematic structure in that
they essentially constitute that structure—or they do not, in which
case they belong to some other structure, or to non-sense. In either
case, Husserl's Desire sustains the assumption of repetition. It is
here, however, that ideality and representation clash, for the colla-
tion of profiles that establishes the true nature of a thing inevitably
requires temporal and variable horizons that are situated in the world
and cannot be taken from it. In other words, the meanings of things
inevitably involve interpretations if they are not to be solipsistic
and purely subjective. Inscribed in meaning are multiples of sedimented features that, when liberated from the assumption of ideality
that constitutes their totality and unity, take on the character of
singularities that do not necessarily cohere as a particular meaning
structure.

This inability to cohere holds not only for the noematic
structure of objectivity but also for the integrity of the noetic
structure of subjectivity. The elaboration of the latter is what the
Surrealists sought in asserting the crisis of the subject and the
object, which Dali endlessly intensified. The rupture of repetition is the Nietzschean Camembert Dali substitutes as a crutch
for Husserl's phenomenology, whose essences are even more pure
than the convulsive essences Surrealism offers on the plate of its
shiny optimism.

A Dalinian *epoché* makes it obvious that Husserl's *epoché* and subsequent imaginative variation constitute a "voluntary hallucination"[93] that, in "seeking refuge in an ideal world," manifests a "swinish . . . hatred of reality."[94] The subjugation of flux and chance to the "fossilization" or "ossification" of essentializing coherence was for Dali not only arbitrary, but "premature." In *Premature Ossification of a Railway Station* (1930), for instance, there is the sense that what identity seeks to stabilize, other ambient phantoms are already decomposing. A dialectic of stabilization/destabilization is not at work, however, only endless "obscenity"[95] whose surplus postpones the closure of essence. The forestalling of closure relegates the rules by which essences coagulate to a future that never arrives (cf. Lyotard's "postmodern art"), making any presentation of their contours premature. Dali's "perversion," then, consists not so much in what psychoanalysis can lend to his various desecrations. It lies instead in the sodomizing of universals and essential structures, in the ravishing of the borders of certainty, and in the exhibitionism of what LIES at those very margins.

Dalinian hyperderealization thus proceeds genealogically as a destructive retrieval of singularities that liberates them from the arbitrary conscription that combines them as profiles of a particular unity, and instead celebrates them as the very particularities that they are: singularities that are ineluctably *con-fused*. But that is not all. To these *con-fused* singularities that are a counterpoint to Husserl's phenomenologically reduced particulars that exist as singularities joining to form distinct essential structures, Dali conjoined the false reality of mundane consciousness. That is to say, Dalinian derealization juxtaposes the "real" (that which is arrived at by *epoché*) with the "false real" (the reality of everyday, unreflective awareness). The net effect of this doubling is to obscure the distinctiveness of any given reality, whether in the phenomenologically reduced sphere or in the sphere of the mundane. This *con-fusion* of the "really real" with the "false real" ruptures the rupture sought by Husserl (and by the Synchromists and by Kandinsky). This amounts to Dali's unique version of the death of God, reinscribed here as the death of the essence and of the clarity dwelling within. As Kolakowski has submitted, for Husserl to suggest the attainability of certitude independent of our biological and sociohistorical existence makes of us Gods.[96] It is the ontotheology of Husserlian-like thought Dali profanes, just as Desnos had profaned Breton's thought. Out of Dalinian phenomenology emerges another sense of immanence—the arrival of colliquative "essences" and their solicitations of phantom meaning.

More, though, than just a desecration of logical intuitionism and abstraction, such a parodic approach also inevitably set Dali outside Surrealism. The juxtaposition of the "really real" and the "false real" inserted an exorbitant alterity into the essential ambivalence of existence celebrated by Surrealism. Because Surrealist derealization required a negation of negation in order to avoid nihilism, relativism, and eclecticism and to enhance the encounter with the surreality of existence, i.e., humans as they "really are," Dali's program went from being an ally to being a heresy. Dali introjected another negation, a third negation, into Surrealist derealization, making it forever impossible to exclude or include the question of an unrelievable (*relever*) alterity from their hope of a reconciliation that would overcome all other contradictions or separations. The development of the paranoiac-critical method, particularly between 1930 and 1938, is the story of just this movement. It is a story of the insertion of the death of God into the ontotheology of Surrealism—into the soul of the necessity of the symbolically functioning object—into the soul of necessity resident in a crisis-laden (furthered also by Surrealism's own work) subjectivity that somehow (for the Surrealists) dialectically thwarted the forces of *an-arche*.

By the time of *Endless Enigma* (1938), the subversion of Surrealism's ontotheology was accomplished. Dali had succeeded in destabilizing the swinish architecture of modern art, architecture, and aesthetics and its "hatred of reality." Although he apparently espoused an idealism with no ideals, which Breton applauded, he also managed to espouse an anti-architectural (as in Bataille's reading of Hegel) and countermemorial strategy that would nonteleologically blossom as a sunflower in the dark blue light of *nonsavoir*. Dali was expelled from Surrealism in 1939. Coincidentally, Husserl died in 1938.

Dali had succeeded in scandalizing Surrealism by displacing the utopia of the marvelous and installing in its place the heterotopia of diversity and surplus. The profanation of the dialectic as the God of embrace (of contradictory singularities) and the opening of a rupturous, a-signifying delay and deferral, situated a silence in the dialectic that would forever be exterior to it. This silence, however, sublime and awe-ful, resists simple reduction to nihilism. It marks the space within which the new can emerge—"news" that were (was) not already located or implied within the conciliatory hold of automatism's essence or necessity. A daimonic space—intermezzo—unfinished—where vagabond "essences" roam, affirming their difference, taking endless time to become. For Dali, as for Nietzsche and de Chirico, this is a space of alterity, a time for a creativity and affirmation other than that necessitated within the sublative circuitry of dialectical eventing. Nor is this a banishing of hope, nor is it a blasphemy, as Breton had received it. Nor is it nihilism or anarchy. Instead, a celebration of the surplus fecundity of chance and plentitude.

THE STINKING ESSENCE

The special concern here is to reread the place of Salvador Dali within the Surrealist movement. In particular, the focus is on the years 1929–38, the years spanning Dali's most intensely creative and outrageous artistic and philosophical/theoretical production. Situating Dali, or *dalilectics*,[1] outside of the Hegelian and psycho-analytic discourses so commonly deployed to circumscribe his work, is an intervention in textual politics. Exploring the subversiveness of *dalilectics* reveals the perilous nature of Dali's discourse for the Surrealists. Dali's surrealism succeeded in pushing Surrealist thought to such an advanced degree that it was forced to stand outside its own project. The genesis of the most advanced and diabolically allusive surrealist object/contrivance, phantom meaning, took Surrealism out of the discourse of modernity and situated it about its borders. This frenzied advance's struggle to assert its voice, silent all these years, can now be told, again.

Dali's surreality was a hemophiliac bleeding in the soul of Surrealism. All the bandages and crutches applied to its flows were but so many masks whose eyes and lips oozed the reasons and justifications of constraint and inhibition, all of them warranted from some ideology of purity. All of them were fictions that tried to hide a motion, fictions that could not reveal their own truth for fear of falling from their phantom carts, under whose absent wheels they would have been silenced.

Surrealism assaulted reality in order to place its own overlay on the magical, mysterious vagaries of transformation it celebrated. Reading from a postmodern site loosens the ossifying forces covered over in Surrealism's official histories of Dali. With its divine annunciation of essence-of-metamorphosis doctrines, Royal Surrealism ironically endangered its own intended deranging of identity and representation. A rereading reveals this endangering by advancing a dangerous reading of Dali. For it was Dali who exacerbated and amplified the scandal already at work in Surrealism's cretinization of consciousness and reality. Such a reading thus raises the question of Surrealism's subversion of itself by its denuding of the mechanism by which this negative productivity occurred. It discloses, as do Nietzsche's and Foucault's genealogies, that desire, power, and knowledge both produce and suppress voices in favor of a Voice. It reveals how Dali's voice was quieted in favor of Surrealism's obsessing desire for Essence.

Within Dali's work are located the suppressed traces of a future discourse, one that would inevitably return to vindicate the hyperlucid delirium of his radical phenomenology of immanence and its discourse of alterity and exteriority, of excess and transgression. Dali's discourse was suppressed by critiques that substituted for its unruliness fables of embrace and recuperation. Dangerous in that it freed the force(s) of change, his discourse endlessly surpassed the dream of identity.

No effort is made here to force on Dali the semiotics of postmodern discourse. To do so would suggest identifying him—a ploy sure to self-destruct. No attempt is made to develop a theory or to attribute an interiority. Those too would quickly slide in the soft, spreadable cheese of excessive alterity, just as philosophy and science had earlier stumbled about on the viscous skids of Dalinian words and images. Instead, Dali is taken seriously, focusing particularly on the years 1929 to 1938, the period prior to what Breton termed Dali's "self-kleptomania." Dali's incandescence is tendered as more and other than what Finkelstein suggested as "an ambience-forming element" that carries "hidden" meanings.[2] Specifically, then, this reading of Dali is a liberation of the hyperreal lucidity of delirious nomadism—a digestible crutch sure to dissolve as the first rays of representation appear in the night of analysis.

As is well known, the Surrealists maintained that anyone can be a surrealist. Herein lies its revolutionary contribution to the metamorphosis and emancipation of human existence. To be a Surrealist, however, was quite another matter. This status was either decided by or strongly influenced by the proclamations of Breton, articulator of the movement's canon. The history of invitation and exclusion has been documented.

Without recounting the whole of Dali and Breton's direct and indirect communications, it is important to note some significant differences that compelled Breton to admonish or refuse Dali. Among their differences were controversies concerning Dali's discrediting of automatism in favor of active intervention, his scatology, his fascinations with monarchy, aristocracy, Catholicism, Franco, and Hitler, his refusal to join various political groups, his promotion of himself as the "primary surrealist" and the competitive threat this posed to Breton, his arrogance, his disturbing eccentricity, the humor and "cretinization" directed at the Surrealists themselves, the use of his art for personal exultation, his adoration of Meissonier, his excessive self-exploration and its relation to his exhibitionism, and a variety of other factors related to his exuberant manipulations and perversions of psychoanalysis, the ego, politics, money, religion, sex, aesthetics, humor, surrealist methods and goals, and whatever else (he) taunted (with) his wild imagination. All the latter were intolerable for Breton.

Dali's relationship with Surrealism, however, was not always combative and acrimonious. Dali saw Breton, initially, as his "new father." After the release of *Un Chien andalou* and for his first exhibition of paintings in 1929, Breton praised Dali as one with whom, for the first time, the windows of the mind were thrown wide open. He also suggested Dali was *une veritable menace*, not fully knowing how prophetic his description would be. The latter notes on Dali's and Breton's reciprocity are important, for they underscore the great admiration one had for the other, and they note Dali's fleeting embrace of and by the Surrealists. The success in 1929 of *Un Chien andalou*, as well as that of such paintings as *Illumined Pleasures*, *Accommodations of Desire*, *The First Days of Spring*, and *Portrait of Paul Eluard*, and Dali's illustration of the final number of *La Revolution Surréaliste*, which contained the *Second Surrealist Manifesto*, solidified the relationship.

The year 1929 was, however, also the year of two other paintings, *The Lugubrious Game* and *The Great Masturbator*, and together they began to threaten the bond between Dali and Breton. Not until 1930 did Dali propose the "paranoiac-critical method" in *La Femme visible*. In 1930 the poem "The Great Masturbator" also appeared. In 1931, Dali suggested that the surrealist object is an irrational object with symbolic function that is to be preferred to the earlier surrealist objects that arrive on the passive, nocturnal avenues of automatism and dreams. These paintings and writings articulated ideas already very much present in 1929, particularly those related to psychoanalysis and dialectical thought. The notions of excrement and ejaculation, central foci in *The Lugubrious Game* and *The Great Masturbator*, respectively, were heavily laden with Freudian symbolism, which was as much an effect of Dali's interest in psychoanalysis as it was the interpretive grid of his audiences.

Operative in these two paintings of 1929, and inscribed upon Dali's advance (and already a sign of its discontinuity), was the "rule" Dali and Bunuel had agreed upon as a guide for developing the script and imagery for *Un Chien andalou*: No idea or image that could lend itself to rational explanation would be acceptable. Only surprising images made available by opening the "doors to the irrational" would be permissible. The symbolic function of excrement, coprophagia, or masturbation, for instance, was an irrationality that intended to both assume and parody the dialectics of the soluble, communicating vessels of the conscious and unconscious mind(s). For psychoanalysis such actions are inevitably tied to the dynamics and symbolism of parental domination, rebellion, fear, anger, insecurity, neurosis, obsession, and the like. From a hermeneutic/alchemical vantage they can be seen as symbols intimating transition and metamorphosis, preludes to ascendance.

In neither case, however, are excrement or seminal fluid simply taken as that which stands outside of and is other than the body, be it the psychophysical or the textual-imaginal body. Dali argued with Breton repeatedly that such images were perfectly natural in that they emanate from the libidinous recesses of the psyche and from the body's own biological unconscious. Nonetheless, they took on for Breton and the Surrealists a sense of filth and a falling from ascendance—a negative metamorphosis. Breton attempted to overcome this threatening notion by insisting on a binary analysis that forever linked objects in paradoxical yet symbolic couplets. Binary analysis was essential to assure the operation of the dialectic in favor of the ascendance he envisioned as the essence of surreality. The poetics and logic of "the one in the other" asserted the symbol over the sign, substituted depth for laterality, imposed continuity over fragmentation, and promoted sublation and interiority over alterity and egress. The effect of Breton's code was to bring all stray motion and entities into a nonidealized ideal—a totality—that could transcend and transform singularities and incoherence. Metamorphosis was something, though elusive, that should never have its sense delayed or deferred any longer than necessary. Though it is true that Breton's "phantom object" was laden with a content that would surface in the conscious mind only at a point later in time, it was nonetheless cast in a dialectical framework—i.e., Freud's dialectic of the unconscious/conscious mind, or Marx's notion of the falsely conscious mind—that would assure its revolutionary activity.

Not until the early 1930s did Dali's relentless erosion and elision of the symbolic function of the irrational object become obvious. It appeared in two concurrent motions: the development of "psycho-atmospheric anamorphic objects" and the "paranoiac-critical method." The stirrings of these motions, evident in *The Great Masturbator* and later in *Premature Ossification of a Station* (1930), *The Persistence of Memory* (1931), *The Average Fine and Invisible Harp* (1932), *Myself at Age 10 when I Was the Grasshopper Child* (1933), *Average Atmospherocephalic Bureaucrat Milking a Cranial Harp* (1933), and *Atomspheric Skull Sodomizing a Grand Piano* (1934), did not reach a full level of crisis until 1938, the year of *Endless Enigma*, the year preceding Dali's final expulsion from the Surrealist circle.

In these works, emblematic of the work of the early to mid 1930s, symbols are soft, limp, tumescent. The Bataillean anti-architecture[3] of the symbol is not yet in full force, but clocks, skulls, penises, pianos, and other swollen objects push against edges and boundaries that keep them within the orbit of (a) form, within the possibility of an ascendant symbolization. Symbolization, as boundary formation/location, as essentializing, itself is stretched in works such as *Diurnal Fantasies* (1932), *Surrealist Architecture* (1933), *Atavistic Vestiges After the Rain* (1934), and *Hysterical and Aerodynamic Nude* (1934). Fluid Heraclitean fires (*Lighted Giraffes* 1936–37) burn at the borders of the molten symbolic, foretelling of their liquidation (*cf. The Birth of Liquid Desires*, 1932; *The Birth of Liquid Anguish*, 1932).

Distended, distorted skulls implicate the deformation of knowledge and the collapse of reflexivity. Such deformation stems from the liquidation and putrefaction of essences whose soft, viscous forms cannot but shift and flow in the turbulence of toxic time and the effervescense of profiles that fail to coalesce coherently. For time itself is liquid, soft and elusive, mercury on shiny mirror glass. Visible in *The Persistence of Memory* (1931) and *Soft Watches* (1933), as well as in *The Archeological Reminiscence of Millet's Angelus* (1933–35), is the slide of decomposing time, its relativity. Dali most eloquently illuminates this flow in the phantom cart paintings of 1933 (*Phantom Cart*) and 1934 (*The Moment of Transition*). The cart, a double image and a phantom object, disappears in the moment of transition. The moment of transition itself is the hero in the liberation of intensity from form. It is also the accomplice or culprit in the decay of boundaries and their failure to stem effluence. The moment of transition is the space of desire, both beautiful and violent, ugly and soft; these dyads Dali loved to fondle and profane.

Signs of the collapse of boundary and identity appear in the turning of anamorphism and deformity toward decomposition and effluence. In these paintings, rot intimates evanescence, rupture suggests incandescence. Images of death, mutilation, castration, and excrement appear in the physiognomy of distended membranes. Weak and unable to hold back the incursive onslaught of a desire for *hors-de-soi*,[4] "elsewhere" and "otherwise" shatter and eclipse interiority. *Autumn Cannibalism* (1936–37) and *Metamorphosis of Narcissus* (1936–37) suggest transformation, but *Autumn Cannibalism* reveals a mutilated reflexivity and referentiality that later breaks open in the *Endless Enigma. The Specter of Sex Appeal* (1934) and *The Rider of Death* (1935) revisit the site of the putrefying corpses (*Putrefied Bird* [1928] and *The Stinking Ass* [1928]). Only the comestible crutches of a futile Cartesian rationalism stand between the ectoplasmic, intrauterine substance of interiority of the symbolic and the terrible, undulant-convulsive hysteria of free signifiers. The film *L'Age d'Or* (1930), however, was the site of a supreme moment of rupture. Its disconnected signifiers cannibalized representative sense, resulting in an upheaval in both the virtual space of the symbol and the actual space of the theater, where riots and destruction accompanied its showing in movie houses.

Both pleasurable and painful, moral and immoral, surplus overwhelms the extensibility that images of protrusion would appear to contain. The transgression of (symbolic) membranes and limits is as much a moment of wonder as of desire, a fact/question to be phathomed, much as one would wonder about an *Average French Bread with Two Fried Eggs without a Plate, on Horseback, Trying to Sodomize a Crumb of Portuguese Bread* (1932). Mutilation, war, and destruction inscribe themselves as tears and openings in these membranes, visible in *Cannibalism of Objects* (1932 and 1937), *Soft Construction* (1936), and *Autumn Cannibalism* (1936–37). Benign time is exceeded by a treacherous loosening and violence.

Vividly apparent in the latter deformation and decomposition are the simulacra of transmutation and metamorphosis that utter no promises of conciliation or union. A consideration of the paranoiac-critical method and its implications for symbols and simulacra illuminates the latter. In *The Stinking Ass*, Dali promoted paranoiac activity as a means of discrediting reality. Paranoiac activity, admitting of "control and recognition," and thus differentiating itself from hallucination, is an "active advance" of the mind where images do not come solely from the unconscious. Springing rather from a mechanism "swiftly and subtly" making associations, paranoia uses the world to assert its dominating idea.[5] The effect is a delirium of interpretation systematizing confusion: a *con-fusion* of images, objects, and understanding. The process is not purely automatic and unconscious; rather it is coterminous with the active functioning of the mind. This paranoiac activity is the genesis of (at least) double images. Through a fearless continuation of the paranoiac advance, multiple images are made to appear. The "violent" disparity and lack of interpenetration between reality and images permits images (and desire) to assert themselves, hiding the many appearances of the concrete, engendering a crisis in both consciousness and objects, and thus in reality.

Indigenous to the action of the mind, according to Dali, the advance of paranoia is available for use by the unconscious. The paranoiac advance, itself a simulacrum of desire, situated in and between the passive and the active, was explored by Dali in his obsessive meditations on Millet's *Angelus* and on the legend of William Tell. Each meditation was accompanied by a variety of paintings, illustrations, and writings. Through works such as *William Tell* (1930), *The Old Age of William Tell* (1931), and *Enigma of William Tell* (1933), Dali overtly gave desire the names of eroticism and sexuality. Here themes of incestuous mutilation are raised, questions that can be raised only in a familial context. An inversion of the father/son relationship in the legend of William Tell and the Oedipus legend provides the space in which the authoritarian relationship of signifier and signified is challenged. What is to name and contain is confronted by what is eventful and inexorably singular. Their order is cut loose. Meaning is distended and opened to new possibilities. The accent of signification is liberated, free to visit according to the play of random, magnetic tensions. Who/what the author is and what the meaning is to be, if any at all, is the I of sense cut open by a violent slash, the repetition of the cutting motion that opened *Un Chien andalou*, much as it had earlier opened the eyes of Oedipus.

Perhaps Dali's most notorious obsession, other than Gala, was his paranoiac-critical appropriation of Millet's *Angelus*. Among the more celebrated images are *Meditation on the Harp* (1932–34), *Architectural Angelus of Millet* (1933), *Atavism at Twilight* (1933–34), and a series of drawings appearing in the illustration of *Les Chants de Maldoror* (1934). Together with the essay "Interpretation paranoiaque-critique de l'image obsedante L'Angelus de Millet," Dali deeply disturbed the entrenched, complacent eroticism of the subject-object binary. Just as active erection and ready receptacle had been exposed in a paranoiac fury, so too had the repressive duplicity of subject/object and signifier/signified. The paranoiac advance that denuded their shame and exposed their desire put them in a state of disarray. Automutilating in their desire to display and shelter desire, symbols and meanings expanded, the mortality and fragility of their corporeality (morphology) protruding and everywhere evident. Anamorphic, they lost their shape. Forms became engorged, distorted, and deranged by the libidinous force of a delirium of phantasmic silences and alternatives: singularities intimating the terrible possibilities of dissemination and excess.

Dali's liquid desires (masturbation, excretion, bleeding, putrefaction, blasphemy)[6] were not vulgar ropes cast across abysses of lack that solicit satiation and completion. Breton, though, took them to be the misguided, random emissions of physical automatism, and thus they were not beautiful among other Surrealist secretions. For Dali, however, they are not the detritus of the dialectic elevated to the status of "found objects"; rather, they are nothing less than waste and unproductiveness simulating the productivity and utility of evolution. The latter could be read psychoanalytically, as Rojas has so cleverly done, where Dali's masturbatory obsessions are taken as deriving doubly from his perverse virginity and his tortured "spitting" on his mother's grave. Such a reading, however, conveniently absorbs effluence and waste into the elasticity of a dialectical grid. Liquidation, perverse or not, is not here simply melting or liquefying, but a rupture of interiority and a rending of latency by *non-savoir* and useless expenditure. Already Bataille, Blanchot, Levinas, and others were assembling in the vicinity of an alta(e)r where essences would be sacrificed for a new aesthetics and ethics.

With the development of multiple and anamorphic images and meanings, Dali furiously and incessantly unleashed delirium and irrationality. Continually asserting himself as the only real Surrealist, his ebullience became problematic. At the tail end of *The Stinking Ass*, Dali proclaimed that surrealist images will "follow the free bent of desire at the same time as they are vigorously repressed." Nothing need be expected from these images but "disappointment, distaste, and repulsion," for they will take on the "forms and colours of demoralization and confusion."[7] It was not, however, simply Dali's shenanigans that aroused horror and anxiety. His sabotage and decomposition of symbols, meanings, and sense into an unrecuperable flow of disjunctions and delirium played a much larger role. His attack on consciousness and its imagery and meanings was paralleled only by the desire for the "destruction of reality . . . which, through infamous and abominable ideals of all kinds, aesthetic, humanitarian, philosophical, etc., brings us back to the clear springs of masturbation, exhibitionism, crime and love."[8] Later in his life Dali noted that Surrealism was the only space in which he could have unleashed these springs. Yet in the early 1930s, Dali put himself in the service of the Surrealist revolution, accepting such cretinizing activity as operating outside all aesthetic or moral preoccupations. He took this matter seriously, so much so that his interpreters and critics alike were forced to convert the seriousness into humor and weird eccentricity in order to contain it, simultaneously violating his seriousness and the humor embedded within it.

Surrealism finds its life and force in the moment and space of the object, be it image or verbal or physical object. From the time of the first manifesto, where Breton extolled Reverdy's juxtaposition of distant realities, the bipolarity of meaning was extremely important. Breton, codifier of Surrealist discourse, had always been enamored with a dualistic ontology and with a metaphysics colored by the reconciliation of dualities. Although multiplicity and plentitude preside over the mysteries of life, Surrealists tended to cauterize and form out of them a dualistic universe: man/nature, irrational/rational, marvelous/mundane, agony/ecstasy, dream/waking, conscious/unconscious, space/time, spirit/desire, automatic/intervention, and the like. Heraclitus, the cabalists, hermetics, alchemists, Hegelians, and Freudians, all saw opposites as being held in a vital tension. In the electric, magnetic space of this tension, a finite field coheres in which an infinite variety of permutations and metamorphoses are possible. Transformations occur through a capillary tissue, where the stuff of one pole or vessel flows into and communicates with that of the other.[9] Yet however loose or taught the disparities or contradictions between the dualities might be, a reconciliation or *point suprême* was always taken to be possible and the appropriate path to seek. The hope of resolution of opposites (the *exercise dialectique essentiel*) in a miraculous and liberating embrace occupied Breton from the *Second Manifesto* to the very last lines of his last poems. The need to mend contradictions or differences was as much a part of Breton, the healer/physician, as it was of the man in *Nadja*, who in the opening lines of the novel asked, "Who am I?" and who assumed, however convulsive its beauty might be, that he would find a marvelous identity that would make him whole.

As Carrouges has eloquently shown, Breton always took the arrival of the *point suprême* to be the recovery (refinding and healing) of the "lost colors of the time of the ancient suns." What happens in surreality is a moment, already long in motion and known to a "unique original faculty," that was derailed by "dissociative" traumas.[10] When Breton announced that the subjective and objective were once one, "to which the eidetic image bears witness," he was, reminiscent of Husserl, uniting the noetic and the noematic in a moment of transparent self-presence. He was also, more than Husserl would have dared, though Kandinsky would have cheered it, placing an original unity—an ontotheology, an available noumenal *savoir*—at the core of what it means to be human. The essence of the experience of the surreal and its materiality in objects, persons, events, etc., becomes substantial in a ray of the time and space of lost suns. Here light and origin travel with vision and *savoir*, as in Breton's claim, in *Communicating Vessels*, that the goal is "to bring to the light of day . . . a glimpse of [the] structure" of the capillary tissue that guarantees exchange and continuity.[11] The dialectic of the subjective and the objective—the one-in-the-other—is a replay of a universal automatism. Its elastic dialectic of past and present is a lovely moment of *anamnesis* and mimesis. The latter, of course, figure prominently in the production of Surrealist objects and images, whether those of pure psychic automatism or those where automatism is enhanced by active intervention (e.g., paranoiac-critical activity).

In the thought of Hegel, Breton found perhaps the richest expression of the dynamics of the *contradiction surmontée*.[12] The motion of the dialectic, in particular the moment of sublation (*Aufhebung*), was the key to the moment of crystallization in the *point suprême*, the metamorphisizing turn of the universe. For "the true strength of Surrealism lay in the fact that, at its best, it sought to raise consciousness and expand understanding of existence as a fluid state in which chaos and contradiction are resolved by transformation and metamorphosis."[13]

Returning to Dali, it is noteworthy that after his surrealist breakthrough in the paintings of 1929 and in *Un Chien andalou*, not to mention the outbursts of imagination, irrationality, and scandal they indexed, Breton saw a need to codify them. To locate them within the discourse of Surrealism was to control and channel their effervescence. Such a situating responded to the incantations of the Hegelian recuperative strategy. Prior to the publication of *The Visible Woman* in late 1930, Dali had already placed its most important essay, "The Stinking Ass," in an edition of *Le Surréalisme a.s.d.l.r.* earlier that same year. Dali's various activities and productions prompted Breton (with Eluard) to declare, in the foreword to *The Visible Woman*, that paranoiac-critical thought was, in effect, the alliance of dialectical and psychoanalytic thought. The year 1930 also saw the appearance of the *Second Manifesto of Surrealism*, in which the dialectics of Hegel and Marx were integrated into alchemical and psychoanalytic dialectics. And then in 1932 appeared *Communicating Vessels*, itself a classic celebration of sublation. The latter publications, while not designed as containers for Dali, as was the foreword to *The Visible Woman*, nonetheless accentuated the sanctification of the conciliatory embrace of tense opposites.

Breton's discourse invoked Hegel's dialectic of subject/object and also Freud's polyvalent dialectics of the conscious/unconscious, libidinous-erotic/moral, rational/irrational, and dreaming/waking mind. Not only did this mold the plentitude of directions and energies in Dali into a bifurcation, it also provided the means for their conciliation and possible comprehension. Desire and imagination were thus both celebrated and harnessed to the grid of the revolutionary apparatus of Surrealism's canon. So too were vertigo and the irrational elevated, and appropriated. Through the structure of the dialectic, Breton assigned a finitude to the occurrence of *le hasard objectif*, tempering Dali's reveling in the delirium of the endless enigma of the unknowable and incommunicable.

The latter is quite clearly illustrated in Dali's observations in "The Object as Revealed in Surrealist Experiment" (1932). He suggested here that paranoiac-criticism is an advance over the earlier "nocturnal" phase of Surrealism (its concern with automatism and dream) and even over Breton and Eluard's active intervention in the automatic process in their experimental-poetic simulation of mental disorder in *The Immaculate Conception* (1930). What struck Dali about this active process, also articulated in "Interpretion Paranoiaque-critique de l'image obsedante 'L'Angelus' de Millet" (1933), and in *Metamorphosis of Narcissus* (1936–37), was that the *drame poetique* between passive and active confusion could be fused in a *conciliation dialectique*.[14] The full realization of this reconciliation would be profound in that it would move surrealist objects/meaning from a state of *l'irrationalité générale* toward one of *l'irrationalité concrète* (which would not be fully proclaimed a success until *The Conquest of the Irrational* in 1935). This appealed immensely to Dali, for it not only contributed to the desire to disrupt the workings of consciousness, it also introjected a real uncertainty and awe-ful dread into human experience. "We are seized with a new fear," he rejoiced, for we are "deprived of the company of our former habitual *phantoms*, which only too well ensured our peace of mind."[15] Following the "free bent of desire,"[16] and "at the limit of the emerging cultivation of desire . . . we perceive the existence of a thousand bodies of objects we feel we have forgotten."[17] The release of multiple phantoms, which once animated Ernst's 1,000 chimerical projects, which were yet to visit Cixous's 1,000 flames and Deleuze and Guattari's 1,000 plateaus, and would again and again visit Dali 1,000 times,[18] threatened the recuperative power of dialectics, for as "new shivers running through the intellectual atmosphere,"[19] they would soon be more of a "storm rising from within this tea-cup" than Breton would desire.[20] For this particular time, however, the time prior to the full blooming of concrete irrationality in 1935, Dali only intimated hyperdelirium (i.e., anamorphic symbolization) and remained within the orbit of dialectical thought. Aside, then, from the debate about the significance of paranoiac-criticism vis-à-vis automatism, Dali did not always strenuously object to Breton's dialectical discourse. In seeking a solution to his growing problems with Breton, Dali acceded and worked out a "conciliation dialectique" that both "liberated" automatism and regulated "the system of interferences" between automatism and "the road to the object."[21] Perhaps because of his desire to be counted among the Surrealists, Dali also submitted to the dialectics of psychoanalysis. This is evident particularly in his analyses of Millet's *Angelus* and the legend of William Tell. Both analyses are heavily indebted to the tensions between unconscious and conscious mind, libidinous desire and morality, internal and external reality, scatology and convention, and dream and waking. Even in his method of analysis Dali adopted the method Freud used to analyze Leonardo da Vinci, where a dialectic was set up between the visually grasped world, on the one hand, and the mental world of images and *hallucination volontaire*, on the other. This strategy was particularly evident in his analysis of the eroticism of Millet's *Angelus*. Also at work in Dali's approach at this time was the dialectic he himself set in motion between Freud and Lacan, as well as between Lacan and himself concerning the active structuring of delirium and delusion.

It is also significant to consider, however, that Dali, though drawing upon Kraepelin and Bleuler,[22] as well as Freud and Lacan, very much insisted on defying psychoanalysis. Irrationalities and delirium that could be brought into systems of codification and classification lost their status as irrational. For, dialectics not withstanding, Dali expressed a sympathy for a Nietzschean becoming, an eternal return of unmitigated irrationality and singularities capable of exceeding any and all boundaries and safety nets. Explicitly invoking psychoanalytic dialectics, Dali implicitly evoked the "depth psychology" of Nietzsche that was embedded within but continuously suppressed by Freudian discourse. Of course, in Hegelian dialectics there is a moment of refusal and release—a dialectical unrest. Even

though Dali moved in the transitional space of dialectics, he always
left open the question of the destiny of this unrest and refusal.
Always present were the traces of excess and alterity—the phantoms of Nietzsche and Bataille—and an endless disruption of canonic
crystallization.

The trace of this trajectory becomes ever more visible with
other considerations of Dali's celebrations of becoming. Not only
was 1929 the beginning of Dali's major painting, it was also the year
of "crisis," which included the expulsion of a number of renegade
Surrealists. According to Chadwick,[23] Surrealism, in 1929, needed a
means to reach out to an ever larger number of people on a more universal plane, and turned to mythology, in particular the preclassical
and classical myths of Dionysius, Oedipus, Theseus, Narcissus,
Leda, and Daphne. In the figures of Loplop and Gradiva, Surrealist
images were also treated as mythologies.

Dali too became enthralled with mythology, so much so that he
has even been referred to as a "mythomaniac."[24] Marcel Jean has
suggested that Dali "provoked" mythologies that were both fantastic
and artificial.[25] All Surrealist mythology intended to induce ambiguity and enigma that would stir and elevate imaginations and souls,
but Dali's provocation was much more dangerous. Mythologies are
by nature already fantastic and artificial, and also "real," emblematic
as they are of human experiences sedimented in histories and in a
collective unconscious. Dali, however, forced a disturbing distinction
in the realm of myth, the realm of the already fictive/real, between
what is myth and what is "myth." Such inc(s)itation is certainly
problematic in that its irrationalities and exteriorities are not easily
synthesized. Dali promulgated a new myth that extolled plentitude
over system, and openness and dissemination over a possible *point
suprême*.

The myth Dali advanced was akin to Aragon's about Telemachus
(and de Chirico's about Hebdomeros), where objective chance and
objective necessity collude to assert the objective over the heroic
subjective. This is no Hegelian or Marxian objectivity, however, and
the issue is not one of domination and alienation. Instead, objectivity is suffused and *con-fused* with a simulacrum of subjectivity that
effaces subjectivity. The simulation of subjectivity, in the form of an
apparition or phantom, is so subjected to the radical immanence of
chance that teleology and communication are impossible. Objectivity is not a moment of a dialectical tension, but rather is its ruina-
tion. The possibility of subjectivity's exercising a will to know in the
face of the Eternal Return is supplanted by a sovereignty that cannot
be harnessed to subjectivity. Objectivity, as chance, returns as inter-

ference. The myth of triumphant, heroic overcoming, simulated in the complacent philanthropically smiling face of *Endless Enigma*, is but an abysmal myth. Law is exposed as and juxtaposed with fiction. Instead of closure, space opens, and in radical time, the linear (though convulsive, according to Surrealism) temporality necessary for identity and progress collapses. The apparition of subjectivity here is but a simulacrum of a feigned image that arrives in a sublime moment (see *Transparent Simulacrum of a Feigned Image* [1938] and *The Sublime Moment* [1938]) that is endlessly exterior to the hope of peace. A simulated face is only virtually present in a scene where substantiality and synchrony are erased at the moment they apparently appear.

The myth of the myth, of which *Endless Enigma* is the featured story, occasions an intense experience of time that subjectivity cannot manage, a time where everything that exists cancels itself, consumes itself, and disappears, "each instant producing itself only the annihilation of the preceding one, and itself existing only as mortally wounded."[26] *Endless Enigma* does not participate in the hatred of becoming that Nietzsche smashed in *Twilight of the Idols*, nor does it practice the rage of idealism Adorno slashed in *Prisms*. The smile on the face of *Endless Enigma* is not that of one who projects a beautiful future out of a reconstructed past but rather is that of one who lives by chance and in ignorance of the future.[27]

Here, where *amor fati* displaces *amour fou*, objective necessity so catastrophically[28] multiplies capillary tissues that they metastasize as rhizomatic flows, postponing the emergent *point suprême*. Ascendance becomes multidirectional, non-linear lateralization and dispersion. This motion, however, is not the Surrealist convulsive slippage between fissures that stitches those fissures together so as to make possible the transport of meaning. Instead it is a *con-fusion* with those fissures such that a relay or delay irrupts to forestall the arrival of orders and forms that arrest becoming. In place of a subjectivity "biting directly into objectivity . . . marking man's comportment with new impulses,"[29] *Endless Enigma* simulates an unusual totality where accretion, syncretism, and all manner of evolution and ascendance are exiled. Possibility is put forth as myth, its residence everywhere and nowhere, cyborgian and virtual.

As Chadwick noted, Surrealist myths are myths of heros who overcome the polarities of life.[30] They alone transcend the limitations of consciousness and social reality and achieve elevation. Dali's version of a "mythical" text, such as Millet's *Angelus*, while promoting the Surrealists' infatuation with paranoiac-critical activity as a vitalizing force for the movement, also placed it outside the movement. It is a mythology in excess of itself and of its ability to channel its evanescence in favor of the *signe ascendant* and marvelous revelation. Dali sabotaged and usurped the power of metamorphosis to synthesize disjunctions, situating instead a terrifying, running opening, an abysmal immanence, in the place of a miraculous sublation. Dali's mythomaniacal desire thus consisted in his doubling of myth. This mythology—the myth of the myth—denuded conciliation. Here another phantom's creed is announced, exhorting the development of action, thought, and desire by proliferation, juxtaposition, and disjunction, and not by subdivision and pyramidal or spiraling hierarchicalization.[31]

The rending of overripe anamorphic forms as a subterfuge of the symbolic, the defiance of psychoanalysis, and the overdetermination of myth were powerful moments in the Dalinian desecration of dialectical meaning and in the liberation of the suppressed discourse of delirium, profusion, and alterity. Further intensifying them was Dali's publication in 1935 of *The Conquest of the Irrational*, in which he presented the most advanced statement of his theoretical and painterly work. It is crucial to highlight here that conquest is not *of* the irrational, but *by* the irrational. This conquest is predicated on the very notion, which Surrealism's appropriation of it suppressed, that the dialectical tension between passive and active delirium has been shattered.

From the site of this disjunction, an active delirium asserts itself, only to be infinitely multiplied by critical analysis as that analysis struggles, however futilely, to grasp its sense. In this action, concrete irrationality passes "tangibly onto the plane of reality."[32] This is to say that external reality and paranoiac apprehension are both delirious. By dint of *le hasard objectif*, reality is already imbued with a vital necessity whose coincidental occurrences always surprise and confound reason and human design. Likewise the mind's advance is also imbued with interpretive associations that are delirio-synthetic. Phenomenologically,[33] the noematic is already deliriously *con-fused*, and the noetic, its correlative moment, is also involuntarily, yet actively and systematically, delirious. The latter are consubstantial.

But that is not all. Irrational knowledge is further "based upon the interpretive-critical association of delirious phenomena."[34] Here the active, critical/interpretive intervention of the artist/thinker is introduced. Critical/interpretive intervention, injected into what is *already* a delirious knowing, significantly intensifies it such that its objectivity occurs *a posteriori* (it "only becomes objective *a posteriori* by critical intervention").[35] In other words, critical intervention too becomes consubstantial with prior knowledge, the only thing significant is that it moves perceived reality onto the plane of objective, "tangible" reality. Critical activity "intervenes solely as liquid revealer"[36] and "discovers new and objective 'significances' in the irrational."[37] Irrational phenomena, as "concrete" or "objective" irrationality," are "significant events in the authentic domain of our immediate and practical experience of life."[38] They "surpass the domain of phantasms and 'virtual,' psycho-analyzable representations"[39] and are "at the service of . . . the concrete irrational subject"[40] for the sake of appeasing "irrational hungers."[41] Irrational phenomena are "neither explicable nor reducible by systems of logical intuition or by the rational mechanisms. The images of concrete irrationality are thus authentically *unknown* images."[42] According to Dali, echoing his earlier thought on Lacan, paranoiac thought itself is already a "delirium of interpretive association" whose "active and systematic" elements are not "voluntarily directed thought."[43] In paranoia, this active and systematic structure is "consubstantial with the delirious phenomenon itself."[44] "Consubstantiality" in the latter statement is actually refigured here as *con-fusion*—disjunction and conjunction are juxtaposed so as to simulate a confusion that could be usefully deployed by a Surrealist as a prelude to illumination.

The full force of the Dalinian deconstruction of dialectics shows itself in "giving objective value on the plane of the real to the delirious unknown world of our irrational experiences."[45] Not only does this signal the elevation of active, delirio-critical activity over the earlier "nocturnal"/passive phase of surrealism, but it does it with such a fury that undecidable simulacra are grafted onto symbols, supplementing their alchemy. In *The Conquest of the Irrational*, Dali celebrated further what was in motion in the work of the early thirties—the "liquidation" of "surrealist objects functioning symbolically."[46] Those who ignore this, or deny it by insisting on the folly of a dialectical recuperation of this liquidation, continue to see Surrealists as "mystics of fantasy and fanatics of the marvelous."[47] They fail to see that the irrational delirium that is the messenger of Surrealism is also its ironic and elegant saboteur. For the images and meanings of concrete irrationality are authentically unknown. They are but traces or phantasms that brush by the soul in eloquent and silent anonymity.

It would be a mistake, however, to assume that these quiet voices are buried or hidden, as in the notions of "depth" or "under" or "in" that are so common to dialectical and psychoanalytic discourse, or to esoteric discourses, as in Kandinsky's "unknown voice." Rather, that these meanings are unknown stems from the failure of symbols to withstand the frenzy of the hyperirrationality of which humans are the apparatus (Dali himself being the "precise" apparatus).[48] For humans are both the object and "irrational subject" of this hyperirrationality. Together *con-fused*, they (we!) "with the most imperialist fury" pursue this concrete irrationality such that it might be "as objectively evident, of the same consistency, of the same durability, of the same persuasive, cognoscitive and communicable thickness as that of the exterior world of phenomenal reality."[49] Hyperlucid irrationality defies symbolization by destabilizing symbolic couplets. For the latter to be effective, ambiguity and enigma must in some way attach themselves to or open onto the conventional or the collective. This was the intent of Surrealist objects, in particular Breton's "phantom-object," functioning symbolically—that its paradoxical meaning would "surface" later and would effect a metamorphosis capable of altering the individual in whose consciousness it arose, as well as the course of humanity as a whole. (Concern with the universal or the collective was, of course, embodied in the Surrealists' turn to mythology.)

As symbols became hypertrophic, and eventually yawned and tore, the symbolic couplet became a precession of simulacra. With the arc or conduit linking the polar communicating vessels having been compromised, the possibility of their unity-providing sense and meaning as a symbolic event was canceled. Symbols collapsed and reformed as singularities, as signs and signals open to the free play of desire and objective chance—an endless foreplay without a climax.

A return to Dali's phenomenology illuminates this precession. In the essay "The Stinking Ass," Dali had more or less equated symbolically functioning surrealist objects and simulacra. By 1935, however, the conquest of (by) the irrational had made this equation untenable, and a more radical stance became apparent. Concrete irrationality, as a phenomenology of radical immanence, generated a *con-fused* succession of profiles of singularities that were organized in a systematic association. Yet, on the other hand, this sequence of profiles is one of disjunctive singularities capable of systematization only when a gratuitous act of critical intervention "stops" the eventing-forth of these profiles and presents them as a "thought" or "symbol" or "object." The lucidity of hyperirrational objective chance operates in both external reality and in the workings of consciousness (as paranoiac systematization and active intervention), and Dali elaborates the mechanism by which concrete irrationality occurs. It consists in a reflexive turn of a delirious, gratuitous consciousness on a coincidentally arranged external reality. The autoreferential nature of this reflexivity amounts to a self-mutilating reflexivity (eg., *Autumn Cannibalism*, 1936) that leaves singularities symbolically unsynthesized. Thus, the paranoiac advance of consciousness and its critical intervention, both agitated by desire, were always in excess of themselves, denuding and deceiving symbols of their mission. The juxtaposition of truly disparate realities—multiples of them, a "thousand bodies" of them—surpasses the ability of symbolic appropriation and communication.

The consubstantiality of which Dali speaks is thus a conjunction of disparate and discontinuous images and realities. The confusion he had always intended to precipitate falls out now as an a-mazing *con-fusion* of simulacra b(e)aring unreal semblances. The delirious simulacra ("simulacrum-notion")[50] he advocates move as intense singularities or lateralities, suggested by the painting *Singularities* (1935–36), where paranoiac doubles are erased in favor of individual, isolated forms and objects fragmented and separated from each other. Their only unity is the field they share. Perhaps, too, it is ironic that Dali is playing upon Breton's inversion of Hegel's suppression of the individual in favor of the universal.[51] It will be remembered that the humanism of Breton's Surrealism reasserted the space of the individual in the universal. A psychological interpretation might suggest that this is an assertion of personalism, but it is as much a celebration of ecstatic singularities circulating in an infinite field of desire. *Singularities* is thus emblematic of the wresting of simulacra from symbolic structures in such a fashion that they not only stand on their own, but also carry with them absent or feigned meanings (e.g., *The Transparent Simulacrum of the Feigned Image*, 1938). Simulacra are always in motion, drifting on the slippery, ephemeral skids of putrefaction, bleeding, and excretion, the three great simulacra.[52]

One effect of the *con-fusion* of objects, images, and meanings is that meaning and identity themselves remain hidden. Psychoanalytic interpretations cannot retrieve this hiddenness. Neither can the Hegelian logic of history, nor the occultation Breton called for in the *Second Manifesto*. Nor is it made sensible, as Finkelstein suggests, by simply considering it as merely "gratuitous."[53] The hidden nature of meanings stems rather from a precession of fragments, each of which, and all of which as a non-totalized field, implode the possibility of coherent meaning by overdetermining it. As each arrives to deliver its promise of meaning and essence, it metamor-

phosizes into another, and another, *ad infinitum*. So many conjunctions: . . . and . . . and . . . and. . . . Delirious diachrony a-mazes
meaning, and it recedes, is canceled, or at best is deferred. No origin
or destination is implicated. Meaning is occluded without reference
to tropes of verticality, latency, submersion, or depth. There is no
isolable suggestive mechanism hidden underneath or within paranoiac delirium that is to be ferreted out.[54]

Whereas Surrealism did advocate to some degree the freeing of
signifiers from signifieds with its emphasis on chance and the juxtaposition of different realities, it did so in such a way as to create a
dynamic and surprising tension capable of transformation. Surrealism's reliance on an exchange between distant, bipolar realities
formed a boundary capable of prevailing over limitless vertigo and
enigma. Even though the question was left open as to what was signifier and what was signified, a symbolic arc was generated whose
sense was revealed in the encounter with the marvelous. Dali broke
open the loop of signs by introducing, onto the same plane of surreality, a plentitude of signs, all free, and together, beyond this arc.
For the *signe ascendant* he substituted alterities that transgressed
the very possibility of ascendance.

A Luddite tendency operates here in Dali's work. The particular
machinery against which he directs his energies is that of Surrealist
symbolization. His dismantling, however, not simply a destructive
smashing, advances on two related fronts. One motion consists in an
exhibitionist denuding of symbols, the other in the hystericization of
the symbol. Dali presents symbols as overzealous, overheated, and
incontinent vases for transporting meaning. Images/objects seduce
and interrupt each other in a frenzied commotion whose effect is
to strip from symbols the transcendence of their singularity that
would make possible identity and coherence.

This latter transsignification of meaning amounts to an "absence" of meaning. Dali's apparent odes to Surrealism could just as
well be read as a preamble to the irony of modernism Berman so
poignantly captured with the notion of the solid melting into air.[55]
For symbols become volatile in the hyperspace of multiplicity and
plentitude, symbols melt down (liquefy, decompose) into a torrent of
magnetic, serial, partial meanings, marked only by their instability
and concupiscence. Solicitation is *con-fused* with metamorphosis
engendering an a-signifying deterrence. Symbols become but preludes to provisional meanings, which themselves quickly flee in the
agitated "face" of *Endless Enigma*'s hyperreal delirium.

Reminiscent of Rimbaud's "deranged" alchemy, Dali's surrealism (dalilectics) also marks the hystericization of the symbol. The

"hysterical symbol" is one whose sense is exterior and alterior to the womb of sense that gives birth to its meaningfulness. Because of this hystericization, the intrauterine ovial stuff that could form as yolk (symbol-substance), or interiority, cannot. It instead remains slippery, nomadic, plasmatic potentiality whose frenetic, pixilated meaning alludes and runs freely, as did Humpty-Dumpty's yolk when he (sic) fell from the membrane of meaning. Indeed, it could be said that in his inimitable, mythomaniacal fashion, Dali has recreated the allegory of Humpty-Dumpty so as to narrate the story of the demise of symbols in the form of shattered scraps and liquid intraovial stuff.

Breton became increasingly disturbed by Dali's disordering of Surrealist metaphysics, which is not surprising for one whose edifice rested so firmly on the saving grace of the dialectic. Breton was very much in favor of paradox and enigma, but irony was to have only a small role in the latter's magic. For, following Hegel, Breton admitted to irony only as an opening gambit, a first point of departure, a transitional point in the dialectical unrest that is infinite absolute negativity. To give more to irony would be to involve oneself in an endless slippage that would lead only to incessant contradiction and illusion. Irony, if unleashed too fully or resourcefully, would undermine synthesis, and just as Hegel saw Schlegel as a buffoon,[56] Breton came to see Dali similarly. For Dali saw this sublime, convulsive unrest as a persistent opening that yields no promises or echoes. Breton worried about the limitlessness of this motion, as is evident in his 1936 essay "Le Merveilleux contre le mystere." He warned here about the tendency to confound chance and marvelous metamorphosis by intentionally infusing obscurity and mysteriousness into life and art. For Breton, such action was a terrible sign of weakness and ignorance and a sabotage of Surrealism's mission. Uttering the rhetoric of purity, he invoked the substantiality of essences, and perhaps more significantly, their implications for self-understanding and self-preservation.

Any attempt to reduce Dali to the excesses of a gratuitous, masturbatory imagination or to a disturbed mind,[57] or to a private mythology, succumbs to the "fear" that Nietzsche and Bataille suggested terrorizes humans. Such trembling requires systems of causality and hierarchy to contain chance and the uncanny. The conquest of (by) the irrational is that it slathers the slippery, accidental Camembert and transient grease of objective chance on the plane of reality. Such an approach suspends notions of causality and connectedness in favor of coincidental con-fusions that could, by quirk of human intervention, be subject to fictive systematization! Excrement and erection then would not have to symbolize anything, and would not necessarily be tied to anything symbolic. Rather, they would occur as so many disseminations and supplements. In its most radical and ironically disturbing sense, Dali's delirio-critical activity is *not* paranoiac, for it asserts that nothing is connected![58] Once again we are returned to *The Lugubrious Game* and to the shit stain. Excrement is simply there—symbolizing nothing—a simulacrum of itself, a trace of an impossible meaning.

That excrement is just there, minus any capacity to symbolize, is a sign of the atrophy of dialectics and remembrance. Although Dali subscribed to Bunuel's *Golden Age Manifesto*, where Bunuel highlighted the Surrealist interest in "the crucial point at which the simulacrum substitutes realities,"[59] the unleashing of other hazards (*hasards*) of chance, augmented by delerio-critical activity, was already well under way. Dali's discourse intensified the status of the simulacrum as well as the notion of substitution. Also already evident was that simulacrum would no longer substitute for symbol and that substitution itself would be stripped of its powers to endow economies of mimesis, memory, and transformation. Shit is shit is shit! Later, however, when simulation becomes ecstatic, shit is a rose is Hebdomeros is a great cyclopean cretin is *amour fou* is *amor fati*, ad infinitum. With the latter move, Dali would pursue the "avid will to be" of a sorcerer's apprentice,[60] but it would not be Breton for whom he would apprentice. Instead, signs would appear that Dali would assent to that same *élan* as did Bataille when he proclaimed the fundamental right of humans to mean nothing![61]

From the disjunctions displayed in *The Lugubrious Game* and in *Singularities*, Dali moved toward his most gloriously shocking agitation of particularities—*Endless Enigma* (1938). No less than six complete images comprise this extraordinary work, each a *confusion* of simulacrum and intimated symbol, all operating in the same space simultaneously. Earlier this hyperirrationality had been approached in *Invisible Sleeping Woman, Horse, Lion* (1930). Although seen as a triple image, it too easily decomposes into multiple double images, not fulfilling the furious multiplicity desired in *The Stinking Ass*. With *Endless Enigma*, however, "multiple" images and meaning do initiate an endless movement that surpasses simple dual images. Distinct singularities simultaneously bleed into each other, challenging even gratuitous obsession to slow the pace so that coherent meaning might emerge from or even form a labyrinth. A maelstrom of alterities and excitations prevents imagination from stemming irrational metamorphosis in favor of a sensible fiction. Autoerotically, simulacra refer back onto themselves in search of context and sense, only to be centrifuged, spun away, meaning deferred. Hope, embodied in possibility of sublation, is not destroyed, but rather is delayed, itself becoming part of the circulation of desire. The moment of refusal within the dialectic eternally returns, forestalling any possibility of a coagulation called "identity." The marvelous is displaced by a persistent enigma whose otherness defies and defers souls' desires for elevation by incessantly birthing hungers that demand no satisfaction.

Endless Enigma is an enduring moment of radical immanence, an incarnation of a crisis of meaning beyond the crisis of the object and the crisis of the subject. It is the trace and invocation of the most lyrically sophisticated and undulatingly lovely surrealist creation—phantom meaning. Phantom meaning is sublimely awe-ful and ecstatic in that its *con-fusions* provoke an incorrigible condition of *non-savoir*. It is the space where both everything and nothing is connected. With its concrete irrationality fully realized and blooming in 1938, the stage was set for Dali's departure from Surrealism. At that very same moment, Albert was seen carrying Hegel, that "prince of philosophical geniuses," whose dialectical "lever" would enable him "to lift the earth,"[62] into the *Castle of Argol*, much to Breton's delight and relief. In 1939 Dali was irrevocably banished from the Surrealist cenacle, capitulating a sortie that had already long ago occurred.

> what is to be made of
> a chance encounter,
> on a dissecting table,
> of a sewing machine and
> an umbrella,
> and a croissant,
> a flaming giraffe,
> a talking stick,
> and an iris?

Would this encounter be beautiful? comestible? sartorial? alchemical? erotic? endlessly enigmatic? mute? Or would it only be the phantom blue winds that haunted Breton from his first encounter with Nadja—a convulsiveness not beautiful, though simulating beauty, such that the proclamation "Beauty will be convulsive, or not at all" no longer carries with it the hope of ever knowing the difference?

INTERMEZZO:
THE RHIZOMATIC
HYSTERICIZATION
OF SYMBOL AND POINT

Endless Enigma is written against the face of death.

What is most visible and evident in *Endless Enigma* is what is not visible: the face. What announces itself most emphatically is a fiction. What is most visible and evident is not presence.

At the "center" of *Endless Enigma* is supposedly a "face." But it is not a face. Instead it is a profanation of a face, much as a death mask itself is a desecration of "what is" or what can be "fixed." It seems to resemble a face, but it only simulates a face; it also dissimulates being a death mask. As might be expected when simulation and dissimulation are juxtaposed and conspire, their magnetic field is a space of deception.

That what appears to be a face can be taken as a death mask is suggested in the fact that Dali never mentioned that *Endless Enigma* bears seven images rather than six. He himself mentions only six, and conventional interpretation recognizes only six. One of the six (the visage of the great cyclopean cretin), however, is actually taken to be *more than* it appears to be, i.e., a "face," and this face is a simulacrum of the coalescence of an identity rather than the evanescence of what has escaped identification. That is, an essential identity asserts itself representatively as the congealer of all disparate particulars inhabiting a particular space (here, the canvas of *Endless Enigma*).

In this sense, the seventh image, the "image" of an essence, actually presents itself, but disappears, leaving only six. The effect of its appearance/disappearance is to solidify the notion that a face is actually present (such is the strategy of *trompe l'oeil*). It can be said that, in this manner, Dali offers only six images and is silent on any other. The seventh image, the death mask—the effacement of identity—does not become visible because its possibility appears to have been preempted by the very presence of the face. Thus the observer tends to see only the face, which marvelously appears over and over and over again regardless of any combinations of other figures that inhabit the space of the painting as a whole (e.g., the reclined philosopher, the greyhound, the mythological beast). It does not occur to the observer that the face is *not* there. It does not occur that a fiction is *not* a work here. Nor does it occur that the face is a death mask that undoes the fiction/myth of "presence" or "identity" placed there by another (Breton, Surrealism) as a comforting substitute for a terrifying condition not simply of absence but of *non-savoir*.

What would appear to be Dali's silence on the seventh image (the death mask) is terribly deceptive. This deception is revealed in the juxtaposition of *Endless Enigma* and Breton's *point suprême*. As a multiple image, *Endless Enigma* bares no essential meaning and its phantoms do not together produce a phantom object whose latent meaning can arise later at a surprising moment. The seventh "image" is *a* surprise, however, for it erases the positing of an identity that organizes and names a multiplicity of singulars. Had *Endless Enigma* been a multiple image containing a thousand elements, an additional "image"—the specter of *non-savoir* and undecidability—would have inevitably disturbed the holism that would have pretended to gather them together as a "face."

Dali's silence on the issue of the seventh image, the "image" of no face, is brilliantly strategic, for it suggests that a face is in fact not there even when it appears to be vividly obvious. To say this is not a face is to say this is not an essence, which is to say that the dream of Surrealism is a phantasy. Could this have been what Magritte intended when he inscribed `this is not a pipe' beneath a clearly representative image of a pipe? If the seventh face of the die is chance, as the Surrealists offered, *Endless Enigma* advances that chance returns to delay or cancel or disperse the *point suprême*, thereby liberating the particulars that would otherwise be harvested in its name. What is marvelous, then, is not the appearance of the essential experience of knowledge of "the marvelous," but the marvelous *con-fusion* of simulation and dissimulation and their duplicity in the disappearance of the face. With its disappearance, Dali cleverly masked his critique of Breton's discourse of representation while seemingly espousing Breton's promotion of Surrealism as a critique of modernist representation.

The "face" that is not there is an inscription of silence in the present, saying a farewell to, rather than commemorating, the dream of essential knowledge. The death mask is a *r(h)umor* of a presence whose "essence" surpasses and displaces the possibility of embrace and grasp, substituting in its place a plentitude of phantom meanings.

But it is not death itself that is the issue here. That it is a question here, as everywhere, of course, cannot be dismissed. The death of Dali's brother, for instance, is perhaps relevant in that that event made it possible for Dali to appear. Given his dead brother's name, "Dali" was that which filled a space already evacuated. Formed in the visage of his brother's specter, Dali became a trace, a phantom his own presence could never be. In being that which filled the space already vacated, he himself was displaced. As a double absence, "Dali" is the site (sight) of the mask of death. Thus, the occasion of Dali's appearance, his birth, his "origin," was simultaneously a deferral and a cancellation. That is, Dali was a living simulacrum of an absence opening.[1] Already from the outset phantom meaning animated his exorbitant existence and work; his labor was stirred by phantoms of simulated presence and dissimulated absence. (And so he informed incessantly that "Dali" is Catalonian for "desire.")

The death mask is that which is (w)ritually formed around the physiognomy of the passed. Such a mask, *Endless Enigma*'s voice and eyes do not commemorate loss, but fecundity—a site where traces and phantoms return again and again and again to invest undecidable meaning. In a strange sense, they never leave. A simulacrum of death, the visage of *Endless Enigma* is a tracing of phantasms that promise and foretell yet elide something that has brushed by, vacating memory prior to being fixed there. What is fixed in this transpiration, however, is the very subversion of remembrance, history, and identity, for traces announce something "there" that is "forgotten," having withdrawn prior to forgetting. Memory dislocated, itineration displaces iteration. *Aneconomimesis*[2] is substituted for *anamnesis* in the tricky flash of an I.

Written across the face of death and deployed strategically, *Endless Enigma* is a transparent simulacrum of a feigned image of death. By 1938, when Dali had successfully developed the delirium of the multiple image in *Endless Enigma*, it was also apparent in a set of paintings that accompanied it that he had "faced" the ephemeral phantasmic nature of meaning. While *Apparition of Face and Fruit Dish on a Beach* (1938) and *Invisible Afghan with the Apparition on the Beach of the Face of Garcia Lorca in the Form of a Fruit Dish with Three Figs* (1938) raise the question of the apparitional nature of meaning that exceeds simple *trompe l'oeil*, *The Transparent Simulacra of the Feigned Image* (1938) asserts that the "presence" of these apparitions is the transparency, the simulating medium, through which an absence becomes apparent. No longer was Dali concerned simply with the dialectical relationship of the conscious and the unconscious, imaged so wonderfully in *The Metamorphosis of Narcissus* (c. 1936–37) and later in *The Image Disappears* (1938), a tribute to Freud and a goodbye to *trompe l'oeil* and the restricted economy of the double image. His attention turned away from a celebration of hiding and appearing, of revealing and concealing, toward the evasive motility of the unthought and the incommunicable. He encountered the surplus of the three great simulacra (bleeding, excretion, putrefaction) and moved into the open, slippery spaces of unstable and displaced meaning—those strange spaces where *savoir* and *non-savoir* are *con-fused*.

Dali's discourse no longer centered on the systematization of images and meanings as a phantom object. He turned to the circulation of images and the deferral and dissemination of meaning that exceeded reconciliation and fixation. This surpassing was precisely the point. The very fact that in the six images the animal (greyhound, woman, philosopher), plant (fig, pear, mandolin) and mineral (beach, sea, mountains) kingdoms are *con-fused* with the mythic-imaginary (cyclopean cretin, mythological beast, [philosopher?]) attests to the alterities coursing through spaces that incessantly overreach meaning. With this displacement Dali had effected a major transubstantiation of Surrealism, locating it outside its own system. By 1938 the paranoiac-critical method was a most devastatingly powerful strategy for exploiting multiplicity and hysteria. No longer bounded by a dialectical-structural notion of limited variation in a *finite* field, the paranoiac-critical method, as an overdetermining hyperpresence, became the productive machinery of an infinite, indefinite variation within an open field.

The force of Dali's delirious interpretation resides, on first blush, in its double deployment of *trompe l'oeil* and hysteria. From their machinations irrupts a multiplication of Surrealism's efforts at appropriating Lautréamont's and Reverdy's respective notions of dissociation and juxtaposition. It is this intensification that is the *mise-en-scène* of the unthought/unsaid. *Trompe l'oeil* is itself a site where juxtapositioned continuity and discontinuity exchange with each other. Like the gestalt of Jekyll and Hyde, each negates and affirms the other. For Dali, however, *trompe l'oeil* is only an opening ploy for inc(s)iting a sequence of duplicitous, solicitous traces that substitute a transgressive general economy for the evolution of a restricted economy. Here *trompe l'oeil* simulates a site of contained alterities and interiorized exteriorities. It also simulates a controlled and controllable automatism in the service of the revolution rather than the demise of a subject's *disponibilité*.

The *point suprême* and the marvelous thus ravished, those particulars intended for the dialectic's clasp are now unleashed as intensifications or materializations of something else. Each operates and expresses alone, free to roam, to solicit and interrupt, free to abandon. The promise of each, however, is more fiction than a lie; its identity not a falsehood, but a trace of something evocative passed by. Something, now distant, left a trace whose apparition is a sign of an incommunicable meaning whose saying never settles comfortably into a Said. Each moment of what would otherwise be coupled singularities now stands as disjunctive juxtapositions of different and free singularities. Nothing is "behind" them, they do not belong to any transcendental source, nor do they indicate or represent anything, either by themselves or together. Each "lives on," Derrida suggests, in silence, at each other's borders.[3] The very notion of their togetherness is a fiction exposed by that which LIES at the margins of representation's phantasies. In the same sense that "essences" are fictive simulacra of apparitions, apparitions are simulacra of traces. Silent, these traces (phantoms) both inform and undermine systems and structures of expression. Yet their undecidable nature is not completely outside expression; they form expression's limits and disruptively invest them.

Because of their singularity and resemblance to nothing outside of themselves, there can be no focus on what essences these signs reveal or what meanings they intend. They are solicitations of fiction. Their apparitions are fiction's incantations. Discontinuous and disjunctive, Dali insited them as multiples, conjunctions—. . . and . . . and . . . and. . . . His attention was captivated by the journey of simulacra and by the journey of the tracings that animated them and rendered them *con-fused* signifiers/signifieds. This "journey" is marked by fragmentation and discontinuity. Mimesis and representation, crucial for establishing meaning, are inevitably deferred and displaced by such discontinuity. For each image or simulacrum does not join with the next and the previous to make sense. Their interaction and dependency upon each other, crucial for symbolization and meaning, is inhibited by an instability and undecidability.

One, having enticed an other, interrupts it and sabotages the possibility of meaning. What could possibly be fixed (or essential) becomes a fragment, an innuendo, an impotent promise. Like Nietzsche, Dali intimates that meaning is a space of conflict, an accidental moment of identity that endures only for the time it takes traces to flee. The meaning promised in the juxtaposition of intensive fragments continuously collapses as each delays and cancels the other, returning each to a condition of exorbitance.

The inherence of meaningfulness in fragments and intensities is thus little more than an accident. Only fiction or myth could supply the connective tissue that might bind them together, but Dali's mythomaniacal doubling of myth assured that myth would not produce such meaning. The Surrealists, of course, offered a critique of representation, and were well aware that stable meanings cannot endure as such. This understanding was evident in their notions of "convulsive" identity. Nevertheless, the magnetic forces of identity always prevail, and from such magnetism the stability of transformative meaning is established. Dali's three great simulacra (blood, excretion, putrefaction), and their multiple apparati, however, are cast otherwise as traces of mysterious, incommunicable becoming. Simulacra work their magic by breaking down, and only when they break down and are broken down do they circulate and seductively make their empty promises.

The face, then, is the face of effacement. The visage or apparition only feigns a face. Placed under erasure, the face is only an adventitious site where traces and phantasms intersect to celebrate the absence of the face. As a simulacrum of a meaningful, coherent site, as a womb of sense, the face is displaced at the very moment it appears to appear. It abandons itself (and us) precisely when it appears, and announces that certainty and fixity are the delusions and phantasies of abstraction, logical intuition and other vagaries of modernity. The countenance that is a death mask is animated by notions too restless to remain yet too entrenched to abandon the site completely.

Trompe l'oeil, as a space of accident and of conflict, conventionally suggests a longing for inhabiting the outside that every coherent, essential structure, as a continent interior, promises. For Dali, however, *trompe l'oeil*, is rendered as a general economy and eventually loses its interiority. Unlike de Chirico, however, there is no nostalgia. For Dali this notion of a communicable interior or essence is a hysterical notion at best. In this sense, the tears, laughter, and screams of Dali are not unlike those of Bataille.

The notion of essence as "hysterical" is revealed in Dali's siting of the face as an exorbitant signified of chance and plentitude. The apparition or the visage is always other than the face. As a dwelling presence the face can never be, but is yet an innuendo of something long gone. The apparition itself is the undoing of the recuperative embrace of singularities that is the face. An appropriative space, the face for Surrealism is a space of mimesis and identity, a site where a convulsive, hysterical staging of knowledge occurs. Dali's juxtaposition, however, of appropriation and hysteria opens an ironic space in which the notion of juxtaposition and displacement, and *trompe l'oeil*, become a space of rupture and departure.

The issue at stake in hysteria is always relative to identity and continence. In that identity assumes repetitive, mimetic appropriation, what Levinas names the Same,[4] it takes for granted that a face, as an essential form, is the overcoming of various disparities in favor of the notion of a signal or symbol. Hysteria threatens identity, for hysteria is an assertion of difference. Difference happens when symbols are broken down into simulacra and singular signs. The eternal return of particulars undermines "systems" or "laws" or"essences." And here the irony appears, for the eternal return *is* repetition. But it is not a repetition of the same. It is a repetition instead that is forever discontinuous, idiosyncratic, and driven by chance. With this repetition, memory is displaced. Much as Nietzsche had done in *Thus Spake Zarathustra*, Dali does in *Endless Enigma*. What meaning there is passes in silence or speaks only in indirect voices. *Endless Enigma*, an incarnation of the eternal return, marks a violent spasm in the convulsiveness of automatism. It generates a forgetting that cancels the ability of language itself to appropriate and represent. *Endless Enigma* is a simulacrum of the puzzling and hysterical silence encountered when what pretends to be essential, fulfillable experiential meaning is experienced, but remains unfulfilled.

The assertion of the incommunicable is not, however, the only or most critical issue in *Endless Enigma*. Also crucial is the endless journey of difference. However, this is not just a spatial issue, relevant to the space of the convulsions of *trompe l'oeil*. Perhaps even more important is the issue of the eventing itself, particularly its alacrity and instantaneity. While the eventing of difference manifests itself as an autochthonous realization of singularities that stand on their own as spatial formations, it also undercuts the possibility of their being anything other than "other." As autochthonous, *metastatic* meanings, each formation itself inhabits a space unable to be colonized or lent out (for symbolization) without transgression. Yet still these formations/sites interact, now though as duplicitous invasions of each other's space—interruptions that aim not to dominate or subsume each other in order to totalize. That they are unstable and bleed into and onto each other is the unavoidable consequence of the hyperactivity of Dalinian delirium. Tearing, excretion, ejaculation, and bleeding stand only for themselves, and at the same time are materializations, or utterances, of automatism. What Dali collapses, then, is the collaborative relation of space and time, whose conspiracy (symbolization) produces an event(ing) capable of the continence necessary to simulate meaning. What would appear on the surface as clever alchemy, supposedly occurring within *trompe l'oeil*, is denuded. In their nakedness, signs stand ready for sterile unions. Their instantaneous, magnetic attractions and repulsions of each other invoke only dissemination, making of transubstantiation a lovely, yet fictional, narrative.

The effect of Dali's furious, imperialist instantaneous juxtapositions[5] is that they make it appear as though symbolic meaning only dissimulates an absence. That is, strange juxtapositions of distant realities, for the Surrealists, aim only at feigning an absent meaning when in fact the surrealist object (e.g., the phantom object) creates the possibility of presence (in the form of the *point suprême*, the marvelous). On the contrary, though, it is presence Dali feigns, for inscribed in each particular sign is a trace of a signifier no longer present. The assumed presence of symbolic meaning, accomplished by the Surrealists' *apparent* joining of signifier and signified, suggests that singularities are not capable of generating meaning. Here, however, lies the possibility of this assumption's being cretinized. For signs resist colonization and persist as localized formations— traces of phantoms already absconded that left only r(h)umors of their presence. What disappears is an assembling grasp, and histories displace history. The deterritorialization of symbols and the resistance of signs render the appropriative embrace of history a multiplicity of *hysteries*.

The Images Disappears (1938), a homage to Freud and psychoanalysis's celebration of the dialectic, thus must be read against *Singularities* (c. 1935–36) or *Enchanted Beach with Three Fluid Graces* (1938). In the latter, *trompe l'oeil* has virtually disappeared, as has any sense of a transformative structure of meaning. The homage to Freud, a double image, itself doubles as a farewell to the double image as a simulacrum of the symbol's power to conflate signifier and signified. When the possibility of symbolic meaning is deferred by multiples that resist an overarching meaning that combines them coherently, meaning must run the gauntlet of chance. Such a scene appears in *Palladio's Corridor of Dramatic Surprise* (1938). Here an undecidable journey lies ahead, or has just been completed. Telephones, signs of imminent signals, are available, but one senses that no messages are arriving, or that, if they are, no one is available to receive them. Peripheral phantoms, Gradiva seemingly among them, ooze desire. But communication fails, the apparent protagonists prostrate and exhausted (Telemachus having stumbled? somnambulatory Hebdomeros now asleep? the reclined philosopher of *Endless Enigma*?). The dramatic surprise of nothing in particular stands in stark contrast to a supreme point where productive metamorphosis would otherwise occur.

With the emphasis on instantaneity and singularity, what Dali valorizes is the *speed* of the eternal returning, the quickness with which traces surpass essences. This is done by juxtapositioning a multiplicity of distant realities as a sequence of lateral signs or sites that are *not* just transformations of each other. In *Endless Enigma* the philosopher is *not* a transformation of a greyhound. A woman seated and mending a sail is *not* a transformation of a great cyclopean monster. A mythological beast is *not* a mandolin or figs or pears. And none of these, together or by themselves, are a face. Nor is even a face a face. Each of the images, rather, functions singularly, and together they constitute the apparition that can be named "face," but is not face. Delirium and frenzy thus suggest an extraordinarily rapid decomposition. Alternatively, the rapidity of the arrival and circulation of individual phantoms occurs with such instantaneity that transformation is canceled and singulars remain singular.

The distinction between transformation and difference is critical. Not only is difference a sign of a disruption of the dialectic's gathering, it is a sign of irony's own "convulsive" eventing of that difference. The hyperactivity of this eventing belies difference as a morphological transition of alternative forms of existence and installs in its place a radical alterity, a rupture where objects and images are truly different from each other and where, their duplicity not withstanding, they cannot be assimilated into a point. With regard to the eternal return, then, what returns are discontinuous, accidental moments that are alterations and destructions of the same. Only fiction and imagination can suppress their difference and make of them an identity. Despite the struggles of the imagination, slippery persistent truths remain and resist expression as anything other than an endless enigma. Symbols and signals are exhausted by the desultory ecstasy of hysterical time. The alacrity with which time is collapsed has as its consequence the postponing of the future in which a possible evolutionary conciliation could be made of agitated commotion and *con-fusion*.

Already this distinction was evident in Dali's work in the late 1920s and early 1930s. From the time of the paintings *The Stinking*

Ass and *Putrefying Bird* (1927–28) through the early 1930s, Dali continuously disabled the symbolic function of surrealist objects at the same time as he promoted them. Early on this took the form of a relentless decomposition and liquefaction of forms and images and the obliteration of symbolic boundaries. With them hope was seriously questioned, if not already rendered stillborn. Though there was visible in this work a reliance on an evolutionary carrying-over of morphological transitions, there was nonetheless the sense, evidenced by the prevalence in the paintings of the late 1930s, of expectant telephones, with mute and absent conducting wires, languishing in solitude.

It was not evident then that Dali was also inscribing metastasis into this eventing of metamorphosis. Prefacing Baudrillard, who would later claim that "immanence left to itself is not all random,"[6] Dali's decompositions double as scenes where things becoming soft and putrid are scenes where molecular linkings, cyborgian mutations, and localizations of objective definitions transpire.[7] The "escalating power"[8] of the running together of singularities does blur their essential qualities, but even more it stands in opposition to narratives and images that metaphorize presence or body.[9] Although Baudrillard suggests that such exponential conduction and transmutation is a form of seduction that leads to "fatal" consequences,[10] he shares with Dali the notion that once transcendence has decomposed, the world is not necessarily only pure accident. Accident and randomness are potent forces for Dali and Baudrillard. When Baudrillard suggests that it is not true that "things left only to themselves produce only their confusion,"[11] one is reminded that Dali too insited *con-fusion* into the communication between things. Immanence is not random; it "deploys a connection of events or disconnection of events altogether unexpected, in particular this singular form which combines connecting and disconnecting, that of the exponential," suggests Baudrillard,[12] with which Dali would concur. Contra Breton, Dali interfaces this *con-fused* exponential connection/disconnection with the marvelous, ascendant magnetism whose exponential energy is automatism. Contra Baudrillard, however, and apparently for Breton, Dali does not imply that such *confusion* necessarily ends in the imploded black hole of the superficial abyss of a totalizing seduction and fatal simulation. Here the undecidability of *Endless Enigma* arises in its strange juxtaposition of Surrealism's lovely transcendence with the potentially escalating fatality of a collapse of difference.

At stake in both Dali's and Baudrillard's discourses is an aesthetics of disappearance, but they do not end in the same fashion.

Baudrillard closes "ending" in the seductive agitation of an escalating code that insures the death of the social. Dali's "ending," however, leaves open the undecidable possibility of a *telos* where simulation works to multiply the undecidability and thus the very deferral of the *telos*. Leaving the latter open has the consequence of liberating singularities and intensifying the undecidability of questions about their connectedness or disconnectedness. Dali thus *confuses* Breton and Baudrillard's ecstasy of communication in a most subtle and brilliant fashion, hiding its alterity in an alterity that Breton and Surrealism took to be essentially knowable.

A failure to fully realize that metastasis was being put forth as metamorphosis was perhaps what permitted Dali to remain within the Surrealist fold even though phantom meaning was at the time already beginning to stir uncomfortably in the souls of Breton and others. That Dali was himself aware of the aura of phantom meaning, though it was not fully obvious as such, and would not be until 1938, is obvious in 1932. He wrote in "The Object as Revealed in Surrealist Experiment" that "a new fear" seizes us (the Surrealists and their beneficiaries) in that "deprived of the company of our former habitual phantoms, which only too well insured our peace of mind . . . [and] . . . at the limit of the emerging cultivations of desire, we seem to be attracted by a new body, we perceive the existence of a thousand bodies of objects we feel we have forgotten."[13]

With this comment Dali indeed noted the crisis of both the subject and the object, which he aimed to amplify *ad infinitum*. Here the paranoiac-critical method reveals the metastatic delirium of its genealogical force, for within the rhizomatically *con-fusing* juxtaposition of objects was not a duality that dissolved into a body of understanding, but a multitude of bodies, a thousand of them, at least. It was this that induced fear, for the "phantom" that assured peace of mind (the dialectical synthesis of disparities) was displaced (and forgotten) by a condition of *non-savoir* that sustained the integrity of objects and signs as things in and of themselves. That this "new body" is a thousand bodies is tantamount to saying this is *not* a body, but bodies, not history, but *hysteries*. Phantom meaning arrives in the wake of its accomplices: fecundity, ecstatic wandering, metastatic individuation, the eternal return of departure, absence, *con-fusion*. And with the arrival of a multitude of bodies appeared the specter of the possibility of at least a thousand subjects. Indeed this was a crisis for Surrealism beyond the pale of its own desire to instigate revolution and to incite a crisis in both subject and object. While Dali did defer to Breton's forthcoming *Communicating Vessels* (1932), it is undeniable that "The Object as Revealed in Surrealist Experiment" evoked the specter of phantom meaning that would arrive soon to dissolve *le poisson soluble.*

Hysteria thus was refigured. Here, however, it must be dissociated from the discourse of psychoanalysis. Breton and Aragon had already suggested a refiguring in 1928, with their celebration of the fiftieth anniversary of the discovery of hysteria. Seizing it as a disruptive strategy, they suggested that hysteria is not pathological, but is a subversive means of expression capable of plundering the moral authority of the world to be ordered in a designated fashion. Their plan was to plant hysteria and its nondelusional delirium of interferences on the plane of reality (e.g., Breton and Eluard's *Immaculate Conception*, 1930). Already in 1928 Dali, however, had begun such resistance, which for him took the form of decomposition and breakdown. *The Putrefying Bird* and *The Stinking Ass* (the painting) were simulacra of the "stinking essence," which for Dali were emblematic of discontinuity and undecidable absence. Just when Dali appeared to be nearest the soul of the Surrealists, he was already farthest from it.

Under the auspices of his own paranoiac-critical multiplications, Dali's celebration of hysteria revitalized the notion of hysteria as a "wandering womb." It will be remembered that hysteria, as a complex of physical and behavioral disorders, was first conceptualized by the Egyptians as a problem related to the position of the womb. As early as 1900 B.C. the *Kahun Papyrus* (and later the *Papyrus Ebersin*, sixteenth century B.C.) noted that the womb had a tendency to migrate and wander from its seat in the pelvis. Thinking of the womb as though it were autonomous, an entity in and of itself, medical practitioners aimed to lure it back into its position. The Greeks, primarily through Hippocrates, continued this tradition, and it was from the word *hustera* ("womb") that the label *hysteria* derived. Later, the Romans even thought the womb to be an animal within an animal, an independent entity capable of aberration.

There is little doubt that this inclination toward the aleatory, and the surprising disorderings and disruptions accompanying it, were what the Surrealists found so appealing. They had no specific desire, however, to focus on the womb or hysteria as a problem associated with women. Rather, hysteria was a trope for aberration, for moving outside what is normal and desirable. Dali, never missing an occasion to scandalize the Surrealist project, doubled the sense of hysteria by radicalizing alterity so that it became exorbitantly ecstatic. This doubling centered on the notion of the womb as the possibility of knowledge, as that which holds and channels signs toward the birth of meaning, as that which bears a story, an allegory. The womb doubles the symbol.

But the symbol, to fully bear the fruit of meaning and intelligibility, must remain associated with the body (of understanding) that bears it and that it ultimately will reproduce. The womb is a mimetic and hermetic/hermeneutic medium that functions to lend coherence to the eternal return of birth. When the womb becomes nomadic, so too does the sense it carries. Dissociating itself from the totality of the body, the womb becomes a free agent, and the paths it traverses deterritorialize the space of the symbol. Surrealism canonized this dissociative tendency and realized it in the juxtaposition of distant and unlike realities. Within its purview, however, it attempted to celebrate only the vagary and the wandering. Dali's hystericization of hysteria and the symbol went beyond this. His intensification amounted to a profanation of the womb, a breach of birth—a miscarriage of the marvelous. His reveling in this disjunction calls to mind Deleuze and Guattari's body without organs.[14] Dali's interest in the hystericization of the symbol and the point reveals an interest in the molecular and in the disjunctive that can be *con-fused*. Deleuze and Guattari later made a similar point in positing the notion of a "disjunctive synthesis." Such a "synthesis" is not "exclusive or restrictive, but fully affirmative, nonrestrictive, inclusive. A disjunction that remains disjunctive, and that still affirms the disjoined terms, that affirms them throughout their entire distance, *without restricting one by the other or excluding the other from the one.*"[15] Herein the marvelous is transvalued.

The wandering of the womb was the simulacrum of the production of singularities within a singular body that exposed that totalized singularity as a repressive fancy. Dali's brilliant and radical sense of *trompe l'oeil* is glimpsed here in its declaration that the body is bodies and that totality has forced associations of what would otherwise be disconnected. As early as 1926–28, the years preceding *The Lugubrious Game* and *The Great Masturbator*, the expression of singularities and the desire to exceed were evident. In *Blood Is Sweeter than Honey* (1926), *Apparatus and Hand* (1927), and especially *Little Cinders* (1927–28), Dali detailed the various "apparati" or "instantaneous facts" that were the simulacra of individuation, disequilibrium, putrefaction, becoming, corrosion, delirium, and ecstasy. In these works, and even through others where ecstatic particulars are thematized (e.g., *Combinations* [1931] and *Singularities* [1937]), there is simply the assertion of their instantaneous individuality. Elided in these works, though, is the radicalization of absence that various singular apparati affirm. For instance, *Combinations*, appearing on the eve of both Dali's own "The Object Revealed in Surrealist Experiment" and Breton's *Communicating Vessels*, hinted at the specters of difference and individuality with its fracturing of the body and its siting of multiple apparati. While particulars are put forth as individual entities, there is also a sense of continence sustained by an outer membrane or border that promotes the hope that this womb might give birth to ascendant coherence.

Only with *Endless Enigma* is the radicalization of absence completed. For only here does Dali succeed in juxtapositioning *trompe l'oeil and* hysteria in a way that a feigned apparition of singularity (the totalizing effect of the visage) produces singularities by being broken down by them.

Herein lies the power of *Endless Enigma*: its ability to situate plentitude and totality in an postdialectical fashion that both sustains and displaces the fiction of unity and coherent meaning. The awe-ful ability of symbols to resemble and colonize the bodies of signs is offset by the ability of signs, as particular bodies, to escape through the very circuits that circumscribe them.

Endless Enigma is a provocation, a war machine railing against complacency and devolution, against the globalization and systematization of local, minor bodies, forces, and histories. These entities, celebrated in Surrealism's beautiful dream as accomplices capable of forming marvelous, metamorphosizing allegiances, were unleashed by Dali to circulate as saboteurs, as *commotion*, according to their own aboriginal, incommunicable phantom desires.

Dali's discourse during the period prior to 1938 and *Endless Enigma* is hyphenated and discontinuous. This was taken by Breton, and many others, even today, as a stream of inconsistent, incoherently frivolous, and wasted gestures. Alternatively, it is a time of experimentation and play during which phantom meaning is substituted for the phantom object. It is a time during which the (supreme) point and the symbol are rendered hysterical and rhizomatic. The lateral juxtapositioning of particulars is stripped of "the company of our former habitual phantoms" of latency and depth, rendering the space of the point a wide-open window from whose vantage multitudes of different individualities can be seen wandering about. The "instantaneous juxtapositions" Dali deploys work on a doubling of the principle of *trompe l'oeil* and on the speed with which *trompe l'oeil's* deceptions and dislocations occur. Reaching their fullest fury in *Endless Enigma, Endless Enigma* figures not as a denouement of prior disparities in a moment of Surrealist glory, but as a decapitation of the symbolic function of the Surrealist object and the point in which it surfaces.

The discontinuous apparati Dali "furiously" releases during this period anticipate well notions to be articulated later by Virilio in his considerations of speed, war, and disappearance (which also informs Deleuze and Guattari's notions of rhizomatic and nomadic dispersion). In his discussions of war and cinema, Virilio notes that the nature of current war machinery is such that it functions only if it is clouded with uncertainty (e.g., the Stealth fighter jet). Efforts to accomplish such uncertainty have generated an "aesthetics of disappearance" that necessitates the deployment of "indeterminate and unfamiliar" systems whose credibility is no more assured than is its visibility.[16] Putting into play such systems highlights the significance of the "logistics of perception," which are intensified when new images replace prior objects ("weapons") and war is waged at the level of the invisible. It is precisely this space in which *Endless Enigma* wages war. Here *Endless Enigma* is a stealthy point that is a simulacrum of a stinking essence that is a simulacrum of a face that is a simulacrum of an essence. The *con-fusion* put forth in the frenzied simulations of the aesthetics of disappearance makes of *Endless Enigma* a most deceptive Surrealist object.

Virilio offered that deception and concealment are necessary now because modernity's capabilities have made "what is perceived . . . already lost." Citing a contemporary war strategist who stated that "once you can see the target, you expect to destroy it,"[17] Virilio observes that "ocular" watching machinery becomes crucial both offensively and defensively. It will be remembered that in *The Conquest of the Irrational* Dali promoted his works as "hand-done color photography." He had, however, already experimented with the cinematic ocular with *Un Chien andalou. Endless Enigma's* situation vis-à-vis Surrealism's systematization of hysteria and alterity may be explored in this context because for Dali, once an essence is "sighted" (sited), what consists in it is appropriated and, in a sense, destroyed—in his terms "ossified" or "fossilized." As a death mask, *Endless Enigma*, via its double deployment of *trompe l'oeil* and hysteria, simulates the Surrealist project of destroying complacent bourgeois representation all the while concealing its dissimulation of its embrace of a radical exteriority.

Here we turn again to Dali's focus on speed and "instantaneous juxtapositions." Speed lends itself to a sense of the instantaneous. The "instant" is the moment in which time and space are collapsed. The instant in *trompe l'oeil* is crucial, as it is the temporal and spatial hinge upon which "the surreal" both plays and depends. If, however, that moment becomes so immediate as to obliterate the collaboration of space and time, then, for all intents and purposes, objects and motion are fixed, caught in a freeze-frame, as were the passengers and trains in Einstein's example of passing trains where all movement ceased.[18] The cessation of movement, however, was actually a function of speed and coincidence. The sense of stillness and the allusion of fixity is actually an illusion that betrays the speed that makes it possible. But the speed that makes it possible, plus coincidence, is what freezes the moment.[19]

It is this speed Dali pursues in the hystericization of the symbol and the point. The speed that makes possible various illusions is the intervention of the paranoiac-critical activity of the subject, and "coincidence" is none other than the objective necessity of chance. Their juxtaposition effects a sense of a visage or essence that is not there but appears as if it were. Here *trompe l'oeil* is pushed to a new level of deception. In paintings such as *The Phantom Cart* (1933) and *The Moment of Transition* (1934), *trompe l'oeil* generates a detectable point, and this detectability in turn generates the dialectical surprise that transforms. In *Endless Enigma*, however, *trompe l'oeil* is rendered silent by the instantaneous motion of eternally returning multiple singulars. What happens in *Endless Enigma*, then, is that multiple moments of transition *do* occur, but they do so with such speed that they cancel each other out. The effect is that a "face" appears to be a face and the notion of bipolar communicating vessels appears to be sustained. That is, the multiple image is supposedly an ensemble of double images. What makes the latter possible, though, is only the binary logic of the fictional law of *trompe l'oeil*. Only this logic argues that phantom meaning is NOT there. Only this logic argues that a phantom object has conjoined various disparities in a latency that will surface at some POINT in time. But the speed and deception this logic usurps return to transform the point into a line.[20] This line simulates a consolidation of particulars in a "state" of organization. Such simulation camouflages, protects, and promotes their singularity. Resistance to a point-that-gathers permits difference to spread rhizomatically and nomadically.

As noted previously, *Combinations* (1931) hinted at such a rhizomatic movement, but it presented singularities within an environment that too easily organized parts into a body or identity. *Combinations* was not by any means an effort at a double image, and as a gesture toward multiplicity, it was a weak move, but a move nonetheless. Paintings such as *Little Cinders* (1927–28), *Singularities* (1937), and *Enchanted Beach with Three Fluid Graces* (1938), however, accommodate particulars without any effort to play on double images or restricted economies. They announce the status of particulars as free signifiers that have already resisted or are ready to

foil being fixed in a system of references. Not taken seriously by
Surrealism, such paintings have fallen into oblivion or have become
just curious pieces irrelevant in any way to Surrealism. *Endless
Enigma* picks up their anthem and carries it into the territory of
Surrealism by camouflaging itself as a sequence of *trompe l'oeil*
images. What in effect occurs is a spreading out of space—a freezing
of the time of identification—and a multiplication of differences
that do not form a face.

So, *Endless Enigma*—face, or not? And if so, of what? *Endless
Enigma's* incandescence is its ability to *con-fuse* the "logic of appearance" with the "aesthetics of disappearance" in a marvelous display of undecidability. This hysterical motion serves to prevent the
Royal Science of Surrealism from systematizing delirium and difference. Cleverly concealed within Dali's claims of his own efforts to
systematize delirium was his "systematic" dissimulative undoing of
Surrealism. The effect of this undoing was that signs and singularities were not forced into the service of a Signal or Symbol. The latter
cast a pall of silence over the POINT of Surrealism. For in the delirious space of *Endless Enigma*, the POINT becomes .   .

PHANTOM MEANING

At the beginning of chapter 2 it was mentioned that this reading situates Dali *après modern*. To more fully explore this siting, as well as the import of *Endless Enigma*, it is necessary to recognize this reading as *après coup*. *Après coup* because *Endless Enigma* has never been fully appreciated for what it meant for Surrealism. It has typically been treated with silence (though Rojas has recently given attention to this work).[1] Perhaps this silence arose because it was received as clever chicanery? was not understood? was taken as evidence of Dali's failure? That it might have been a failure, as well as misunderstood, is a point of departure, for in another way it did succeed, and that was its failure.

Dali's surrealism was more subtle and insidious (vis-à-vis Surrealism) than was Dada, in the sense that it did not assert a new aesthetic at the limits of language, image, and meaning, as did Dada (e.g., Tzara's *Seven Dada Manifestos*). Rather it asserted a supplement to the magnetic circuitry of Surrealism's antidote to the negativity of Dada rupture. *Endless Enigma* is a revisitation of certain Dada sites (e.g., collage and derisive laughter), but it *con-fuses* the latter with *trompe l'oeil* and paranoiac-criticism. The result is a *pharmakon* or a *parergon* doubling as some perverse alchemist's or philosopher's stone (in the *Second Manifesto* Breton had anointed the philosopher's stone as what would permit the imagination to take stunning revenge on things). *Endless Enigma*'s *alchimie du symbole* casts its spell by *con-fusing* convulsive identity with convulsive writing, resulting in a visual inscription that operates transgressively rather than *parergonally* (in Kant's sense) or dialectically.

The phantom meaning traveling with *Endless Enigma* is so diabolical because it takes Surrealism's lyricism to extreme limits beyond hope of respite or recompense. Its delay and displacement of any ascendance that could ever earn the name *surreal* inscribes a heterology in the machinic code of Surrealism. This heterology irrupts as a rhapsody of flows and releases. The latter, traces only of an automatism Royal Surrealism aimed to memorialize, play in the presumed binary spaces of *trompe l'oeil* and the dialectic. Their play occurs as secretions that make it secret that the Point of Surrealism is in indeed a myth.

Breton attempted to do for Surrealism what Derrida suggested Kant had done for aesthetics: to construct a frame—a set of margins, a vessel—that would distinguish what is "intrinsic[ally] constituent in the complete representation of an object" from what is only an "adjunct."[2] For Kant the *parergon* is the frame constituted at the borders of the interior and exterior, but it nonetheless remains external to the *ergon* in the sense that only the *ergon* possesses what is essential to make the aesthetic the beautiful thing or experience that it is. Breton too identified a frame around the *ergon* of Surrealism's conceptions of beautiful, marvelous things and experiences. This he did, much as Derrida suggests Kant did, by importing determinations and judgments from his philosophical anthropology. These judgments (e.g., diatribes against painters like de Chirico, various excommunications, verdicts about Nadja or "X's" character) establish the space of SurrealISM by delineating its interiority vis-à-vis that which is only adjunct.

But there are complex parasitic and ironic relations between the inside and outside. Derrida submits that had Kant not inserted his own constructions and positionings, there would be no way to decide just where and what is interior or exterior. Within Kant's and Breton's framework, theory creates certain closures that make identification and representation possible. Only such theoretical positioning stabilizes the relation between the *ergon* and the *parergon*, and only as long as that theory holds sway can the legal space of an essence or interior itself remain stable. When determinate judgments are contested, as Derrida contested Kant's, the tension pairing *parergon* and *ergon* loosens, slides, and opens. Here the *parergon* becomes the supplement of the *ergon* rather than its consort. As a supplement it loses its ability to be distinguished from the *ergon*, or from that which is exterior to the *parergon* itself. The question about beauty, then, as a judgment about knowledge, becomes terribly difficult. For now it is possible that the site of beauty (or knowledge) is not interior space; it may well be exterior, or even elsewhere and otherwise.

In a manner akin to Derrida's commentary on Kant, "Dali" became a similar commentary on Surrealism (cf. his comments on "sticky and retarded Kantians"). (It is important to note here that Dali was on no more certain grounds than was Breton in deciding what is beautiful or transformative. What is crucial, though, is that Breton was quite sure, not withstanding the vagaries of a convulsive universe, of where delineations were to be made. Dali's catastrophic, antitheoretical "method," however, remained open to alterity and difference.) Dali was, from his first promising moments, gathered within the *ergon* of Surrealism even though Breton had premonitions of his potentially menacing unruliness. Through the 1930s Dali eroded the coherence of the *ergon/parergon* couplet. Continually an irritant to its apparatus, which that apparatus could not transform into the "pearl" Breton so longed for, his untoward activities were received as vulgarity, waste, and trickery. Over these years, and prior to his expulsion, he moved from the *ergon* to the *parergon*—not yet dispossessed by Breton, as he still accorded Dali the status of a darkness-before-illumination that was crucial to the *ergon* of Surrealism. That is, Dali's aesthetics still served the project of knowledge Breton set forth. Various of Dali's paintings and writings took on a supplemental character, and their anamorphic marginality vigorously contested the identity Breton cast over the necessities and chance of psychic and universal automatism.

But with *Endless Enigma* everything changed. Its paroxysms shattered the tenuous *tissue capillaire* connecting the *parergon* and *ergon*. Its agitated indeterminacy no longer permitted a tension between the one-and-the-other to endure so as to produce an economy of inclusion/exclusion. For instance, no longer could the mimetic circuitry of *trompe l'oeil* form a binary out of the lost wholeness of the time of ancient suns and certain surprising experiences. *Endless Enigma* is a site of effacement[3] where frames, interiors, and exteriors wither and are erased, surpassed by an endless exteriority Breton would himself later admit even he had overlooked. It is most problematic thus to say any more whether *Endless Enigma* is *parergonal* or whether it is simply other. Conventional criticism would suggest it is *parergonal*. In this reading, however, it is received, reminiscent of Blanchot, as a step not beyond.

Such a stance can be offered only if the *parergon/ergon* duet no longer holds the status of an issue or question. That is, once "the beautiful" is no longer associated with knowledge, the whole matter of positioning slips away. For Kant (especially via Lyotard) such a situation exists when the sublime arrives, for it renders all questions of borders moot. *Endless Enigma* is such a scene. (Is it not surprising that Dali often referred to himself as sublime as well as divine?) Its irruption raises the specter of the "non-logical difference" between *savoir* and *non-savoir* Bataille so struggled with. Here is where *Endless Enigma*'s disastrous *con-fusion* of interiority and exteriority insites a rupture into which both Dali and Breton tumbled, never to be seen together again, though conjoined forever in some strangely transgressive surreal space.

To glimpse the workings of this activity, *Endless Enigma* can be taken conjunctively as silence, laughter/joke, and, ironically, communication. Considerations of this ensemble permit an opportunity to assess that smile on the face of *Endless Enigma*.

SILENCE

Breton had trepidations and premonitions about Dali from the earliest moments of Dali's "insinuation" of himself into Surrealism.[4] Perhaps that began in 1919 when Breton acknowledged the significance of "fragmentary phrases," of which it was impossible to say what "shaped or framed them." This acknowledgment he published in "Entrance of the Mediums," an essay on Desnos's surrealist speech in <u>Les Pas perdu</u>.[5] At this time Breton had already made his break with Dada Tzara. Yet he was still enchanted by both the fragmentary and its mediumistic quality. Because the mediums enter "tapping at the window,"[6] in an other voice, they tend to assume (though not yet articulated as such by Breton)[7] the character of the "phantom object."

It can be said in no uncertain terms that Dali was a phantom object, whom Breton would later acknowledge, in 1929, as one with whom for "perhaps the first time that the mental windows have been opened really wide."[8] Dali was the fragmentary, veiled in Desnos-like surrealspeak, who had been knocking at Breton's window. But with the premonition came a rumbling that would later blossom as the sunflower in the night of phantom meaning, whose exorbitant radiance would reveal the extent to which the sky was a trap entered without gliding upward.[9]

Initially, though, Dali had none of the evil Maldoror's aura about him. Breton received the multiple fragments as positive evidence of the hope he placed in Surrealism, a hope that for him was synonymous with ascendance. Not yet apparent were the rips in the "conducting wire" and the tears in the "capillary tissue" imprinted by the phantom object's phantom meaning. The convulsive beauty of the marvelous seemed immanent, as did its veiled eroticism, but desire had not yet been freed from Freud, from Marx, from Hegel, or even from Heraclitus or the elder esoterics (all of whom harnessed desire to destiny). Early on with Dali, Breton took the *point suprême* to be ever so imminent, Dali hailed as a medium of its presencing. The *point suprême*, Breton's mad love, still celebrated in 1937 against the seductive wiles of particularities and fragments, was a point that could be attained with some finality. Though one could not repose there, Breton acknowledged, that moment of coalescence, of essential fusion, was still what Breton's Surrealist lived for. Mad love is that essential clarity where all profiles align in one glorious embrace that marks a cessation of enigmatic egress and excess.

Nonetheless, by dint of objective chance, phantom meaning, perhaps on the wings of Nadja's future breath, had insinuated itself into Breton's life. But Dali would not forsake his own mad love. For this he was to be expropriated—a heretic. For Breton the binary (e.g., "convulsive beauty will be veiled-erotic, fixed-explosive, magic-circumstantial, or it will not be")[10] is the minimalistic *l'age d'or*—the simplest, truest path through the labyrinth. Indeed, *Mad Love*, published in 1937 on the eve of *Endless Enigma*, can be read as an ode to love, objective chance, and desire, all of which service the automatism of fusion. It is also, however, a profusion of certainty and clarity where the disarrays of fragments, and their negations, embrace, at least for a moment, even though the restlessness of the dialectic is destined to continue.

For Dali desire is extravagantly perfidious and ironic, and endless—without a recuperable coherence. This is evident when considering the noisy silence emanating from *Endless Enigma* (see chapter 3). This silence is quite different from that described by Breton in *Communicating Vessels*. For instance, in his discussion of the phantom object,[11] which manifested itself during the game of the "exquisite corpse," it is clear that it came to him not only as "silence" (a concurrence of *cils* and *anse*, items that were part of his drawings in the game), but in the silence only the nocturnality of automatism could ensure. The literal, the auditory, and the spectral conspired quietly and surreptitiously to gratuitously posit a surprising pun that was the archetype of the phantom object (here the "silence-envelop"—a communicating vessel).[12] Its very being is its *modus operandi*—the medium is the message. But this does not at all prevent it from speaking very loudly and clearly. This it does from within the sublimity of the *point suprême*—a fleeting, unstable moment of mad love, of totality, of reconciliation of difference, where awe is full.

Breton not only was sure to highlight the unsettling consequences of the irruptive meaning(s) of the phantom object, but also

noted that it inhabits and obsesses the one who by chance encounters it. He invoked the spectacle of Lautréamont's umbrella and
sewing machine in establishing this obsession, but even more promi-
nent was his invocation of the symbology of Freudian sexual desire.
The point Breton advocated was indebted to that made by Dali (and
Giacometti) with his "symbolically functioning objects" in 1931.[13]
Via various psychic circuitry, stimulated by objective chance and
external necessity, and by phantoms,[14] it is possible for disruptive
and transformative meaning to irrupt. This is the *signe ascendant*—
the hope of Surrealism—a materialization of truth already available
within the universe, awaiting only a spark to reveal it.

While Breton continued to defend this position, however, Dali
went another direction. The divergence arose over differences concerning the degree to which it was permissible to intercede in the
workings of automatic processes. In the *Second Manifesto* and
Communicating Vessels Breton showed a certain openness to per-
mitting subjective intervention, in that he deemed it part of the
process of the subject's self-understanding (concomitant with the
Hegelianism of both Marx and Freud). But he remained suspicious
about tampering with the nocturnal means by which phantom(s)
(objects) perform. Fabricated objects, whose latent content is decided
in advance, are still explosive and beautiful, but when "too particularly conceived, too personal [they] will always lack the astonish-
ingly suggestive power that certain almost everyday objects are able
to acquire by chance."[15] Breton's primary concern here is that imaginative intervention opens a "narrower field for interpretation" than
objects not determined so systematically. Dali's paranoiac-criticism
was intervention par excellence, but more, it was the site of an other
silence.

Though Breton vigorously promoted the uncontrived realities
of automatism over voluntary hallucination (which he advanced in
1929 as Dali's promise),[16] there is a convulsive twist of chance Breton
overlooked: Dali ironically supported Breton's argument! *Endless
Enigma* is ostensibly presented as a phantom object—a feigned symbolically functioning object. The unexpected surprise that leaps from
it is none other than phantom meaning. There is no doubt Dali
labored over the construction of the various images constituting
Endless Enigma, but it cannot be ruled out that they did not come to
him via automatic paths by chance. It can even be said that Breton's
famous lines/images that commence *Surrealism and Painting* ("The
eye exists in its savage state . . . the wild eye that traces all its colors
back to the rainbow")[17] were themselves a phantom object that sur-
faced in *Endless Enigma*. That is, having already noted the existence

of six (seven?) images in *Endless Enigma*, is it not surprising that rainbows have six color bands/rays (and in some esoteric renderings seven)? In a circuitous way, was Breton not part of the production of *Endless Enigma*? Did he not have a premonition, in anticipating in 1929, that Dali's art is a "menace . . . new and visibly malintentioned beings hereupon enter into play . . . with a sinister joy we watch them . . . and realize, from the way in which they multiply and swoop down, that they are beings of prey?"[18] Is it strange then that these colors, these six rays, these fragments, never join to make of *Endless Enigma* a rainbow?

Further, is it not strange that Giacometti's surrealist objects, published in *Le Surréalisme au service de la révolution* in 1931, are seven in number, as are the phantoms circulating in *Endless Enigma*? And more so, that Giacometti's objects are mute as well as mobile (*objets mobiles et muets*)? The phantoms whose movements reverberate silently in Breton's (phantom) objects are likewise mute in Giacometti's noisy automatist inscription under *les objets mobiles et muets*: "all things . . . near, far, all those that passed and the others, in front, moving; and my lady friends—they change (we pass, very near, they are far away); others approach, ascend, descend."[19]

But it is not a gentle, vessel-like silence that envelops possibility stirring in Giacometti's objects or lines, nor is it in Dali. It is an exorbitant meaning, an exploding, violent silence occasioned by hyperdetermined alterities that cannot be made binary. Inscribed instead is a general economy rather than a restricted economy[20] from which silence relentlessly pours and returns eternally to interfere with the phantom object.

Silence then becomes convulsive. It would be too easy, though, to say that the silence arising from Giacometti's mute objects or Dali's *Endless Enigma* is a matter of "lack." To make of silence lack is to rush in with theory in hopes of stemming an egress whose advance cannot be forced into the binary apparition of "two distant realities." Here desire does not bare the respite or recompense of a *telos*, however ephemeral, that Breton had conceived of in *Mad Love*. Rather, desire's obsession is pure—for its own movement—and not for a moment of satisfaction, interiority, or transparency. The event of a *mise-en-abîme*, the desire operative in *Endless Enigma* is more akin to what Levinas, in *Totality and Infinity*, named "the caress." In the caress, the "essentially hidden throws itself toward the light, without becoming signification. Not nothingness—but what is not yet."[21] The what-is-not-yet, Levinas suggests, is a "clandestinity," which, though agitated, does not bring about a possibility or accomplish an objective. Rather, as Lingis notes, "it returns obsessively

over the surface fondled, as over ever-virgin territory . . . [it] moves
without knowing what it wants or what it is doing . . . limp and
passive, it is without will, without program."[22] The endless enigma
of this furtive returning incites a silence in the heart of the silence
Breton took to be so sacred. And, as in the movement of desire noted
by Levinas, there is a profanation[23] of a secret (here Breton's myth—
that desire would end in a fleeting consummation of mad love).

For Breton this was nothing less than a scandal, a revisitation of
the Dada corridors he said went nowhere, of de Chirico's repetitive
wandering in his own confusion. That desire and obsession yield no
flashes or order and induce only evacuation instead of aleatory wandering were but treason and impertinence of the highest order. And
perhaps even more dangerous was that a surrealist object such as
Endless Enigma would raise again, and intensify, the specter of collage (which Ernst identified as "convulsive identity"), whose purpose
it was to disturb "the principle of identity" and to abolish the
"author."[24] For Breton this amounted to a crisis in the subject and in
the object outside anything he was willing to entertain. It is one
thing for an object to "disturb us within our memory,"[25] but it is
quite another for that object to render memory and the unconscious
passive and irrelevant. For Dali, anticipating Foucault's "counter-
memory," on the other hand, to not liberate as many singular phantoms as possible, at once, and to permit only two at a time to express
themselves, under the regime of the dialectic, was simply un-
phathom-able. Wrote Dali, "I hate simplicity in all its forms."[26]

What we have with *Endless Enigma* is little else than the utter
transvaluation of the phantom object as phantom meaning.

JOKE

It would be an error to assume that the silence incited by *Endless
Enigma* is the only consequence of the stirrings of multiple and different phantoms who interrupt each other's autonomy as well as
that of the "whole" of which they might be taken as messengers.
There is still the smile or smirk or innocent smugness on the face of
Endless Enigma to be reckoned with. A consideration of Dali's jux-
taposing of *trompe l'oeil*, convulsive beauty/identity, and the joke
speaks to the disruptive powers of *Endless Enigma*, for beyond all
else is the notion that the meaning, identity, and representation of
truth are a joke.

Lest this be taken too cynically or nihilistically, let us locate
discussion of *Endless Enigma* near Cottom's recent inquiry about the

relationship between jokes and the politics of interpretation. In particular, his notion of the "sceptical joke"[27] is important as *Endless Enigma* operates as its accomplice. Such a rendition makes of Surrealism itself a joke, rather than humor, and it exposes aspects of the politics existent between Dali and Breton/Surrealism.

Cottom's provisional notion of a joke is "text in a context that allows someone to take it as an occasion of humor—that is, as conveying a non-serious or playful meaning, usually inspiring smiles or laughter."[28] In that a joke is in fact a discourse that invokes a historically contingent realm of signification, it is inevitable that the meaning of a joke requires a particular identity to be represented that simultaneously operates to repress differences. In the presentation of them as a totality that locates things relationally, power and rhetoric conspire to produce the context and conventions ("culture") upon which the joke relies. Of particular interest to Cottom is the "rhetorical authority" of the "imaginary law" a joke requires, and constructs, in order to have meaning.[29] What the latter suggests is that the culture invoked to provide a context for meaning is never entirely present or universal or transcendent. Truth and meaning are thus deeply political and not necessarily about "the world."

Crucial to the mechanics by which the materiality of rhetorical practices/discourses become operative is the "rule of irony." The rule of irony is an apparatus deployed to insure that everything does not become ironic, that is, "subject to endless qualification from different contexts and yet maintaining no identity through these changes, as in the phantasmagoric and hallucinatory moments"[30] of various writings or other presentations of reality. Central to the rule of irony is that it displaces rules of origin.[31] Thus, when questions of origin are problematic, as they certainly are in surreality, the rule of irony functions to give some sense of coherence, order, and identity,[32] as well as some sense of subjectivity and desire.[33] (Quoting Breton in relation to the latter, "At least it [Surrealism] will have tried, perhaps inefficaciously, but tried, to leave no question without answer and to have cared a little about the coherence of the answers given.")[34] The rule of irony thus performs as a rule of order.[35] It does so not by way of a dialectical process, but rather as an "enchantment"[36] that presides over the genesis of meaning.

As an instigator of the imaginary law of culture, the rule of irony presides over a text's production of differences. These very differences provide the possibility of an economy in which identification can occur by marking boundaries that constitute the real, the meaningful, the moral, etc. This is as much true for making linguistic and artistic conventions as it is for any other cultural productions. The rule of irony operates as power and knowledge and sets all within its sway on solid ground.[37] And ever so crucial to its machination is that its performance is the unconscious, unrecognized compulsion that marks the invisibility of custom and protocol.[38] Unleashing his own version of the revenge of imagination, Dali's insistences, as subjective intervention, showed Breton's automatism to have been, as Cardinal also notes,[39] never much more than an ideological construct. The legal space of its essence was more a matter of juridical fiat than anything substantial, more a matter of hope than elixir. Cardinal's observations are especially interesting and relevant here in that he is comparing the automatism of the visionary and the mad with that of the contrived automatism of Breton, which Breton himself distinguished from premeditated intervention or voluntary hallucination (cf. Dali, Bellmer, Magritte).

Thus, when Breton articulated in his various writings and images a sense of what surreality is, and how experiences of it are to be prepared for, and especially when he promoted its humorous and radical challenge to conventionality, he secreted an oppositional, but nonetheless structured, discourse. For this discourse to be effective and stable it necessarily drew upon and constituted a community. Here community is understood as both the social actors of the Surrealist group and the community represented and identified as existing within surreal space. Any jokes, strategies, objects, or other ploys utilized within this community were under the aegis of, and at the same time produced by, that very community. A strategy of joking *non gratis*, which Dali deployed, was the sceptical joke. Cottom considers the sceptical joke "rare."[40] It is also pernicious in its ability to undermine constructed truths and to expose the capillary routes power takes and the machinery it forms. Sceptical jokes raise questions and doubts about "the certainty of knowledge itself." At the heart of the sceptical joke is a confusion of truth and lie such that one lies only when telling the truth and the truth is told by means of a lie. Referring to a discussion (see chapter 3) where *Endless Enigma* was considered to possess a "metastatic truth," Cottom likewise suggests that in the sceptical joke "truth is always a neoplasm, "genuine truth," a trope; in which there always remain other possibilities for laughter, for a new victory; in which the conditions of truth are always only possible."[41]

With *Endless Enigma* Dali slipped a sceptical joke into the device of Surrealism. Ever the irreverent Luddite, Dali sidestepped the rhetorical unconsciousness necessary for Surrealism and did not forfeit the occasion to challenge, and advocate a new reading of, the imaginary law(s) that gave Surrealism its force and meaning.[42] He defied Breton's reading of the "ur-scene" or "ur-reality" that became instituted in text and image as s-ur-reality. Dali's strategy, which in no way escapes the problem of the politics of reading and writing, seeks no universal, utopian, or idealized freedom. Rather it takes freedom always to be mobile, local, provisional, and open to contestation. *Endless Enigma*'s peculiar rhetorical strategy amounts to a form of periphrasis: various incarnations of beasts, vegetation, mineral, and spirit swirl about a visage that never forms. Neither *arche* nor *telos* is immanent, and meaning never ceases to slide or escape elision. The hysterical present is not able to cast a veil of identity over what would seem to be ever so possible.

Endless Enigma thus posed a serious challenge to the meanings of *trompe l'oeil*, convulsive beauty, and laughter within the Surrealist canon. The convulsive *trompe l'oeil* of *Endless Enigma* is an ur-scene where the marvelous is displaced by phantom meaning, which simulates and operates as an imaginary law, as a rule of irony, and at the same time doubles as the phantom object (or the rule of order). The *mise-en-abîme* of *Endless Enigma* produces wondrous *con-fusions*.

Quite a joke! That there is an innocuous, childlike smile or smirk (or perhaps a mischievous grin)[43] on the face of *Endless Enigma* is accidental? and that this final reading of Surrealism by Dali as a member of its community, on the very eve of his expulsion from that community, is coincidental? Perhaps not. Had Baudrillard been there, he might have consoled and reminded Breton, who himself said that the marvelous isn't what it was before, that neither is the real anymore what it used to be!

But here, where the real and the marvelous are no longer what they once were, the joke turns serious. When, for instance, Baudrillard confronted the same canonical truths of Marxism to which Breton has also pledged allegiance, he observed that "canonical representation" sets itself up as expressing an "objective reality . . . a 'real' signified."[44] The problem Baudrillard identified in the Marxian canon was that it had fallen, however earnestly it had tried not to take concepts for reality, into the *imaginary of the sign*, or the *sphere of truth*.[45]

The same Nietzschean critique of imaginary truth that Baudrillard applied to Royal Marxism, Dali applied to Breton's Surrealism, locating in it an imaginary law whose rhetorical authority demands a rule of irony that functions in favor of power and domination. On the conventions that arise here, Baudrillard offers: "When the real is no longer what it used to be, nostalgia assumes its full meaning. There is a proliferation of myths of origin and signs of reality; of second-hand truth, objectivity, and authenticity."[46]

Endless Enigma forces its viewer to consider how humor was transformed into a joke whose received laughter doubled as the punch line of a critical discourse, in operation almost a decade, whose aims included the destabilization of the imaginary and the substitution for it of multiplicity. And if Bataille could be heard laughing in the background, is it perhaps because he could recognize a certain uselessness and *non-savoir* created by *Endless Enigma*? This for Bataille, of course, would have meant that the sun and its radiance had been repositioned in the scheme of things, if not inverted, as he himself had done with the pineal eye and the solar anus.[47]

COMMUNICATION

So what then does *Endless Enigma* communicate? Or does it communicate anything? Because it is a journey, reminiscent of de Chirico's iteration of Nietzsche in *Endless Voyage*, let us begin by recalling that *by chance* Dali, in pursuing Breton's exhortation to find Surrealist objects, encountered phantom meaning feigning being the phantom object. His enchanted celebration of phantom meaning, however, amounted to a liberation of the sense of hazard and peril glossed over and suppressed within Breton's assertion of the meaning of *l'objet hasard*. *Endless Enigma* does not forget that hazard is as much a *necessity* as is chance in Breton's notion of objective chance. Is then marvelous, mad love, whose gathering renders a reality more sublime than either the object found or the desiring subject, perhaps forced, after all, to exist side by side with hazard and jeopardy, in a transgressive rather than a contradictory relation? That is, is hazard perhaps the limit experience, the extreme limit of the encounter with the marvelous? Perhaps *Endless Enigma* is, by chance, a strange twist of that same convulsive event that meandered through Apollinaire's discovery of himself in a de Chirico painting (in which his head formed a target; he was later wounded in the head)? through Victor Brauner's *Self-Portrait with Enucleated Eye*, 1931 (later in 1938 he lost an eye in a brawl)? through Breton and Giacometti's flea market discoveries and subsequent writings and sculptures (e.g., see *Mad Love*, pp. 19–38)? through the vector that slashed the I of a possible subjectivity-transformed-and-elevated-by-the-ascending-marvelous first celebrated in *Un Chien andulou* by Dali and Bunuel now come back to haunt Breton's premonitions with all the unkempt fury of Nadja? And is "X," after all, the sign of erasure, disaster, and catastrophe?

Breton, of course, never projected such a destiny for objective chance. In 1937, for instance, shortly after the International Surrealist Exhibition in London, he offered the view that objective chance and objective humor are "the two poles between which Surrealism will be able to flash a current of the highest tension."[48] Considering, however, the way the joke embedded in *Endless Enigma* advanced itself, objective chance and objective humor could not be the dialectically paired "black and white sphinxes" whose "embrace," Breton predicted, would produce the offspring that would be "all further human creation(s)."[49] Breton had warned that a collapse or nonarrival of dialectical fusion was a pitfall to be avoided, as if it were a *fait accompli* that such avoidance could occur. He had, for instance, rejected Nadja's sirens, as well as those of X, and had rebuked de Chirico for having not the slightest idea of what he was doing and for coming to "wretched conclusions" where "inspiration is totally lacking . . . and a shameless cynicism is flagrantly evident."[50] Indeed, it is precisely in the diatribe against de Chirico, which was a forerunner of those yet to come (e.g., see the *Second Manifesto*), that Breton, considering particularly the role of painters as Surrealists, identified Surrealism as having a "fundamental moral code."[51] In his zeal to retrieve "the pearl . . . from the dung heap of absolute idealism,"[52] Breton exalted an idealism whose denials betrayed the objective necessity of hazard.

The particular form this idealism assumed was not for Breton the nauseating terminology of mysticism or spiritualism but rather the worldly lived-experiences of material occurrences. Manifesting themselves as things (images, objects, writings, meetings, events, etc.), they consisted in material appearances (consistent with the objectives of Surrealism and Hegelian Marxism in the *Second Manifesto*). These materialities operate, according to Breton, as Chenieux-Gendron astutely notes, as "traces" within a "grid,"[53] with each trace or -gram sufficing to be the occasion of a movement toward the next, and so on, until, via convulsion, the beautiful and marvelous *point suprême* shows signs of coalescing. Automatism and the role of the subject collude to set the stage for the *signe ascendant*'s movements. The "lyricism of the uncontrollable" (in 1923 a name for Surrealism) thus depended, in no uncertain terms, on a material presencing. This presence was always subjugated to being a "manifest identity" within the "universal elasticity" of dialectical reality.[54]

Breton, however, had always resisted a too active role for the subjective despite his somewhat duplicitous insistence on the place of the subjective in preserving interiority from a precipitous slide into the abysmal. In 1933, under the spell of "endless bad fortune," Breton gave in to the notion that certain "premeditated intentions"[55] are permissible—a concession to Dali's arguments against the passivity of automatism. Breton admitted to two possibilities for Surrealist praxis: (1) pure automatism, and (2) the mimetic recording, via *trompe l'oeil* and strange literary and visual juxtapositions of the one-in-the-other, of the experiences of the artist. This mimetic activity is actually the analogue of a remembrance of a more primal *ur-scene*, prior to the dissociation of subjectivity and objectivity, that is preserved in the eidetic image and in the primitivism of the child. Here Breton preserves, though assenting to a tactic such as paranoiac-criticism, the authorial authenticity of the conjunction of psychic and universal automatism. Dali, of course, with his trump of *trompe l'oeil*, revealed that automatism is not automatic but subject to interruption and deferral.

Hazard, then, has an obstinately exorbitant material necessity that forces itself into the dynamics of the *signe ascendant*. This much is intimated, but still suppressed, in the distinction made between objective humor and black humor. Black humor is an advance over objective humor in that objective humor, following Hegel's notion, tends to materialize in the world in the form of temporal disruptions of reality that transform the destiny of things and meanings. Black humor, on the other hand, is the ego's province, for in the work of the artist, poet, or painter, representational schemes and semiotic systems, which too affect the destiny of meaning, can be unsettled (here also is the political import of this notion, which resulted in *The Anthology of Black Humor* being banned for a period of time). Is it not uncanny that Breton, having referred to black humor in earlier writings in the 1930s, did not use the name *black* until 1937, the same time as the appearance of *Endless Enigma*? And is it not strange that much of its conceptualization by Breton drew on Freud's *Jokes and Their Relation to the Unconscious* (studied in *Le Surrealisme au service de la revolution*, no. 2, 1930), to which Cottom appended the sceptical joke that, I have suggested, informs the mechanism of *Endless Enigma*? Further, is it not uncanny that "black" also involves the specter of death (which Breton also found in Freud), not death as tragedy, but as overcoming and liberation from a host of social ills affecting both world and consciousness? Chenieux-Gendron notes that for Breton black is the "color of exaltation: it is the color of the flag of Anarchy."[56]

What a pity then that the figure of Dali, here as the hazard incarnate, was met with charges of error, insubordination, and turpitude. What a pity that liberation could be envisioned only as a *point suprême* rather than as a plentitude of differences and particulars. What a pity that such plentitude would be construed as negativity and tragedy rather than as fecundity. In all this, too, one notes carefully that Nietzsche is suspiciously absent in Breton's discourses on mad love and ascendance, for from such a vantage as his, only the tragedy of a madman's hebephrenic nihilism would be heard, its other possibilities lost in the glare of a dark sun Breton encountered with Bataille. What a shame, then, that Breton did not see *Endless Enigma* as a death mask that valorized not ending and misery but beginning and opening. Beginning and opening are not necessarily coterminate with the rhetoric of hope, but then again, they do not necessarily preclude or deny hope.

The "original" sin of Dali, materialized at last in *Endless Enigma*, is the divulgence that at the heart of Breton's carnival of objective humor and black humor resides an idealism that revered subjectivity despite Breton's multiple insistences that the objective nature of Surrealist humor overcomes and corrects any obsessions with subjective desire. What Dali recognized in Surrealism was not a break (*coupure*) but a hinge (*brisure*) on which it was warping. What Dali exposed was an advanced form of subjective revolution, which affirmed the sovereignty of bourgeois and modernist interiority and individualism despite its simulation of collective desire and objective necessity (e.g., mad love's embrace, where in the amorous encounter of lovers or the collectivity of Marxist/socialist society). Dali recognized that such subjectivism and materialism carried tendencies similar to those Bataille had noted when he wrote:

> Most materialists, even though they may have wanted to do away with all spiritual entities, ended up positing an order of things whose hierarchical relations mark it as specifically idealist. They situated dead matter at the summit of a conventional hierarchy of diverse facts, without perceiving that in this way they gave in to an obsession with the *ideal* form of matter, with a form that was closer than any other to what matter *should be*.[57]

Dali's "exhibitionism," for which he was roundly critiqued by Breton, consisted not only in his own excessive subjectivism, but in his exposure of a general economy repressed within Breton's restricted Surrealist economy. Asserted pictorially, it consisted in his argument that traces mask themselves as signs, expose themselves as simulacra of symbols, and thereby erode their chastity in denuding both themselves and the very meanings whose destiny they were to transport and transform. In a cruel inversion of Breton's use of Freud's notions of condensation, and especially displacement, Dali dislodged Breton's subjectivism by undercutting its own advocacy of metaphoric and metonymic transfigurations. For as we see in *Endless Enigma*, the endless enigma is instigated not by mystical obfuscation or by marvelous convulsion, but by a precession of simulacra.

The mediums advancing in the materiality of Dali and *Endless Enigma*, and Breton's associated premonitions, were echoed again in Breton's claim that Dali was "one of those who arrive from so far off that when you see them enter, *and only enter*, you have no time to see them. He places himself, without saying a word, in a system of interferences."[58] The interferences, as Caws intimates,[59] are indeed already part of the elastic grid of the time of ancient suns Breton posited as hidden behind appearances. These interferences permit recovery of the seemingly lost rays of those ancient suns and ground the possibility of sight and *savoir*. But the interferences in *Endless Enigma* are different. They are the inescapable hazards of chance suns whose rays diverge and disappear. The face of *Endless Enigma* is not the face of "Dali" placed in a system of interferences.

What is communicated by *Endless Enigma* must be understood not in terms of metaphoric or metonymic transformations, that is, not in terms of what *Endless Enigma* contains, but rather in terms of the medium by which it expresses. The medium is a message, and the medium is more than a *trompe l'oeil*; it is also a clever trump of the I that deeply alters both the I (subjective) and the world (objective). The trump of the I, an accomplice and acolyte of phantom meaning, simulates *trompe l'oeil* thereby maintaining a certain invisibility vis-à-vis the dialectic of representation to which Surrealism assents. The effect of this trump is transformation, but a cyborgian transformation named better by fission that by fusion, better by rapture or a-lasticity than by elasticity.

Via this trump of *le trompe*, Dali transvalues the Surrealist crisis of the subject and the object. The subject, now committed to being a relay, which is different from, or *con-fused* with, the "conducting wire," never quite emerges with an identity, never is able to extract a "pearl" from overabundant convulsiveness. Those moments where a spectral I feigns appearance are little more that chimeric accidents. As accidents, though, they are sites of conflict where each ray or facet that could coalesce as identity disrupts the autonomous field of the other rays or facets' sensibilities. The endless journey (also an alternative translation of the title of *Endless Enigma*) is one of interruption, delay, deferral. Without Dali's drawings to make them visible, one would scarcely even know what phantoms inhabit the spaces of the painting.[60] Yet even in noticing them, one is at a loss to make sense of their juxtapositions.

Because phantom meaning performs as a *supplement* to the phantom object, there is a ceaseless, tireless dissemination of meanings. The olive branches in the forefront of *Endless Enigma* may signify a hope for meaningfulness, or perhaps just for its impossible possibility. In other paintings of the same period, the telephone minus the mouthpiece (e.g., *The Enigma of Hitler*, 1937; *The Sublime Moment*, 1938) also intimates the silence and impotence of circulating signs that cannot communicate to or with each other—a sort of the Baudrillardian "death of the social" inscribed in the *signe ascendant con-fused* with the irruption of the sublime. As they assert their differences, reminiscent of Nietzsche's singularities and Jarry's pataphysical particulars, and premonitions of Lyotard's paralogies, the philosopher does not communicate well with the woman seated on the beach, nor does she communicate well with the greyhound or the mythological beast, and the cretin does not see the fruit of the world. Perhaps, as Descharnes suggests, this is Dali's comment denouncing the cretinization of humans.[61] Just as much, though, it is Dali's cretinization of human possibility. At once a celebration of paranoia and antiparanoia, everything, and nothing, is connected, and the *point suprême* (e.g., *The Sublime Moment*, 1938) is without voice or ear, razored by a feigning portraying itself as transparency (Husserl's mad love; e.g., *The Transparent Simulacrum of the Feigned Image*, 1938), the very razing of the I of *Un Chien andulou*.

The possibility suggested by the olive branch is perhaps hope. But hope is necessarily and unavoidably supplemented by hazard, as in the wandering of Hebdomeros, or in Telemachus's dive onto the rocks, after a series of delays and interferences, in search of his father and Homeland.[62] *Endless Enigma*, cryptically EE, is Dali's version of Mentor's "Dd system" in Aragon's *The Adventures of Telemachus*. A "white and black janus" (a parodic predecessor to Breton's black and white sphinx?), the Dd system promotes both "doubt and faith."[63] Doubt is associated with breaking and smashing everything, which then prepares a way for belief and "wisdom."[64] But alas the "system" (which was perhaps for Aragon Dada on the cusp of Surrealism?) is much like EE is a "system." It feigns being a system, just as phantom meaning simulates being a phantom object (which *does* reveal a system.) But in the end living and dying, meaning and nonmeaning (due to absence or excess) are indistinguishable. When Mentor proclaims Telemachus a "fool" for having opted for freedom,[65] and having thus denied the necessity of chance, he too himself perishes, by of all things, chance, in a rockslide. And

> Distaffs danced while shedding their silvery locks. Great rotary presses copulated on the pebbled beaches. Jackhammers strolled prettily in the squares, and while metals, howling with pleasure, petted one another, the lord our God astride his steeds of tenderness burst into wild guffaws.[66]

Perhaps the smile on the face of *Endless Enigma* is the ripple of this laughter, smug in its trump of systems of becoming? Perhaps Tzara, ever suspicious of automatism due to its invocation of essences or orders of truth (whether unconscious or transcendent) that emerge when conscious control is banished,[67] was that reclined philosopher, or mythological beast, in *Endless Enigma*? Perhaps Breton knew finally Dali was Telemachus? And given Dali's frequent comments that when he first met Breton he took him to be his "new father," what a perverse twist this would be on the father/son relationship (in that Breton had at one time somewhat revered Tzara as a father figure, the twist would be even more interesting)!

With *Endless Enigma* Dali smashed the Surrealist object, at the same time subverting the subject Surrealism had proclaimed would replace the bankrupt and corrupt subjectivity of mundane, worldly existence. But he did not do this in a fashion that simply reiterated Dada, thus *Endless Enigma* is not Dada, i.e., EE ≠ Dd. That Dali attacked representation via simulation and silence, supplementation and difference, while still promoting cut-up and collage and laughter, is an advance over Dada that nonetheless shares with Dada some foreshadowing of what is now generically referred to as a "postmodernist/poststructuralist" critique.

Endless Enigma's transvaluation of the Surrealist object forces the question: Are the particular multiples constituting EE just Dali's excessive subjectivism, or are they in fact a precession of phantoms that come from somewhere beyond, or elsewhere, to shatter the very possibility of a coherently convulsive identity? Because each image/figure interrupts the next, and the next the next, ad infinitum, the subject, like the scribe of the bottled messages brought to Telemachus on the waves of time, "could [not] return to [a] point of departure."[68] In *Endless Enigma* desire breaks free from lack and from the grid of destiny from which it could later emerge, as would the phantom object, and affirms itself as endless movement, as slippage, as play and joke, not circumscribed by the Surrealist play of chance, desire, and humour.

Desire, laughter, and silence combine to make of phantom meaning not just a site of multiplicity and conflict, but also a scene of slippage and leakage. As such, *Endless Enigma* is curiously aligned with
Bataille's writings on "communication"[69] and its relation to the destiny[70] of the "total man,"[71] which is "impossible."[72] Communication,
which for Bataille necessitates excess and death, is where humans
attempt to be whole by surmounting the dissociative features of a
servile life grounded in production, accumulation, preservation, and
identity. This is done by engaging the impossible and unincludable,
i.e., those things that venerate sacrifice, loss, death, the crossing of
extreme limits, ecstasy, and *non-savoir*. Communication, quickened
by an "avid and powerful will to be," espouses a heterology or expenditure that expresses the "fundamental right of man to signify nothing."[73] To signify nothing is to become party to the "principle of slipping"[74] where the self, and all its objects and projects (including those
of Surrealism which cling fervently to convulsive identity), are gratuitously forfeited. In particular, in seeking the impossible and *non-
savoir*, whose transgressions open a general economy of "interior experience," Bataille found it necessary to contest language and knowledge
with "slipping words."

Among the slipping words Bataille advocated were *silence* and
formless.[75] The significance of slipping words is that they contain
within themselves the limits of words themselves, in general, to
voice or visualize the passion or desire that makes humans whole.
That is, slipping words contain within themselves the ironic possibility of naming that which cannot be named, not for the purpose of
doing something in particular, such as naming the unnameable, but
rather for demonstrating that purpose, goal, *telos*, etc, are dependent upon forces of difference and dispersion they cannot represent
or identify. Bataille chose *silence* as a slipping word capable of decapitating the architecture of language as a coherent system by which to
present the word and/or experience. It does not reveal anything hidden, signify any idea, or represent any thing, as does Breton's *silence*.

What slipping words and the principle of slippage do invoke
though is the "extreme limit of the possible." For Bataille, "without
the extreme limit, life is only a long deception, a series of defeats
without combat followed by impotent retreat . . . degradation . . .
Every human not going to the limit is the servant or enemy of
man."[76] The extreme limit is "the essential,"[77] but here the essential
is impossible because inscribed within it is an interminable condition of *non-savoir* ("I see what knowledge was hiding up to that
point, but if I see, I know. Indeed I know but non-knowledge again
lays bare what I have known . . . (without possible end)."[78]

The specters moving about in *Endless Enigma* are signs of a heterogeneous reality whose "force or shock presents itself as a charge, a value, passing from one object to another."[79] But unlike the Bretonian flash of current of the highest tension passing between objective chance and objective humor, this movement is "incapable of stopping at a particular being . . . rapidly passing from one to another."[80] It is there, in this movement "where you would like to grasp your timeless substance, [that] you encounter only the poorly coordinated play of your perishable elements."[81] The trump of *le trompe* of *Endless Enigma* is that subject and object are dissolved, and there is passage, but not from one to the other, as in dialectical reconciliation: "the one and the other have lost their separate existence"; there is only "open yawning gap" and the "unintelligible sky [where] everything is reconciled in a final irreconciliation."[82]

Endless Enigma fragments and effaces itself as a vessel and reconstitutes communication such that the I becomes, "in the vast flow of things, only a stopping point in favor of a resurgence."[83] Because though the impossible and the unincludable operate as part of an "advanced dialectic"[84] (transgression), there is a strange "continuity"[85] that emerges. Contrary to Breton's claim that Dali's extreme subjectivism is ultimately privatization and isolation, there is instead Bataille's claim that "the fragile walls of your isolation, which comprised the multiple starting points, the obstacles of consciousness, will have served only to reflect for an instant the flash of those universes in the heart of which you could never cease to be lost."[86]

The flash that is *Endless Enigma* is the attaining of the extreme limit of the Surrealist object and experience. The crisis, or rather the "catastrophe,"[87] opened in the Surrealist-instigated crisis of the subject and object, is the "disheveled joy of communication" whose "laughter, dizziness, vertigo, nausea, loss of self to the point of death" is "not a point in empty space."[88] Within the lexicon of Surrealist discourse, which included silence, along with hope, the *point suprême*, the *signe ascendant*, etc., another silence now intervenes that limits their possibilities. As a limit experience, *Endless Enigma's* meanings are the silence of Bataillean communication, and are undecidable at the level of the oracular, rhetorical/linguistic, and spectral. *Endless Enigma*, as phantom meaning, is a *slipping surrealist object*.

Not a Dada object, EE nevertheless, like Mentor's Dd system, functions to "unhook the sun, to extinguish enthusiasms sporting tiny full blown bellies."[89] The spectacle of philosopher, mythological beast, etc., is perhaps no different from that including "Aunt Sally, bowling, knives, roulette, hobby horses, rhetoric, politics, poems, religions, loves, auction bridge."[90] For in their wake, and with them,

> Everything slides, quoit of smoke, nimble quicksilver. Torrential centuries escape from mountains of shadow. Jostled by the sands of hours, *I* no longer knows whether 'soon' lies just around the corner or arrived here a moment ago; and *just now* designates what eludes me.[91]

That the I no longer knows situates an irrepressible condition of *non-savoir* within the grid of the phantom object's automatism. Phantom meaning, in place of the phantom object, assumes the status of an "object"—catastrophic and ecstatic. With it time is "unhinged."[92] Having become "toxic" and "deleterious,"[93] time is annulled, and the temporality necessary for convulsive subjective transformation within the dialectic/labyrinth is rendered moot. Space too, necessary for the emergence of identifiable materiality, becomes unhinged. "Whirl, the celestial canopy spreads its milky rivers, I succumb, I roll a long, long time numb in the waves of my own flesh unfurling over the earth."[94] Discontinuous time and space disperse the aural magnetism of the multiple fields and vessels profiling about in *Endless Enigma*, rendering their possible communications of meaning mute.

With *Endless Enigma*, Dali confronts Surrealism with a tumultuous reordering of the world and consciousness. *Endless Enigma* stands, in Bataillean terms, as a sovereign act. Against a certain subjectivist idealism and utopianism, and contra Dali himself as an extreme subjectivist, *Endless Enigma* lends flesh and breath to the human right to signify nothing. As a "projectless project,"[95] it is a "questioning undertaken endlessly in a new direction."[96] Not written under the sign of the dialectic, it is an exercise in transgression, an "advanced dialectic" in which loss, excess, and *non-savoir* are impossibly "reconciled" with hope, elevation, and identity. *Endless Enigma* transfigures dialectical alchemy as "obscenity,"[97] as "acrobatics,"[98] and as "ridiculousness."[99]

It is crucial to understand *Endless Enigma*'s affinities to the latter notions, for Breton, at the end of the *Second Manifesto*, rendered Bataille as one incapable of approaching the world in ways that were not sordid, vile, and depraved. Though Dali's obsession with the three great simulacra—blood, excrement, putrefaction—would seem to suggest a similar interest in impurity and uselessness, this rereading offers that "impurity" here is not aligned with filth, but a sense of what Bataille meant by "inner experience."

Impurity, then, must be refigured so that what is at issue is Dali's questioning of another impurity—that which encloses and orders the contents of interiority. The interior model of Surrealism is what is under attack, and, of course, the revelation of its borders and frames as a "stinking essence" would seem to lend credence to the notion that rot and flies alone are of significance. *Endless Enigma* exacerbates what Carrouges calls "surrealist anguish" whose "excess of being . . . [and] sense of fatality . . . pierces the depth of [one's] being."[100] As a celebration of sovereignty, *Endless Enigma's* phantom meaning evokes the specter of Klossowski's phantasm, whose "interiority" and "dialectic," unlike Surrealism's, are incommunicable, elliptical, and silent.[101]

Herein resides the denuding blasphemy of Dali. *Endless Enigma* anticipates Derrida's exposure of the "white mythology" as well as Pynchon's "creative paranoia" and "anti-paranoia," all of which, as fictions, like Husserl's, order and structure the world and lend it an accent of "truth." The interiority of automatism and the labyrinth are revealed to be fables. In Kantian terms, *Endless Enigma* is a *Rhapsodie*—something stitched together (recall the earlier mention of symbol as *symbaellin*). *Rhapsodie* was problematic for Kant, as it is here for Surrealism, because it disturbs the possibility of *Einfassung* (framing, setting borders) and the generation of coherent knowledge operating as identity, form and system; it exposes what LIES at the borders and margins of such systems.[102] Perhaps *Endless Enigma* can be dismissed *pastiche* or *bricolage*, but more aptly, it is the impossible wholeness or "totality" Bataille contested with slipping words and Dali contested pictorially with his own version of slippage.

With meaning simulated, promised, and deferred by the fecund, evanescent caress of *Endless Enigma*, the marvelous is opened and "set adrift forever."[103] Its movement, incapable of composure or repose, is more akin to the hyperactivity Deleuze and Guattari name a "schizophrenic experience" ("intensive qualities in their pure state . . . a cry suspended between life and death, an intense feeling of transition, states of pure naked intensity stripped of all shape and form")[104] than to the hysteria celebrated by Surrealism (in 1928 the Surrealists celebrated the fiftieth anniversary of the discovery of hysteria). Though both hysteria and Deleuze and Guattari's "schizophrenia" operate with notions of an unconscious and desire, schizophrenia cannot be tracked into a meaning-giving system such as psychoanalysis. *Endless Enigma* thus is more a "nomad" following an unknowable vectorial field across which singularities are scattered as so many "accidents."[105] Compelled by forces for which there is no account, or end, *Endless Enigma* "moves between the cloths" of those forces' "furnishing air," which forces it to "sculpted gestures."[106]

So sculpted, *Endless Enigma* is not without form or content; its silence is not that of nothingness or absence. It is instead the disquietude of a system of knowing that has collapsed, overburdened by the noisy hauntings of numerous particulars whose persistent memories restrict them to localities not conducive to a general coalescence or ascendance. Like the unnamed narrator in Cixous's *Souffles*, *Endless Enigma* induces a breathlessness and panting, and the I experiencing it, excited by phantom meaning and tumbling into the abyss of *non-savoir* that makes it complete, knows only "I was burning, I knew that in the flood a fire can burst? which flows without pain and lights up each nerve . . . the flesh is then internally sparkling with a thousand flames which do not mingle, but separately produce a sweet blazing."[107]

The apparition of tranquility, whose simulacrum appears on the face, belies the perpetual commotion that defers the fixity of an essentializing moment the opportunity to offer shelter or respite. What Shaviro so sensitively recognized about Bataille's "catastrophe" and Blanchot's "disaster" is that they do not simply oppose projects of synthesis and harmony with their contrary.[108] To do so would make possible a third term that could cure. Instead the venture is to slip an insidiously repetitive conjunction into such projects so that they become the event of slippage—a self-dissolving act that forever sets things in motion. The smile now shows itself as the lassitude of the face.

Reminiscent of de Chirico's *Disquietude and Uncertainty of the Poet*, this lassitude, however, is born of an incessant effort to fervently assent to heterogeneous life and to the impossible totality of being whole. Rather than the languor of the struggle with indeterminacy that irrupts in Nietzschean abysmal thought, Dali takes a journey somewhat similar to Bataille's. Whereas Bataille confronted fascism and other cultural deformations more directly than did Dali, Dali engaged the same dynamic, but within the politics of Surrealist purity. Little wonder his self-effacing, autoerotic surrealism would end in excommunication, which psychoanalysis would later misread as a death wish. But death and excommunication, as apocalyptic closure, are not equivalent responses to the silence of *Endless Enigma*, for its silence is not that of destruction. Rather it is only catastrophe and disaster, a thrusting of oneself headlong into that which has no foundation. That a foundation would appear to be there is only the work of phantom meaning.

Shaviro suggests of Bataille that his effort to live an intense, heterogeneous life was a "paradoxical intervention" in the stabilized orders of language and hierarchicalized society from which it was excluded. As "performative utterances of a particularly radical sort," they were the simulation of an action that is consumed by its enactment.[109] Dali, espousing *l'amour fou* doubling as *amor fati*, likewise delivered similar performatives, except on the pictorial plane. Simulation was also active here, but because it was inscribed within the already tricky space of *trompe l'oeil*, its effects were ever so difficult to explicate. Whether or not Breton identified them as such—as decapitating gestures—he nonetheless understood their threat to the creative subjectivity of Surrealist praxis. In the strangeness of heterotopic space,

face=seer, project=fetish, he(ad)gemony, yet face=decapitation . . .
silence, joke: phantom meaning . . .

Suppressed, yet in motion within the grid of identity, phantom meaning effects resistance and *sortie*. That same desire that drains Surrealism's breath, as well as that of *Souffles* narrator, phantom meaning

> is the voice which opens my eyes, its light opens my mouth, makes me shout. And I am born from it . . . There is a link between this kind of star and the eruption of my soul. Thus it spreads in the air that makes it move, and from a mixture of its beams and my breath is born a field of star's blood and panting.[110]

The reclining philosopher, name and face repressed though reeking of Nietzsche simulating Lautréamont, and the face of *Endless Enigma*, mark the entrance of a medium more faceted than a janus minotaur (Janus the god of origins and transitions) into the halls of Breton's castle—the *acephalic surrealist*. Phantom meaning, materialized as a slipping, breathless surrealist object not functioning symbolically, is other than, beyond, and more perfidious than a Dada object. For what it advances is just this acephalic surrealist. Acephalic because the face exists under erasure. Acephalic because the I, the symbolic bearer of consciousness, knowledge, goals, projects, etc. (i.e., as "headedness")[111] is decapitated, but feigns not being so. Yet it is the sundered member that once graced Masson's drawing (*Acephale*, 1935). It would thus be too easy and too sterile to assume the face of *Endless Enigma* is in fact *a* face. To attribute to *Endless Enigma* a monocephalic character (via the dialectical embrace of oppositions; the minotaur, the Surrealist mascot, was in fact a bicephalic creature embracing the various binaries of dream/waking, conscious/unconscious, etc.) would be a "crushing atrophy."[112] *Endless Enigma* cannot be forced into this serenity because it is a polycephalic space, a rich zone where difference and discord are given their due as that which ironically invigorates the "total" I, the whole human. The simulation of the head as the sign of the possibility of system and essence, a grid from which the marvelous could arise, *con-fuses* the condition of ascendance with that of a deleterious fall. *Endless Enigma*: a luminous warp of *trompe l'oeil*, a surprisingly scandalous limning of automatist revelation. Another story of the I.

The face of *Endless Enigma*, however, unlike the death skull in Masson's drawing for Bataille and Klossowski's journal (*Acephale*), is not inverted as it was in Bataille's conception of Acephalic man.[113] That is, the head is not located at the site of sexual and excretory organs, which effects this inversion and the destruction of identity formation and continuity. *Endless Enigma* is not as overt an attack on Surrealist notions of dialectics as were the well-known attacks of Bataille against Breton. But there is one similarity between *Endless Enigma* and Acephalic man. The body (base matter) of the Acephalic man, for Bataille, is the site of a labyrinth in which move not only life and death, but savoir and *non-savoir*, desire and difference, and waste and coherence, none of the latter of which are dialectically tensed pairings, but rather moments of "non-logical difference" within a general economy in which exchanges producing a continuity of meaning and identity founder. Dali, on the other hand, retains the notion of the head, which appears to promise what is lost in Acephalic man. Yet the head, a feigned representation of a symbol, is a simulacrum of the acephalic body. *Endless Enigma's* *trompe l'oeil*, playing on the one-in-the-other dynamic, locates the face/head, on the one hand, as the possibility of continuity and identity, and, on the other, as a menage of singularities that do not form a "one" that can exchange and transmute in the one-in-the-other dynamic. The effect of this trump of *le trompe* is to substitute the body for the head so as to retain a feigned sense of the Surrealist ontological and aesthetic machinery while simultaneously rendering it impossible. The face of *Endless Enigma* thus becomes the face, and symbolization collapses. We are to be reminded again of Dali's remark that shit is a simulacrum of shit—it points to nothing, offers nothing, nothing is returned to it, and it is devoid of the magnetism necessary for symbolic formations. Without this magnetism, things (e.g., phantom objects) that could form symbols or signals disperse into a rhapsody of free signifiers. That a smile, not yet a full-blown guffaw, emerges in this silence attests to a sovereign act of counter-memory and counterprophecy. The smile is the prelude to an irrepressible laughter—a meaningless sign of an impossible, incommunicable interiority whose phantoms already tickle and cajole the face of *Endless Enigma*, itself a feigned simulacrum of teleology, transcendence, and wholeness. The slipping surrealist object engages in an act of automutilation that ins(c)ites phantom meaning and its desublimated alterities and excesses.

The death mask *Endless Enigma* forms thus communicates death, but assents to death as an exuberance of life.[114] *Endless Enigma* is a sacrificial site where the marvelous is expended and lost in favor of fervent life, a sorcerous ploy escaping the servility of essentialization. That Dali said so many times even he did not understand or know from whence his images came attests to a desire to celebrate life and destiny as an irreconcilable whole, a lost totality. Again Bataille, "the one who sacrifices is himself affected by the blow he strikes, he succumbs and loses himself with his victim . . . in . . . an incomplete world, incompletable and forever unintelligible."[115] Such exuberance in the face of superabundance, even in death, raises the specter of desire without origin or *telos*—an eroticism not traceable to a banal sexuality or to psychoanalytic, Hegelian, Heraclitean, or occultated dialectics. It raises also the specter of the sacred—of a "knowing" and of a mad love of an other ilk or sort(ie).

And that smile? There is in divine things a transparency so great that one slips into the illumined depths of laughter beginning even with opaque intentions.[116]

X: WHO'S? ETHICS, AND DISASTER

If dissimulation and simulation are the artifice of phantom meaning, what can be said to be "behind" it? For Breton, as for Husserl and Kandinsky, despite their differences on transcendance, what-is-behind is something to which one can be present, if only for one gloriously necessary and curiously essential moment. For chance "mysteriously manifests to man a kind of necessity, a necessity which eluded him even though he vividly experiences it."[1]

Phantom meaning reveals, however, that an imperialist fiction operates in such moments, a fiction Dali parodied with his own "imperialistic rage." Dali's practice discloses that what-is-behind *Endless Enigma* is not of the Same as what-is-behind Surrealism. The "causality" of the universe recognized and articulated by Breton assumes another face, immemorial, in the event of the endless journey. Surrealism does, however, promote a particular sense of the Other, but *Endless Enigma* forces further questioning of this Other. Doing so leads not to its essence (whether convulsive-elastic or

Acknowledging that he was haunted by forces and "relations"[67] beyond human control, Breton noted that chance is an accomplice in life. In order, however, that chance might not render life or identity accidental, inconsequential, or isolated without revelation, Breton believed that the I, via "elective sensations," is complicit with chance so that it is never incapacitated by enigma or *non-savoir*.[68] Elective sensations, a form of active recognition, choice, and resignation (the Surrealists' sense of

not) but to the very alterity of the Other. Indeed, Breton himself even admitted and took responsibility for the "impropriety" of not even entertaining "the question of the *exteriority* of, let us say again for simplicity, the 'voice'"[2] which unifies the psyche of the human.

At the outset of chapter 1 the role of the imagination was highlighted concerning its relation to knowledge and the world. Breton, too, accented the imagination, as a "voluntary hallucination" that would permit the Surrealist to take revenge on things/objects as they are, without going mad. To take such revenge is to discredit the conventional status of objects and render them part of the magnetic circuitry that would transform both them and the world. An aspect of objects Breton carefully excluded, however, which he controlled by locating it within the domain of madness, is that objects tend to exact a certain revenge of their own. In their surging forth, compelled by the necessity of necessity (of chance), objects point to destinies unknown and unknowable. Although Breton recognized this, he viewed "pure mental representation" (which extends beyond perception but is separated, however "poorly," from mad hallucination) as the domain of the Surrealist's representations, and he assumed Presence was possible. That is, while he sought to go beyond, in a "visionary fashion," the "closed system" of earlier modernist art, he aimed to surpass the ego and the id and achieve greater dominance of the pleasure principle over the reality principle. This surpassing and domination was possible, though, only within another system of representation Breton presumed to be open, not closed, which recalled what children and primitives once knew.[3]

disponibilité), permit a sense of power over chance that makes it appear as if a particular destiny had always already been inevitable.

Elective activity, a brightness irradiating the path both excited and contaminated by risk and recklessness, Breton asserts, "is *in my own eye* and . . . saves me all collision in the darkness."[69] The complicity of chance, subjectivity, and knowledge further permits the recognition of the ideal, as portrayed in Breton's ode to "X" in *Nadja*, an epiphany later reiterated in *Mad Love* and *Arcane 17*.

With objective chance Breton recognizes a "voice from the outside"[70] and even intimates that its manifestations can be ordered in a scheme progressing from simple to complex and from surprising to so disturbing as to necessitate an invocation of "our very instinct for self-preservation."[71]

That Dali also knew this is born out by his numerous proclamations that the difference between himself and a madman was that he was not mad. And when he stated in "The Conquest of the Irrational" that "concrete irrationality" is "authentically unknowable," that it is past the domain[s] of psychoanalysis, virtual representation, and logical and rational mechanisms,[4] he similarly acknowledged the revenge in which objects revel.

It is important, given this concern with the revenge of objects, that these remarks not be taken as suggesting that *Endless Enigma* portends the early arrival of Baudrillard's "fatal strategy," where subjective agency is completely obliterated by its absorption into the ruses of objects. Rather, a revisiting of the "ambition on the pictorial plane" that animates *Endless Enigma* permits a closer examination of the revenge Dali exacts. This ambition is none other than a materialization of the trace of the Other and its consequence for the I, the subject to be transformed.

Because phantom meaning is otherwise than being, and beyond essence,[5] it cannot be known. Its utter alterity and surplus make any totalizing projects of epistemology or ontology, including Surrealist aesthetics as surrogates of the latter, useless. That is, phantom meaning cannot be rendered in any essential form (despite homages to such essence's elusiveness), nor can it be circumscribed within the synchronic presencing of Being, nor is it available to any Surrealist-incited warps in the movement of Hegelian *Bildung* or Platonic *anamnesis*, nor does it come to presence via the alchemy of any other philosopher's stone. Rather, only in turning toward the Other, of which the other is a phantom, is any sense possible. But

Named "slope facts" (*faites-glissades*) and "cliff facts" (*faites-precipices*),[72] the I/eye sees and knows such occurrences as "signals,"[73] and despite the number of inconsequential jolts and shocks, discerns, in their perpetual solicitations,[74] those that are "destined to produce one *Shock*."[75] Breton was always at pains to preserve the essential, the ideal, without sacrificing the convulsiveness by which it events. The aleatory posture of the eye/I is necessary, for only in such openness can the cryptograms of reality and identity be deciphered. The series of signals and signs that produce a Shock form constellations where subjectivity and objectivity are conjoined in the name of the marvelous.

With *Endless Enigma*, however, this constellation becomes a grid of conflation where subjectivity and objectivity are *con-*

even this "knowledge" will be haunted by a condition of *non-savoir* and counter-memory.

Turning toward the Other—the Endless, the Infinite—is occasioned in concrete situations in encounters with the other. Here for Dali, the other—persons, as well as things and objects, which are the echoes of persons—only sets the stage for a journey that never has the marvelous at its end. Rather, the adventure ends only in diachrony. Because the other is the trace[6] of the Other, it can be no other way. The trace is the *an-archic*, pre-originary movement of the Endless, which exceeds any and all initiatives of the I, including discourses that seek to locate the Endless within a grid. The experience of the trace is one that forces the I to evacuate itself as a site of knowing and continuity. It evacuates itself in response to an evocative call ("voice") that shatters the ability of the I to remain in *chez-soi*[7] where it can experience the Same.[8] The most moving encounters with the alterity of the Other pass in the encounter of the face of the other.

The face of the other is the naked face of the other before the I, but it is more. Face, or visage, also names the excess that destroys the idea "I" has or hopes to gain of the other. It is an uncancellable exteriority incapable of being brought into the fold of the Same. The I is thus made vulnerable and fragile, no longer possessing the power to collapse (via conducting wire, capillary tissue, etc.) the distance marked by the alterity of the other.

But there is even more. In the face of the other lurks the very site where subjectivity itself is constituted. To be faced by the alterity of the other is to be contested and magnetically summoned by the other.

fused, their differences indistinguishable, their sublation refused. In such a space, the ability of the I to preserve itself, as well as the possibility of beauty, is lost. Having plunged over the precipice of a shocking cliff, the I's capacity to mediate the call and play of alterity becomes inconsequential. The insufficiency of the I to rise above insubstantiality and achieve organicity[76] relegates the I to mystery, terror, and panic. Perhaps nowhere is this more poignant than in the very opening of *Nadja*, where Breton—asking Who am I?—mused if he were a phantom haunting *some other no longer present*. He soon realized, however, that the haunting phantom is none other than the alterity of his conventional identity that recedes and remains allusive when confronted with his worldly identity. The idea of escaping such

Such an encounter is deeply disturbing because what was once assumed to be active, creative, and spontaneous is now rendered passive and susceptible. The other that "I" finds in front of itself arises in a way it cannot identify or account for in itself, seriously undercutting Surrealist autoanalysis. So forceful and evocative is the call of the other that it is even closer and more immediate than objects! When I apprehends objects, it still has a stance that permits a distance through which it can grasp the object or thing. But the alterity of the other ambushes the I, overwhelming it and rendering impossible the distance necessary for "vessels" of signification or meaning. Such closeness, or "juxtaposition," Levinas names "proximity."⁹

Because proximity instills a sense that the past has already happened (accessible though, according to Breton, in the "eidetic image" perceived by the "savage eye"), consciousness's ability to be present to itself, as a condition of knowing the other, is disrupted. Instead a trace inhabits the moment assumed to be filled by a self-identifying act of subjectivity. In this moment, in the space of the trace, phantom meaning performs. In its radical automatism, it calls out, evokes, with the very "exterior voice" Breton acknowledged "does not even arise."¹⁰

Within the space of proximity, the I is shattered, as is the dialectical tension that makes possible conciliation with alterity. Paraphrasing Levinas, the I and the other do not form "a number,"¹¹ and "we" ends only as juxtaposition. There is no collectivity, no Same, where plurality and difference are overcome or lifted up together in a moment of ascendance.

And still there is more. The passivity of the I and its inability to know are not an

worldly servility and assenting to the allure of this alterity formed the basis of Surrealist revolution. Yet assent could be meaningful and productive only if conflict and difference were cast in a dialectical grid where binaries would prevent alterity from positing an utterly inescapable alterity whose consequences, as decided by Breton, would be mystery and randomness.

Equally as poignant as Breton's query—Who am I?— was his answer near the conclusion of *Nadja*, where he told of what he had found in his new love, "X." Despite noting the convulsiveness of love and beauty and the numerous dangers and fictions that speckle its street, Breton recognized the reality of the ideality of mad love. "X," the embodiment of this mad love, Breton offered, is "not an enigma" and she (i.e., mad love, essential knowledge, ideality,

affliction of subjectivity, nor are they facets of finitude or lack, or even a prelude to death. Rather they are the occasion of a transubstantiation—the subjecting of the subject—the site/event where the subject becomes a subject. For in evacuation (i.e., self-sacrifice), the I becomes separate, passive, open to the provocation and interferences of the other. The I here becomes a sensuousness or sensibility because "sense," or the "sensible," having displaced the known or knowable (via the irruptive meaning of the phantom object), is actually "the other in me, " "the other in the Same," "having the other under one's skin."[12] But ironically, having become an "exile" or "hostage"[13] of the other does not constitute a condition of objectification or alienation. Rather, it is incarnation, inspiration, deliverance.[14] *Endless Enigma* is a space where such alchemy happens.

Thus an interpretation such as that of Rojas,[15] for instance, that takes Dali's relations to his dead brother, his father, his mother, or Lorca, only as instances of alienation, confusion, or pain, overlooks them as a rendezvous with the alterity of those others. It would be tempting to say Dali did search for an identity much to no avail, but this would be a death mask laid over otherness so as to stretch a wire across its abyss. It would be tempting too to make of Dali's eroticism a matter for Freudian shenanigans, but this would eclipse the non-sexual sense of *eros* alive in *Endless Enigma*.

Though involved in an effort to discredit conventional consciousness, Surrealism nonetheless insists upon the integrity of the I as a subject capable of action and meaning. Dialectically woven together, the I and the world are together beauty) has turned him from a succession of terrible and changing enigmas forever.[77] Though "X" herself would soon disappear, attesting to Breton's belief that finality is only transitional and momentary, the ideal, and its possible representation, is established as that for which the Surrealist suffers and lives. While he admits that the signals and sensations of the perpetual solicitations of the beyond bring an "incommunicability [whose] pleasures have no equal,"[78] he intimates that "the beyond" *is* "here in this life," and one *is* capable of knowing it and being present to it. "X" is the presence, the existence, of this ideal that appears. Herself a provisional *telos*, an end to a series that gives meaning to the past and future of the series, "X" is the final "substitution" of intercessors ("You, indeed, ideally beautiful. You whom

a starting point. But because of the *anarche* of the face of the other, and the consequence that juxtapositions can be nothing other than proximate (proximity), it is not possible to assume that the one-in-the-other dynamic, characteristic of surreality, and of such strategies as *trompe l'oeil*, can work to produce a "third term."[16] The third term, the manifest destiny of the phantom object, and the essential moment of dialectics and alchemy, is to be both a denial and lifting up of difference in conciliation and self-presence. But there is no third term in *Endless Enigma* because the one-in-the-other has been displaced by the *other-in-the-one*. The trump of *le trompe* is to substitute, via simulation, the undecidability initiated by the alterity of the other for the interiority of a *point suprême*. *Endless Enigma*'s *trompe l'oeil* doubles as a trick of (not by, but of) the I. The other-in-the-one feigns the one-in-the-other, shattering the I and meaning, decomposing both.

The relation of the Surrealist subject to the alterity of the other is a juxtaposition that itself far exceeds that subject's own juxtaposition (via active intervention or passive finding) of objects in the world. The juxtaposition of the subject and the other pre-originarily precedes, *without being encoded in the elasticity of a convulsive grid*, the juxtaposition of the subject and the other. The consequence of proximate juxtapositions is the one *and* the other(s) where "one" is no longer a system but another particular coexisting with other particulars. Such a stance belies the modernist scaffolding of Surrealism's epistemology and ontology and the innovations of their aesthetic disguise.

The sharp edges of the nomadic vectors slicing across the surface of the new I that everything identifies with daybreak and whom, for this very reason, I may not see again").[79] Though he did not see her again, the vision was regenerated in ever new dawnings whose contingent finalities were documented and celebrated in *Mad Love* and *Arcane 17*.

Upon the bases established in these texts (and others), Breton articulated the moral bases of Surrealism, and here is where Dali utterly founders in Breton's scheme. "X" is more than just a woman Breton loved—she represented an ideal, what Champigny named a "mythic idol."[80] In the presence of such an idol, or icon, ambiguity and failure dissipate in mad love's incandescence. The tribulations, suffering, and enigma Nadja rained on Breton were for him both fascinating allures and failure. "X" symbolized a moment of recuperation and a restoration of hope—

is given sight by Surrealism is not, however, an end to convulsiveness. Here is where *con-fusion* spins its enchanting spell, for it marvelously feigns a threadedness that is the simulation of sublative convulsiveness. Not revealed as such by official Surrealism, however, this endless convulsiveness, born of the enigmatic repetition of difference, appeared to promise moments of identity. Phantom meaning, henceforth conjoined and *con-fused* with the phantom object, mimicked the automatism and occultation prescribed by Breton in the first and second manifestos and never ceased to haunt him. Never able to escape the subterfuge of phantom meaning, Breton projected onto Dali identities diametrically opposed to his own beautiful fictions.

It can be argued, as Rojas has recently done, that one finds in *Endless Enigma* the face of Dali's deceased brother as well as Lorca's visage. Even if one were to grant this, which is plausible given Dali's biography, that "truth" is quickly exceeded by another where the alterity of the other renders mute the convergence of *anamnesis* and the surprise of the future. *Endless Enigma* registers the trace of the other as an apparently obvious "face," and this in turn colors the space within which move the other phantoms comprising the iconography of the painting. They too reveal themselves to be traces, faces of the other, undecidable simulacra that only intimate, without accomplishing, reference or symbolic function. At every turn they unravel Ariadne's thread, showing it to be a pixillated space in which multiple phantoms cavort without sustaining a coherent myth. Or alternatively, they assent to another myth, and an other, and . . .

the very essence of Surrealism, the way of the soul out of the limbo where Nadja herself, admittedly, was mired. Further, Breton averred that the I, complicit with chance, can avert a "fall whose lack of moral basis . . . is indisputable"[81] only in acts of self-preservation (much as Breton had done numerous times with Nadja, epitomized by an episode where she almost caused an "accident" while kissing Breton and wildly depressing the accelerator of the auto he was driving). Only by discerning a destiny in risk that is not a reckless end to destiny can one open oneself to a spontaneity that makes possible the one Shock whose organicity lends it a moral sensibility in which ambiguity has no home. On the other hand, only by going to the extreme limit where such boundaries reside can "the beyond" open upon us.

No negation, but heavy terms, like whole stanzas juxtaposed while remaining without any connection, each one closed in self-sufficiency (but not upon any meaningfulness)—each one immobile and mute, and all of them usurping the sentence their relation, forms a sentence whose significance we would be hard put to explain.—Hard put is an understatement: there passes through this sentence what it can contain only by bursting.[17]

In that the dialectic leads to a one (i.e., the third term), it can be said *Endless Enigma* represents a going beyond the number one, as well as beyond the number two. But following Sulieman, the number one represents unity and identity, and the number two hierarchy and antagonistic opposition.[18] To go beyond both one and two is to go to no number. No number, the sign of endless complication, displaces the "third term," dismantling the dialectic. The undecidability surfacing here (though not from any depth) is an instance of Derrida's "incalculable choreographies"—a "dream" of the innumerable—desire escaping the combinatory.[19] Here the eternal return of the Same finds itself in a space of difference, of no place, the consequence of which is the slipping ground secreted by the slipping surrealist object.

Endless Enigma, parodying Surrealist reverie, plays the dream of the surreal against itself and ends with a "dizzying accumulation of narratives" that go nowhere and everywhere.[20] As such they become other than the other of Reverdy's juxtaposition of two distant realities. The multiplicity arising in the demise of a

With *Endless Enigma* Dali championed an openness and spontaneity that for Breton was truly foolhardy and imprudent. In *Endless Enigma*, Dali abandoned the elective capacity of the I *after* the moment of paranoiac-critical intervention. That move instigated the delirium of interpretation he sought. That is, the I, having acted in concert with chance, evacuated itself in favor of joining the flow of an evocative call it cannot stem. Surrendering to the summon of alterity, the I loses sight of the possibility of one shock and enters into multiple complicities and duplicities that render the home of "real ideality" impossible. Here Abraham, Hebdomeros, and Telemachus (Aragon's) appear as the philosopher, or mythical beast, displacing the mythical icon of mad love. Duplicity displaces binarity, and the dialectic holds no third term suggests that the mythological beast in *Endless Enigma* is Harraway's Cyborg,[21] which Smith-Rosenberg recognizes as the Trickster.[22] The face of the other that feigns the Surrealist hermetic face of the other doubles as *jouissance* that itself feigns the desires associated with both alienation and lack. In that hermetic dialectics always lend themselves to the weaving of a narrative or story, *Endless Enigma* indeed is a dreaming within a hazardous space.

Such a dreaming is materialized in the disjunctively conjunctive writing of *Endless Enigma* where "the voice" that summons does not tell of something marvelous. Instead it asks "useless questions: where are you going? where are you coming from? what are you driving at?"[23] In the very same breath in which it solicits, it inscribes in the answer innumerable rhizomatic conjunctions that conduct only delay in those hallowed openings where variations on the verb *to be* would otherwise work their magical presence.[24]

In the lacunae of these spaces the I or subjectivity celebrated by Surrealism often fails to retain the integrity only a myth of interiority could lend it. The I, now opened, becomes incontinent, and sees Ariadne's threads everywhere. *Endless Enigma*, written in paint under the sign of *amor fati*, rather than *amour fou*, is a site where consciousness languishes endlessly in hope of encountering the "consequence [that] alone gives the nature of truth to a set of accidents that would make no sense unless they were chosen by some human quirk."[25]

Such a reading begs to ask if the identity of the reclined philosopher, or the great cyclopean cretin, is now Jarry, and whether or not *Endless Enigma* is a pata-sway, or alternatively, becomes a swaying and swerving unbecoming to convulsion. Swerving, slipping dialectic: the stinking essence.

Dali, like Nadja, was an anarchist individualist whom Breton was forced to celebrate but whom Breton could not accept without restrictions that harness eccentricity to a constellation in which passion, hope, and liberty collude. Capriciousness, defiance, irrationality, passion, and individuality, though productive of the spasms so crucial to Surrealist ideology, must be capable of innovating a new order of reality, a new *savoir*. This new domain of surreality could be achieved only within the context of how one lives one's life. Just as Nadja's fanciful peculiarity and frailties caused her to slip from Breton's conception of purity, so too did Dali's actions require a pre-

physical joke. This is not a retrograde move to make of Surrealism pataphysics, however, but is a premonition of Lyotard's pagan parologies. The ostensible face of *Endless Enigma*, which is none other than the trace of the other, is also the simulacrum of the Surrealist I. In the face of this I the phantom of Jarry is now seen inscribing a pataphysical element into the circulation of meaning and object such that they are infused with a mysterious ruse enabling them to rule within the space of endless enigma. Counter to these ruses, the I labors heroically to impose designs upon and to effect imaginary solutions within the universe, only to be confronted with the folly of such projects. The play of objects, the very commotion of unknowable interconnections, lends to the universe an aura of uncertainty and surprise. *Endless Enigma*'s effect, though, is not to blaspheme, debase, and shock the I in the manner of Ubu Roi or Faustroll. Rather, the effect is to return to things their uniqueness as eternally returning singularities that become giddy and vertiginous, and somewhat ludicrous, and ultimately silent, when they are forced to join other singularities to produce something meaningfully representable as an essential form.

The "new lyricism," by which Apollinaire described the meanderings of Jarry's laughter as it rose from the "lower regions,"[26] insinuates itself into *Endless Enigma*, but not with a similar sense of misanthropic negativity and depravity. Nonetheless, *Endless Enigma* is inhabited by Jarryesque specters whose mobility renders meaning a restless, perpetual motion that goes everywhere and nowhere. *Endless Enigma* marks a space where each attempt at predication is cipitous fall from grace.

Perhaps, then, the woman seated on the beach in *Endless Enigma* is not the nurturing femininity of ideal Surrealism, but rather Nadja? Or maybe she is Fanny Beznos reading those passages from Nietzsche she did not tell Breton about in their delightful encounter, one that surely would have gone awry had her fuller enchantment with Nietzsche been revealed to him. Or maybe she is the mythic idol, her back turned, not inadvertently, to the notion of the marvelous, reading, and rereading, intently, infinitely, that volume entitled *Enigmatics* that Breton, drawn to also, was compelled to repudiate?[82] Or is that woman "S," the figure in Baudrillard's stories whose actions produce the *eminence grise* (that which steals or erases traces)?[83] And perhaps the philosopher, or mythic beast, was

equivalent to any other, an infinite parody of the myth of meaning where difference takes the form of an absence of contradiction. The smile on the face arises as a lyrical prelude to an insolent hilarity, yet reticent, born of the recognition that truth lies.

The smile also exposes the enjoyment in which singularities revel in finding themselves in a heterogeneous field. Delighting in their own excited motion, they show themselves, vis-à-vis Surrealism's version of their sublimity, to be pagans. "Pagan" here does not refer to a heathen, weak and racked with impiety, one in need of a vision of truth that would permit it to be free of those illusions that perpetuate its insufficiency. Instead, the singularities, the phantoms, are pagans in a Lyotardian sense. Pagans because they resist the piety of the thinker or artist who proclaims an essential truth embedded in a space where knowledge and aesthetics are joined in a convulsively beautiful reconciliation. Pagans because they move with an impiety born of an absence of delimiting criteria that permit determinate judgments.

Juxtaposed to the moral code of Breton's discourse, *Endless Enigma* is a pagan work. Its paganism (which Lyotard also figured later as paralogy) consists in disturbing the rule of irony. The rule of irony is akin to the rule of representation, which requires criteria by which something is known, criteria that transform and add a *telos* to eventing such that it becomes something, i.e., an object of knowledge. To play with the rule of irony, as does *Endless Enigma*, is to dislodge what Lyotard refers to as the rule of truth (i.e., the rules of irony and representation). Dali's play with the latter rules, in the

not the refined, communal anarchist Breton would later salute in *Arcane 17*. Maybe the philosopher or mythic beast was the singular individual whose unrecuperable uniqueness amounted to a negativity, a yawning gap in the constitution of ideal identity? Whether particulars are taken as cyborgian plasma, simulated teleological nodes, or disastrous symbols, the utter undecidability escorting the irruption of *non-savoir* overwhelms one who addresses the queries posed by Breton in *Nadja* and throughout his career-long defining of Surrealism. Undecidability is little less than an insidious chance materialization of a failure of signals to form a constellation from which an identity can be elected. *Les mots glissants*, when inserted into a scheme that begins with *faites-glissades* and ends with *faites-*

form of a slipping surrealist object, bears a similarity to the "drift" of Lyotard's paganism and paralogy. Because *Endless Enigma* is a site where newer and other truths blossom, the conditions of their production amounts to a concern with knowledge. Dali, however, ever interested in *non-savoir*, presented *Endless Enigma* as an invention in which *savoir* and *non-savoir* exist in a relation of non-logical difference. Because invention does not aim at knowledge or truth, it can only be concerned with endless invention. Here the repetition of invention is a repetition of difference that disrupts the mimetic activity that produces truth and identity. *Endless Enigma* is an experimentation that does not rehearse the litany of codified Surreality. Rather it is the epiphany of many truths that such a litany cannot convert into a Truth—stories that do not form a Story. This is the work of the sorcerer's apprentice—to be a pagan perpetuating impiety and making slippery and drifting the ground on which oppositional strategies might set themselves up so as to form a dialectic. The work of the pagan intensifies the enigma of the *parergon*.

Breton, an advocate of the avant garde, presented Surrealism as innovation, which aims to make novel moves (convulsions) within a "game" of art in order to sanctify both the truth of art and the truth that anyone could experience that which would transform them (anyone can be a surrealist). Dali, however, presenting invention as a simulacrum of innovation, displaced innovation in favor of a creativity that was constantly starting out in new directions. As such the eternal return of the instant of invention precluded truth as a possibility, insiting instead impossibility. This is the work of

precipices, ruins the chance of a progressive movement toward complexity, that is, a maneuver in a particular direction where that very movement itself doubly grounds representation and an *ethos*. *Endless Enigma* reveals *ethos* as an inscription of power, knowledge, and desire that propagates a grid of truth rather than an outcropping of surrealist objectivity. The latter disclosure forms the basis of Dali's irritation of Breton's moral sensibilities.

The fuller heresy of *Endless Enigma*'s morality becomes more obvious when it is realized that its annunciation of the great refusal, or failure, of particulars to coalesce into a community (i.e., their *an-arche*) plunges them into the *nomos* from which *polis* and *ethos* derive. *Ethos* and *polis* refer to a particular sense where place, identity, and practice coincide to mark the presence of a com-

the pagan—to make the moves that make the productivity of the rule of irony impossible. The endless enigma is an event to which no truth can be attached; its shifty, roving movement is not dependent upon rules of complementary opposition. In games underwritten by the latter rules, the unsaved weak are opposed to the strong via the opposition of truth and repressive ideological conventions, e.g., the unconscious, rhetorical (w)rites of the rules of irony and truth. Within modernist discourses, such as Surrealism, paganism and paralogy suggest that truth will not do away with illusion or generate freedom. The pious, who seek the truth, are resisted by pagans, not by confronting their ideology adversarially (thus becoming bound to it) but by putting everything in an endless motion where no grounds arise on which opposition can be erected (i.e., the incessant invention of newer and other truths). The pagan never participates in an overcoming of opposition and difference and thus never manifests a true identity. But this does not mean there is no identity, nor does it mean there is no convulsiveness. There is, and it consists in paralogical ruses and trickery. It consists in the pagan being a cyborg.

Here the spectral assumes the posture of the "figural,"[27] and as such, the phantom object becomes phantom meaning by dint of a irreconcilable resistance to totalizing movement. *Endless Enigma* is a testimony to, a manifestation of, an evocation of a process of invention that generates difference resistant to criteria that make possible determinacy and identity. The strange presence of *Endless Enigma* as a "postmodern" event within the modernist project of Surrealism is per-

munity, a shared situation of communicative interaction and consensual knowledge, a place where difference is overcome in favor of a belongingness or oneness that permits the use of words like *we, integration,* or *organic.* Ethics and morality derive from the situatedness of *polis* in a larger context of *ethos,* a space where identity and the delineation of character are defined by shared understandings. What is fitting or right to do (e.g., *kathokonta, askesis,* or *exagoresis*)[84] is located in the *polis.* Here is where concrete rules and norms are applied. This is the realm of the quotidian. *Polis,* however, is sited in a more encompassing sociohistorical formative process, *ethos.* As abode or dwelling place, *ethos* permits essence to appear. Thus the dialectic of subject and object is also hermeneutic as well as hermetic, cap-

haps well suggested by Lyotard when he offered that his use of the word *postmodern* was but a

> provocative way to put the struggle in the foreground of the field of knowledge. Postmodernity is not a new age, it is the rewriting of some features modernity had tried or pretended to gain, particularly in founding its legitimation upon the purpose of the general emancipation of mankind. But such a rewriting . . . was for a long time active in modernity itself.[28]

Already present then within Surrealism, the figural, the Other, surplus, is a beyond beyond "the" beyond Breton had early on wondered about.[29]

The occasions on which Dali referred to himself as "sublime" are too numerous to recount, but suffice it to say he perhaps little understood the full import of his proclamations (which he many times uttered in acknowledging that even he didn't know what he meant or where it came from). There is only a hint he might have really understood his sublim(n)ity in his comments that he was the *only* surrealist. Nonetheless, moving in the waters stirred by Lyotard's critique of the Kantian distinction between the sublime and the beautiful,[30] and their bearing on knowledge, *Endless Enigma* is indeed a sublime event. Contrary to the sublime point of Bretonian Surrealism, *Endless Enigma* portends that knowledge about reality is not possible and that the beautiful cannot be expected.[31]

The notion of the sublime is crucial here because it scores the point where the limits of knowledge are laid bare and all possibilities of determinate representured aptly in the notion of the one-in-the-other upon which *trompe l'oeil* relies. But *ethos* itself is located in *nomos*, a more expansive dwelling also replete with conventions and mores. *Nomos* also carries with it a sense that there is an "author" that possesses a force that beckons and leads.

For Breton, Surrealism, generated by the "voice" of *nomos*, makes a surprising call or demand upon individuals to live in a particular way. Rippling through and instituted in the *polis* of *ethos*, an essence or destiny is articulated for what humans and social relations can and should be. Breton was not at all reluctant to attempt to codify the conventions, methods, and goals defining the right way to live personally and the right way to construct a society, modeled, of course, on the Surrealist cenacle.

tation are exceeded. Knowledge requires that an idea or concept (what is conceived) be matched with an object or thing that represents it (can be presented), and when such a match occurs the faculties of the mind are harmoniously and pleasurably joined. Such occurrences are also "beautiful." For Kant the beautiful and knowledge travel together, whereas the sublime and knowledge do not. The sublime points to a realm beyond knowledge and cognition, a suprasensible realm of intuitive inexpressibility and indeterminacy. Whereas for Breton surreality defines a space where convulsive beauty is a matter of both aesthetics *and* knowledge, for *Endless Enigma* surreality is resisted as such a site. What *Endless Enigma* presents is not amenable to a harmonious joining of ideas and objects that correspond to each other. As a locus of resistance, difference, and heterogeneity, *Endless Enigma* shares with Lyotard the position that sublime events are marvelous for their ability to maintain a disjunction between aesthetics and knowledge. Thus Dali's annunciation of his own sublime nature, coupled with the materialization of that sublim(n)ity in the form of *Endless Enigma*, was just too much for Breton to harness with his system.

To maintain the disjunction, however, does not obliterate the juxtaposition of knowledge and the aesthetic but only the idea that an oppositional tension could unite them. What is left then is not a determinate realm but a

field . . . only determined to a second degree, reflectively, so to speak: not by the commensurability between a pre-

Breton saw himself mysteriously visited by the authorial "voice" of *nomos* and acted selfrighteously as its materiality, as an avatar, to lead a bankrupt social world to the pearls of self-actualization at the personal and collective levels. ("From within and without, it is a pearl worth a thousand times more than the diver's life."[85]) He took this struggle seriously in his own life, having been thoroughly convinced that the arduous path to the marvelous is not only possible but appropriate.

So enchanted by the voice of *nomos* and its perceived gathering embrace was Breton that he constructed his code in a way that excluded the otherness of that voice. In doing so he forfeited the chance to engage that force or energy that compels one to follow the conventions of *nomos*, but that is actually outside those very con-

sentation and a concept, but by the indeterminate commensurability between the capacity for presenting and the capacity for conceptualizing.[32]

Here the sublimity of *Endless Enigma* stands out, for knowledge is delayed and deferred to another point in time that undercuts the possibility of the aesthetic ever being known in the present. Here is where Lyotard suggests that postmodern art has to be understood "according to the future (*post*) anterior (*modo*)."[33] The possibility of determining what-it-is that *Endless Enigma* presents is far exceeded by its own presenting of itself as the eventing of the unpresentable. That is, the happening of the event (the it-happens vs. the what-it-is-that-happens) precedes the rules of irony and truth (e.g., profiles of its essence) that define it. These being unavailable, an aura of indeterminacy accompanies the event that operates as an undisclosable alterity that upsets representation. As Lyotard has argued on numerous occasions, the "figure" operates within discourses or determinate structures not in a way that opposes them but rather in a fashion that opens a space of radical heterogeneity. For Surrealism, however, such a figure is always subjected to convulsive ascendance, via a set of rules that transforms eventhood into thing.

Returning to the earlier discussion of Levinas, the figure operates somewhat as a trace of something other. It must be carefully noted, however, that this trace does not necessarily reside in the spaces Breton suggested were inhabited by spiritualists or mystics. The endless enigma consists in their somehow being here and now in a way that precludes the discourse

ventions. By delimiting *nomos* to the narrower confines of *ethos* and *polis*, Breton attenuated the ecstatic alterity of *nomos*'s authority, substituting in its place the rhetorical authority of an imaginary law and its rule of irony. The consequence of this substitution was to vest that rhetorical authority's power in his own delineations and occultations of "the voice," i.e., his version of the *logos of the nomos-ethos-polis* grid. By doing this Breton achieved what Deleuze identified as the "triumph of the *logos* or the law over the *nomos*"[86] and thereby overcame the cruel irony of the notion that what authorizes and implicates subjectivity and communication also calls for evacuation. Deliverance and salvation, however, are outside of and other than what tradition (the Said) promises. The Saying of *nomos* radically exceeds communica-

of presence from holding sway. *Endless Enigma* thus does not ignore Breton's question, posed in the last lines of Nadja: "Is it true that the beyond, that everything beyond is here in this life?" *Endless Enigma* answers that the beyond, in the specter of the trace and the other, is here.

Had Breton understood more clearly Bataille's notion of "non-logical difference,"[34] perhaps the irony of enigma would not have been lost or deemed a hostile, worthless haunting. Breton's commitment to knowledge-producing aesthetics, however, precluded this. Revising the oedipal relation according to his own needs, Breton put out the I of Dali. Perversely inverting the psychoanalysis of the event celebrated by *Endless Enigma*, Breton returned the favor of a lacerating gesture, first offered by Dali in *Un Chien andulou*. Unlike Dali, however, who sought to unleash the heterogeneous and the incommensurable, Breton's gash sought to excise what he took to be dangerous irrelevancy. For in his own fashion, Dali had put forth an object that, in its presentation, deterred the rise of an idea. With Dali's expulsion by Breton coming subsequent to the appearance of *Endless Enigma*, it can be strongly argued that Breton sought to convert the awe-fulness of the sublime into the awful—a fateful and coercive play of sublimation and displacement.

Knowledge and aesthetics thus not being commensurable, it is not possible to set up discrete boundaries, as Breton suggested, between "pure mental representation . . . perception . . . [and] hallucinations."[35] *Endless Enigma*'s twisting shock is that "voluntary hallucination," which Dali acknowledges is just what its name implies, produces outcomes that demon-

tive praxis in a way such that participants sharing tradition are transubstantiated as nomads.

The return of the excluded wreaked havoc on Breton because he suppressed the intimate connection of *nomos* and nomad. Nomad derives from the pre-Socratic notion of *nomas*, which refers to a range of dwelling, a pasturage. It also more specifically refers to a movement in this space, a searching for and wandering about in. Fixity here is problematic, for what is searched for a(i)llusively exceeds the places in which it is found. *Nomos*, on the other hand, refers to customary usage, which also travels with the notion that such usage is always exceeded by an alterity radically exterior to it. The *polis* of *ethos* thus involves a search for or wandering into what is otherwise than and beyond *polis*. The connection between

strate that Breton's assumed ability to represent that which eluded him is itself a hallucination. As noted above in chapter 1, there is a peculiar connection between fiction and imagination! The aleatory meanderings of the *paysan de Paris*, proceeding in the convulsive labyrinth of Bretonian *savoir*, are transfigured as the *paien de Cadaques' Endless Enigma*!

Breton does, of course, allude to the alterity or unpresentableness of the unpresentable.[36] Driven, however, by an undying nostalgia that forever readied him for Presence of the Referent, he nonetheless argued, as he did so wonderfully in *Surrealism and Painting*, that painting, though not as well as poetry, *can* generate visual presentations of the unpresentable. Such endeavors Lyotard refers to as modernist avant garde.[37] Modernist aesthetics, such as Surrealism, do deal with the sublime, but nostalgically. They put forward the unpresentable as "missing contents" in a "form" that is "recognizable" and offers "solace and pleasure" and hope.[38] The postmodern, however, "puts forward the unpresentable in presentation itself."[39] It does so by denying itself the solace and consensus of good forms and taste that make it possible to "share collectively the nostalgia for the unattainable."[40]

According to Lyotard, the postmodern artist thus works without preestablished rules and produces an "event" in which he/she seeks "the rules of what will have been done."[41] Because such an artist works without rules, but in search of them (where they always come too soon or too late), the process of inventing new rules (vs innovating) can only lead to a jubilant "increase of being."[42]

The terrible "truth" of *Endless Enigma* is that neither painting, nor Surrealism,

nomas and *nomos* is enlarged by their rootedness in *nemo*, a spreading out and distribution of things in space by the gods. *Nomos* is a space of usage that is unnameable, the actual usage itself subject to an uncontainable slipperiness. The *nomos* of the *ethos* of the *polis* is other than the messages Hermes (for Breton, Automatism) brings to mortals, who search desperately for their sense, thinking, only for a mad moment, that they have fixed them in the *polis*.

In facing *polis*, the visage of *nomos* sets in upon individuals. Subjectivity and identity are called out of themselves by the otherness of its voice. This intersection with alterity, an encounter born of a wandering already set in motion by an *an-archic* nomadism, is a point of crisscrossing. The encounter and "touching" of alterities doubles as an invocation of the

can represent the unpresentable. Yet in their earnest efforts to do so they summon a Nietzschean nihilism by shattering belief and by discovering the "'lack of reality' of reality, together with the invention of other realities."[43] *Endless Enigma* was a bold venture that dared to move in the spaces Kant dared to name sublime. Little wonder Dali could say with impunity that he did not understand his own works. Here then we have a reading of Dali that does not lean upon psychobiography or hermeneutics, as do so many works, the most recent of which is Rojas's most interesting treatise on Dali's person and work.

Contra discourses such as those of Rojas, which seek "Dali" in the "meanings" embedded in his works and the particulars of his biography, *Endless Enigma* advances the impossibility of constructing an Identity or a System. To do so would require positing a grand narrative. In the same sense that *Endless Enigma* renders impossible the realization of surreality's marvelousness, so too does it render impossible the realization of Dali's identity. I have been at pains to argue that neither Dali nor his work manifested a *telos* whose trajectories can be assembled in a Story. Already from the outset this was made abundantly clear in *Little Cinders* (1927–29). An assemblage of icons and phantasms, minus grasshoppers, crutches, and Gala, of course, *Little Cinders* is an "apparatus" (as Dali was wont to refer to works of this period) that is not even a beginning of a Story. Rather, *Little Cinders* deploys a grid of little senders, each telling its own story, each story a little narrative so particular as to assume an incommensurability even the most convulsive of Breton's conducting wires could

ethical and as a point of departure: out of *polis/ethos*, into *nomos*, which was the occasion of that *polis/ethos*. In the departure to find what is fitting, what makes sense of being and existence, individuals are drawn out into the open, out into what can never be known or appropriated. Here individuals become relays of desire, singularities "unconsciously" knowing but not knowing whence they go. As nomads they transgress *ethos* and *polis*, tradition and law, consensus and the Same. Transgression suggests a stepping across, but such a sense of violation or rupture carries only one sense of this movement. Another is movement across and around. It is in this movement, in this transduction and transubstantiation, that singularities draw upon, like so many tracings and caresses, the spaces traversed. In transgression what fits is

not stitch into a system of communicating vessels. Indeed, each does communicate, however, each its own saga/fiction. Thus it is but play to wonder if, in *Endless Enigma*, the seated woman is Dali's childhood wetnurse, or Gala, or Fanny Beznos, or Galuixka, or even "S"[44] or any other feminine phantom moving about in paranoiac-critical space. The undecidability of just who or what these phantoms are is exceeded only by the indeterminacy of just how their stories can be woven together so as to reveal the essence of Dali's Identity and/or that of his work's possible narration of the essence of surreality.

Perpetually instigated by the phantoms of his own iconography, Dali resides elsewhere and otherwise than where various schemata have situated him. If there is a "truth" to which "Dali" attests—with regard either to his identity or to the meaning of his work—it is that the incommensurability of grasshoppers and Hitler is at least as equivocal as that of fried eggs and solitude. Their accidental and incandescent enigmatics—anathema to evolution—are a source of conflict that is only gloriously and inexorably exacerbated when it is assumed there is some quiddity to be realized or destiny to be fulfilled.

How could "Dali" not be a pagan vis-à-vis Surrealism when he himself was persistently the conjunction of multiple phantoms, each themselves pagans? With the phantoms emerging as repetitious and different responses to the evocations of the Eternal Return, each could be little more than a trickster or cyborg. Endlessly reinventing themselves in the play of reiteration and disparity that marks the space of the Eternal Return, phantoms inadver-

stumbled upon, only to be abandoned, and neither stumbling nor finding are guided by any definitive destiny. In finding what fits, strange identities and communities of incommensurate difference occur.[87] Along the same paths that are the signs of their containment, identification, and normalization, nomads escape and wander.

Nomads have no choice but to resist. *Nomos* is not simply a righteousness that is constitutionally sedimented in *ethos* and *polis*, it is also a struggle. And struggle is a searching for, an aleatory looking for. *Polis* is a site of power available only for settling disputes, not for canceling alterity. Exorbitant individualism does not necessarily index nihilism or anarchy. It is, rather, a response to the call of *nomos* that no *polis* can represent. In this sense, *Endless Enigma's* postmodernity is its ironic and destabilizing sense

tently engage in a violence and self-sacrifice. The interruptions and excesses arising out of the event of invention renders the return to or the emergence of Utopia a self-mutilating motion. The return of the same and the different never permits time to secrete stable meanings that can overcome their status as fragments and fictions.

As Stoekl has asserted concerning Bataille, Blanchot, Roussel, Lieris, and Ponge,[45] Dali, too, is a site of both a denial of utopia and a return of the specter of utopia. Both the denial and the return, juxtaposed in the space Bataille named "non-logical difference," are highly problematic in their gestures toward identity and difference. Stoekl observed in certain modernist texts a tendency to engage in such inquiry and has suggested that events of automutilation and inner sacrifice are "by no means a dead letter for criticism itself today: in fact it may be the most important one we as "readers" of literature face."[46] Endless Enigma is a moment in such dynamics, and for those who align Surrealism with Breton's utopic dream-vision, there is the problem of reckoning with Endless Enigma's locating of utopia as a site of heterogeneity. Could it then be that the smile on the face is as much a muffled or botched scream, or a concession to silence, as well as a preface to laughter?

If Endless Enigma can be taken as a site of unresolvable conflict rather than as a denigration of, or as a dwelling for a single identity or ideology, then indeed it carries with it a moral force contrary to that morality decided by Breton. This morality consists in an ethical gesturing that necessitates the inclusion of the unincludable, i.e., the inclusion of otherness

that what fits is not where it has been suggested it would be. War machines and "minor sciences" (e.g., "Dali" or "dalilectics") recognize laws are fictions, idols as false and false idols. Yet knowing that they need them, they know also that they must abandon themselves, much as *polis* must abandon itself to *nomos*.

The voice(s) of alterity then is not simply cacophony or noise. Rather it is the sounds of the struggles of excluded, different, and deterritorializing others rising above destitution, combined with the crumbling of the ossified heights that solidify marginalization and exclusion. In these spaces event displaces icon, the sacred surpasses the religious, and the inexorable exceeds the inevitable system. Here the ethical is *con-fused* with the moral and the specter of the Good appears to appear in

and disparity that cannot be forced into what Levinas has called "the Said." The event of invention, the Levinasian "Saying," refigures the sacred or utopia as the irreconcilable juxtaposition of different realities. In Bataillean terms, a "projectless project," *Endless Enigma* is to dogmatic Surrealism little but waste. But as expenditure, or radical negativity, its juxtapositioning of alterities suggests only that Surrealism, like any other utilitarian or representational project, must disappear in the very forces and mysteries it seeks to identify in hopes of deriving its own life and security.

In so sweeping away limitation and the violence of identity, the question of the ethical, of ethics, is resituated. Refigured now as event and invention versus repression and death, considerations of morality and responsibility are opened to novel assessments of encounters with otherness. Being fragmented by the alterity of otherness, I, we, are compelled to move on, but perhaps with a different sense of how we could relate to the evocations of others. Such a rethinking of ethics begs to be considered as emanating from the eventing and reinvention of evocation rather than from the boundaries and limits set up by and around the other-who-is-identified by the Said. In fostering such thought, Dali promoted a morality of inclusion rather than one grounded in the exclusiveness of what can be identified. Here Dali's politics do bear some resemblance to those of Bataille. Bataille's and Benjamin's reactions to the politics of capitalism and fascism in the 1930s recognized the role of "catastrophe" and "shock,"[47] which ignite heterogeneity and its ruptures of rational projects of control and accumulation by "reckless discharge the countenance of *nomos.*

Whereas modernity has assumed a continuity of *nomos* and *polis,* postmodernity has wandered into the fissures glossed by this presumed seamlessness. In this space, ethics become not only sites of mutual crossing and temporary agreement, they also, like the erotic encounters described by Levinas and Irigaray,[88] become the most wanton and fertile of sites of departure. For the rupture of the *polis* is not only the pain of the collapse of a project of propriety and property, it is also the incantation and caress of *nomos,* the seductive withdrawal of meaning whose desire singularities abandon themselves to. They do this no more willingly or cognizantly than does a hand fondling flesh, returning over and over again over the same virgin places, not knowing what trajectory it is on,

and upheaval."[48] Dali similarly realized that Surrealism's opposition to rationality, materialism, and idealism was predicated on a religiosity and militarism that authoritatively excluded otherness and difference via mechanisms it proclaimed to be against. He understood that Surrealist politics are subtended by domination and totalitarianism, an irony for a movement aimed at overcoming Dada and bourgeois culture. Rather than being overcome by dialectical eventing, they (Dada and bourgeois culture) were held in tension together, each feeding off the other.

Bataille's (as well as Benjamin's and Blanchot's) response was to engage in certain "absurdities" and "acrobatics." The projectless project of intense heterogeneous life (vs. Breton's *la vie à perdre haliende*) is an absurdity vis-à-vis teleology. As Shaviro points out, the problem is not how to give meaning to "otherwise absurd or ineffective acts" but how "to prevent sacrifice and expenditure from becoming new grounds of power and signification."[49] *Endless Enigma* must be read in this light. The "failure" of Dali, culminating in the happy coincidence of *Endless Enigma* and his exclusion by Breton, rests not in *Endless Enigma's* insignificance or irrelevance. It resides rather in the positing of an impossible gesture, never to be accomplished, repeated over and over again, by which subjectivity can ironically "free" itself from oppressive sociality.

Always the singular, the pagan *confuses* the pataphysical and the paralogical in an ongoing celebration of the unique and the unstable that collapses the horizons and futures implicated by systems. Pagans "generate blind spots and defer consensus," Lyotard observes.[50] Much like

what *telos*, if any, it seeks.[89] Finding what is fitting is the *jouissance* of ethics—a pleasant trouble and craving, a response to a mysterious voice's call that refuses the Name. The ethical and the fitting are voluptuous, their movements seeking a fecundity whose torments are endlessly enigmatic. *Ethics have their possibility in the nomadic motility of* phantom meaning *that traverses the body without organs— here nomos—without "end(s)" and in excess of fixation and death, which otherwise would consolidate desire.*

Because Breton envisioned Surrealism as utopian revolutionary praxis on the personal and social levels, its aesthetics doubled as a moral system, which, Levinas has forcefully shown, is a form of knowledge and totalitarianism. Nowhere is Breton's moralism better cap-

the nomad, the pagan seeks to return to variables their status as variable, a condition abrogated by Royal Science (Surrealism included) when it makes of variables "constants" in order to chart their habits and destinies.[51]

The blade across the I at the outset of *Un Chien andulou* establishes that, at the very beginning of vision, seeing cannot assume the transparency that knowledge grounds its probable conviction upon. Contrary then to the opening of vision (i.e., Breton's sense the windows of the mind are opened wide with Dali), sight, now slashed wide open, turns into an abysmal seeing. But this is not the blindness that a facile psychoanalysis would offer, as in Dali's being the son blinding his literal father (paranoiac-critically rendered in the William Tell paintings) or his "new" father Breton. Rather it is the sun, the blinding light of the black sun, that dawns with *non-savoir*, that cannot be converted into the photosynthesis of *savoir*. The light that blinds is that which is different from the difference between unseeing and seeing that Breton privileged.

That such events transpire within the discourse of Surrealism attests to the fragmentary tracings phantom meaning ins(c)ites. And these incantations are, as Blanchot has suggested of *des-astre*, catastrophic for Surrealism in that they render "neuter" the I that knows and opaque the eye that sees. The fragmentary, Blanchot tenders, marks

coherence all the firmer in that it has to come undone in order to be reached, and reached not through a dispersed system, or through dispersion as a system, for fragmentation is the pulling to

tured than in his recitation of a quotation from Hegel, in the epilogue to *Nadja*, which claims that "each man hopes and believes he is better than the world which is his, but the man who *is* better merely expresses this same world better than others."[90] Now, given the tenuous nomadic space in which *Endless Enigma* situates such moral claims, does not the *nomos* cast a certain pall on the aleatory air of the Surrealist that seriously questions the superiority and hegemony of such moral claims? And, aleatory now within the *nomos* that refuses reductive inscription rather than safely ensconced within an *ethos/polis* grounded in a spurious complicity of the I with objective chance, does not *Endless Enigma* anticipate Levinas's unsettling question in the preface of *Totality and Infinity*: "Everyone will readily agree

pieces (the tearing) of that which never has preexisted (really or ideally) as a whole, nor can it ever be reassembled in any future presence whatever. Fragmentation is the spacing, the separation effected by a temporalization which can only be understood—fallaciously—as the absence of time.[52]

The "absence of time," Blanchot had suggested earlier in *The Step Not Beyond*, arises in a reworking of Nietzsche and Klossowski's renderings of the eternal return.[53] Relating that the present is the impossibility of situating a line between a past and a future for which no passage, no conducting wire, exists, Blanchot writes,

> The law of the return supposing that "everything" would come again, seems to take time as completed: the circle out of circulation of all circles; but, in as much as it breaks the ring in its middle, it proposes a time not uncompleted, but, on the contrary, finite, except in the present point that alone we think we hold, and that, lacking, introduces rupture into infinity, making us live as in a perpetual state of death.[54]

Dali thus, whether a grasshopper child or the son of William Tell or a substitute for his dead brother, or whatever, never participated in being "present." Hence the repetition of displacement in his works: death, decomposition, efflux, egress, discontinuity, conflict, putrefaction. Yet there is no key here to the essence of Dali anymore than there is in psychoanalysis or occultated hermeneutics. His identity is a "not present" that neither psychoanalysis nor hermeticism, assuming an

that it is of the highest importance to know whether we are not duped by morality"?[91]

Breton, however, unmoved by the evocation of *Endless Enigma*, dismissed and rejected its stirrings as the "wild gallop which can only lead to another wild gallop . . . more frenzied than a snowflake in a blizzard."[92] He preferred that all wild gallops end in one Shock or spasm that could be sensed in silence by the seismographic heart which registers quakes on a scale where convulsiveness, beauty, and love never exceed themselves, never accede to a sublime alterity of which they cannot be the name.

And so parted Dali and Breton—Breton into the embracing shelter of a future "X" that would forever erase the erasure of any other X, and Dali into the magnetic blue winds whose otherness forever gave rise to the

original presence, can be nostalgic about or reconstruct. Always different, without place, Dali, indeed the author, the painter, the I, is neuter, neutral[55]—a plurality, a multiplicity of unnameables that only feign and insinuate their presence via phantom meaning.

Dali's painting and theorizing amount to, in Blanchot's blush, a "writing of disaster." That is, they are a continual effacing of both a system and an opposition to a system. Neutral to systems and oppositions, *Endless Enigma* is situated outside (Blanchot's *le dehors*) the holistics of system/opposition-to-system dynamics. Being outside ends only, endlessly, in the eternal return of the same to no particular place—the collapse of the future, of identity—"to think the disaster is to have no longer any future in which to think it."[56] *Endless Enigma*, an enigma without nostalgia, indeed without even a question, is a writing of disaster. The writing of disaster here names, Blanchot explained in *Death Sentence*, that which does not have the ultimate as a limit—that which is without end—which exceeds end—is outside end. Endlessly returning to unsettle language, texts, paintings, moral codes, disaster effaces what writing writes, painting paints, surrealism surreals, dialectics faces. Hence the face that is not a face at the center of *Endless Enigma*.

A strange thing about disasters, though—they never really change anything! Neither negation nor affirmation, "disaster ruins everything, all the while leaving everything intact."[57] Neither silent nor an overcoming of silence, disaster is a space where, when all is said that can be said, there is still more than cannot possibly be said. Not precisely a space of failure or futility, or even madness, it is

questions "Who/what goes there?" with it already inscribed in the response that "I" is not an appropriate answer. The issue thus is not that Dali is absolutely correct or that Breton was absolutely wrong. Rather it is that Dali challenged Breton's rhetorical authority by recognizing the particular, and by raising the question of phantom meaning, suggesting the impossible relation of dialectics and alterity.

Perhaps when Dali claimed, in "The Stinking Ass," that "the day is not far off when a picture will have the value, and only the value, of a simple moral act,"[93] he was already announcing his challenge to Breton's "fundamental moral code" of Surrealism. And when he asserted that the morality (i.e., the ethical) abiding in such images would be nothing but "disappointment, distaste, and repulsion,"

also not a site of certainty or comfort. It is where *non-savoir* compels writing, or painting, in the face of an impossible future where revelation could occur. Disaster is endless movement, and fragments are its offspring and messengers— phantoms and apparitions who tell only of overwhelming encounters that have taken place but cannot be rendered present.

Again, when Dali says he does not know where his images come from, and that he is not mad, we are to be reminded that his fragmentations are not capable of being divined. He has simply bumped into extreme limits and yet has plunged onward without concern for whether or not he could ever know or even believe what anything could mean.

> Why still more books, if not in order to experience their tranquil, tumultuous end which only the "effort" of writing brings about, when the dispersion of the subject—the proliferation of the multiple—delivers us to that "task of death" . . . [which] cannot be limited . . . to the job of exhausting life—causing life, through the constant renewal of desire, to be lived completely. I recognize in this task rather the passion, the patience, the extreme passivity which open life to dying and which is uneventful in the way that the already crossed out "biography" . . . allows nothing to happen, and guarantees nothing, not even the act of writing. All of this restores to the secretness of the neutral that shade, to whom you assign the secure, quasi-professional appellation: writer.[58]

All this sheds other light on paranoiac-critical activity. Vis-à-vis automa-

it did not mean that scatology would or should be exalted over a new eschatology of an excluded sacred or that the "blinding flash of new gems" is not the new freedom radical pluralism assents to.[94]

Perhaps more poignantly, however, *Endless Enigma* is where catastrophe and disaster do their work. Approached via Levinas's distinction between the Saying and the Said, *Endless Enigma* sites the triumph of the Saying over the Said. The Saying (the trace, the turning toward elsewhere and otherwise, phantom meaning), which is supposedly contained within the Said, according to the proclamations of the I, is the unaccounted-for exteriority of the "voice" encountered in the alterity of the other. Breton's "fundamental moral code," uttered with certainty and authority, assumed that it had excluded this alter-

tism, its intent is not to place the I/eye in a labyrinthine process of knowledge so that it/they might navigate the impasses of various obstacles and later emerge as a marvelous sunflower. Rather it is to sacrifice the I/eye by remaining outside the economy of knowledge and ignorance. *Endless Enigma* is an *aneconomimetic* gesture that can be figured only as passion and patience devoid of memory or destiny.

That there is no awaiting the disaster is true to the extent that waiting is considered always to be the awaiting of something waited for, or else unexpected. But awaiting—just as it is not related to the future any more than to an accessible past—is also the awaiting of awaiting, which does not situate us in a present, for "I" have always already awaited what I will always wait for: the immemorable, the unknown which has no present, and which I can no more remember than I can know whether I am not forgetting the future—the future being my relation with what, in what is coming, does not come and thus does not present, or re-present itself.[59]

Because under these circumstances writing or painting ultimately makes no difference, effects nothing, it can be said that in and of itself it constitutes a radical change. Nothing changes, evolves, or becomes more clear or obvious. The very fact of this condition of reversibility, or no difference, is the subtle turn that enables simulation to set itself up in the margins of Surrealist discourse and thereby confront it with an extreme limit. The more things give the apparition of changing, the

ity, thus locating and controlling it, when in fact it had leaned upon its very quick sands and violet winds to erect its edifice. The Said, in terms of *trompe l'oeil*, for instance, is posited as the one(i.e., the Same)-in-the-other, that is, the other is absorbed into and dialectically adheres in the one. Dali, with his trump of *le trompe*, denuded this dynamic to display the other-in-the-one, effacing the imperialism of the dialectic. By demonstrating pictorially that the Saying cannot be reduced to the Said, *Endless Enigma* proclaimed that the ethical—the responsibility for the other called out by the Endless in the "face" of the Other—is *not* synonymous with a moral code. For morality often violates what is ethical, and the question or demand of the ethical, forever "instituted" in the phantom face of the other, returns con-

more they do not change. Confronted then by the eternal return, sameness and identity only reinvent and displace themselves, and nothing emerges.

The stealthy luminosity of *Endless Enigma* is its capacity, via the trump of *trompe l'oeil*, to slip into another moment that is not a continuation of the one prior to it (regardless of what other plane of reality it might inhabit). Nor is it a vessel to a future. The heresy of *Endless Enigma* is that it is a projectless project, whose goal of vivifying the "total man"[60] is completely beyond any systems of revolution or transformation Breton offered. With Levinas, Lyotard, and Blanchot, as with Bataille, Dali shared an interest in both silencing repressive ideologies and confronting the impossibility of being silent at all.

Perhaps the smile on the face is that of the Buddha?

Various efforts to decide the identity of Dali, or his works' meanings, are misplaced when they clinically conclude that he was a man in turmoil, or that his works are themselves troubled by their obscurity or idiosyncrasy. Such claims overlook his struggles to remain outside or beyond *an* identity. That is, they miss that his aim was not to have an identity; rather, for Dali identity is an impossibility that must be encountered by living intensely, spontaneously, and wholly, even if it means automutilation and sacrifice (not interpreted narrowly, though, as a "death wish").

He's searching, turning and returning with, at the center, this word—and knowing that to find is only to seek again in relation to the center that is the impossible to find.[61]

tinuously to unsettle the essentializing moves of the Said's moral strictures. To demoralize, then, is to reveal the emperor's nudity, and that is what is scatological, for it exhibits (i.e., Dali's alleged "exhibitionism") what LIES at the margins of the emperor's clothing. The "obscenity" of such demoralization is, as Bataille suggested in *Death and Sensuality*, the impossible inclusion of excess, which is useless to the posturing of the Said but is nonetheless crucial to the impossible task of being whole.

The apparition of the face that can be encountered in *Endless Enigma* is that of many that are not one and that emerge from under erasure in their Saying. And that smile is as much that of one who has died quietly with a truth as it is the coy snicker of one who defies the Said. Perhaps the Andalousian moon-

The irony and enigma of such struggle are lost in portraits content with psychoanalyzing Dali. In Rojas's otherwise brilliant profile of Dali, Rojas failed to encounter, as did Breton, those other phantoms that quickened Dali when he recited that Dali himself had discovered that everything was subject to the "law of disaster."[62]

That disaster could be reduced to psychobiographical warps and woofs indeed misses that *desastre* also names a site of enigmatic dislocations and astral disjunctions that incessantly end as multiple conjunctions, interruptions, and liquidations. Much as Levinas's "Saying" is one's offering to and for the other that does not necessarily have as its goal a particular Said or represented, *Endless Enigma*, and the phantom meaning that traces its "face," as well as that of "Dali," are a Saying that does not aim at reciting the Said of the Surrealist canon. An episode of the Saying, rather than an obeisance to the Said, *Endless Enigma* is uttered as a *cri*.[63] Perhaps anguished, perhaps not—anguish is irrelevant—the *cri* of *Endless Enigma* is an epiphany.

One should be warned, though, that *Endless Enigma*'s epiphany is not an invocation of a transcendent being (as could be read into Levinas). The Other of *Endless Enigma* is the "voice" of the Endless, the Infinite, and *Endless Enigma* names only an unnameable, anarchic abyss. This abyss in Levinas is not a being or a presence, yet for him the abysmal Other seems to be the trace or specter of God or the Good. The Other whose voice leaves *Endless Enigma* as its trace similarly summons a sense of the sacred. Here, too, abysmal and anarchic, the sacred, via the alterity of the other, assures the shattering light shows the philosopher, or mythological beast, to be a sorcerer's apprentice who expresses an "avid will to be" and affirms the "fundamental right of man to signify nothing"?[95]

Already at this point it is evident that the stinking ass is the stinking essence of a metaphysics of violent inclusion. The "new dawn of the Golden Age" Dali detected in "shameful, scatologous images" was a hope for the decline of enervating codification. The "demoralization and confusion" he predicted were none other than a non-logical *confusion* of totality and infinity and a demoralization of Breton's *nomos*-refusing *polis*.

Endless Enigma is a scene where the turn toward the other occurs. Its consequence is to return the viewer or reader again and again to Levinas's question of whether or not one is being duped by

of schemes that consolidate singularities in a hold that suppresses their difference. *Endless Enigma* is particularly concerned, however, not with Presence, God, or the Good, but with the alterity of the other and its phantom meaning. Nonetheless, the otherness of Dali's three great simulacra (blood, excrement, putrefaction) marks the movement of disaster and decomposure that issues as a medium of the sacred. That the sacred irrupts as a Saying that redresses the destitution of singularities compressed into a Said does register a nondialectical turning where the ethical confronts the moral code that compresses. The Other of *Endless Enigma*'s Saying is a celebration of Cixous's "furnishing air" whose sculpted gestures do not form the contours of a boundary. Such air, the very breath of that same "voice" that also summoned Breton, instead moves to sweep away limitations, including those Breton sought to impose. In this very turning, *Endless Enigma* challenges the fixed and unimpeachable status of the Signifier or Said of Breton's discourse.

Endless Enigma, thus marking the incursion and departure of nomadic intensities within Breton's regime of signs, insinuates the "face" of the Good and the ethical. This consists in the opening of spaces of difference within which singularities retain their individuality and their ambient intensity. As Guattari suggested, this amounts to a molecular revolution that results in a thousand plateaus.[64] This space of multiplicity is the space of the one *and* the other that is not reducible to the one *in* the other or the one *and* the many. Individuality and alterity are not suppressed here, and their movement may lead to coincidences without convergence.

morality. "Dali" does not promote an alternative moral system. The return to the *nomos*, the turn toward the other, and the incessant concern for a response-ibility for the other names an ethics that disables the epistemological and ontological claims of a system of poetics and knowledge that doubles as a moral code. That "Dali" would posit a difference between the individual nature of the ethical and the collective nature of the moral, and would even empower the ethical over the moral, was for Surrealism the unkindest cut of all. Indeed, the phantom object Breton so cherished did return, but as **phantom meaning**, as it had once before, on a cloudy night bathed in the blue of the moon, to lacerate the sphere of the I.

Dali, however, was a dead letter for Breton's Surrealism. But "He was so calm in dying that he

Any questions about what meanings, if any, might arise here, and whether or not they are in conflict or are capable of resolution, must be left open. Schrag has proposed that communication here may occur "transversally"—across the boundaries of particulars.[65] Here *Endless Enigma* preserves the accidental possibility of a notion of *surreality* at the same time that it erases its congealed body.

Communication may assume, or dissimulate, a binary form, or the form of *trompe l'oeil*, or that of cyborgian movement, or an aesthetics of disappearance, or whatever. Such occurrences, however, are only local and invoke no deep structure or transcendent being or presence.

To persist in the activity of trying to say what is yet to be said that cannot be said is what forces—i.e., "writes"—the precession of phantoms in *Endless Enigma*. Binaries found insufficient and distorting, only a continual precession can attempt, both successfully and fruitlessly, to seek an impossible Said. Of course, *Endless Enigma* does stand as a Said, but it is its Saying that gives it life. That fervent life, sought passionately, and endured with patience and supplication, is the only "essence" of which *Endless Enigma* speaks. And in speaking, it invigorates a risking, an autoeroticism and automutilation whose automatism is not synonymous with the convulsive identity of Royal Surrealism.

In a most unexpected fashion, *Endless Enigma* iterates, and reiterates, as itineration, Breton's wonderment that the "beyond" is here in this life. For Breton's modernism, the trace of the beyond is a path, a wire stretched mysteriously through the most confounding of spaces and abysses. For *Endless Enigma*, the

seemed, before dying, already dead; after and forever, still alive, in this calm of life for which our hearts beat—thus having effaced the limit at the moment in which it is that it effaces."[96]

Yet calm is illusive and never acts alone. If one attempts to live intensely (*la vie à perdre halience*), as Breton advocated at the close of *Nadja*, is it not inevitable that in this fervor the word *I* is but a limit that painting and writing, indeed living, must sweep away, thus erasing it? In such a scene, is there not a strange, *con-fused* juxtaposition, or conjunction, of the future "X" (which Breton awaited) and the "I" such that the I unexpectedly and inevitably emerges as an event that neither painting nor writing can establish? If one is to engage intensely the *mises-en-techne-tou-biou*,[97] must one not

trace is effaced in the moment of writing, only to return again and again with the next strokes of the brush and the pen.

Conjunction only grows. As *Endless Enigma's* meanings disastrously and catastrophically slip, as a surrealist object, it takes a step not beyond. And in taking *le pas au-delà*, this object also becomes a *pas*-sing object "not destined to leave traces, but to erase, by traces, all traces, to disappear in the fragmentary space of writing more definitely than one disappears in the tomb."[66]

Endless Enigma—a most marvelous and delirious surrealist con*trap*tion . . . again . . . and again . . . and . . .

take it seriously that beauty and love, and life itself, are *not* circumscribed by a marvelous reconciliation of extremes, but rather that extremes are, by chance, simply juxtaposed with other instants—nomadic, enigmatic, without constellation or an order of things—though nonetheless magnetic?

NOTES

PREFACE

1. A. Breton, "Surrealist Situation of the Object" and "The Automatic Message," in *The Surrealists Look at Art*, ed. P. Hulten (Venice, Calif.: Lapis Press, 1990), pp. 161, 153 (emphases mine).

2. S. Dali, "The Stinking Ass," in *This Quarter: Surrealist Number*, ed. A. Breton (New York: Arno Press, 1969), pp. 53–54 (emphases mine).

3. A. Breton, "The First Dali Exhibition," in *Andre Breton: What Is Surrealism?* ed. F. Rosement (New York: Monad Press, 1978), p. 45.

4. J. Derrida, *Positions*, trans. A. Bass (Chicago: University of Chicago Press, 1981), p. 26.

5. S. R. Suleiman, "Bataille in the Street: The Search for Virility in the 1930s," *Critical Inquiry* 21 (Autumn 1994): 61–79.

6. D. Hollier, "On Equivocation (Between Literature and Politics)," *October* 55 (Winter 1990): 3–22.

7. For another reading of the perplexing and seemingly inconsistent nature of Dali's productions during the 1930s, see M. LaFountain, "The Irruption of Singularity and Solitude in Dali, 1927–1938: Dali, Blanchot and Surrealism's *Other* Other," paper presented at the International Conference on The Hideous and The Sublime, Atlanta, 1994.

8. M. Foucault, *The Archaeology of Knowledge*, trans. A. M. Sheridan Smith (New York: Harper Colophon, 1976), pp. 220–28.

INTRODUCTION

1. R. Barthes, *Camera Lucida*, trans. R. Howard (New York: Noonday Press, 1981), pp. 77, 115.

2. Ibid., p. 77.

3. Ibid., p. 89.

4. Ibid., pp. 70–71, 73.

5. J. Tagg, *The Burden of Representation: Essays on Photographies and Histories* (Amherst: University of Massachusetts Press, 1988), p. 4.

6. M. Nadeau, *The History of Surrealism*, trans. R. Howard (Cambridge: Harvard University Press, 1989), p. 154.

7. D. Kuspit, "Dispensable Friends Indispensable Ideology: Andre Breton's Surrealism," *Artforum* (December 1983): 56–63; D. Cottom, "Purity," *Critical Inquiry* 16 (Autumn 1989): 173–98.

8. P. Soupault, *Memoires de l'oubli, premiere partie* (Paris: Lachenal & Ritter, 1981), p. 148. See Cottom, "Purity," for a discussion of Soupault and others' stories of Breton's tactics.

9. A. Breton, "Le Bouquet sans Fleurs," *La Revolution surrealiste 2* (January 1925): 25.

10. A. Breton, "Surrealist Situation of the Object [1935]," in *Manifestos of Surrealism*, trans. R. Seaver and H. R. Lane (Ann Arbor: University of Michigan Press, 1972), p. 259.

11. A. Breton, *Point du jour* (Paris: Gallimard, 1934), p. 250, cited in M. Carrouges, *Andre Breton and the Basic Concepts of Surrealism*, trans. M. Prendergast (Tuscaloosa: University of Alabama Press, 1974), p. 25 (emphasis mine).

12. On "guerilla writing," see C. Gutierrez-Jones, "Legal Rhetoric and Cultural Critique: Notes toward a Guerrilla Writing," *diacritics* 20, no. 4 (winter 1990): 62; also see P. Beitchman, *I Am a Process with No Subject* (Gainesville: University of Florida Press, 1988), p. 216, on "nomadic" writing.

13. F. Kittler, *Discourse Networks 1800/1900*, trans. M. Metteer (Stanford: Stanford University Press, 1990).

14. A. Stoekl, *Politics, Writing, Mutilation: The Cases of Bataille, Blanchot, Roussel, Leiris, and Ponge* (Minneapolis: University of Minnesota Press, 1985), p. xii.

15. E. Levinas, *Totality and Infinity: An Essay on Exteriority*, trans. A. Lingis (Pittsburgh: Duquesne University Press, 1969), and *Otherwise than Being or Beyond Essence*, trans. A. Lingis (The Hague: Martinus Nijhoff, 1981).

16. A. Breton and P. Eluard, *The Immaculate Conception*, trans. J. Graham (London: Atlas Press, 1990), pp. 25–26.

17. Note that P. Hulten's translation (in *The Surrealists Look at Art*, p. 163) of Breton's essay "Surrealist Situation of the Object [1935]" includes *phantom* in its delineation of the surrealist object, whereas R. Seaver and H. R. Lane's (in *Manifestoes of Surrealism*, p. 257) does not.

18. M. Nadeau, *Histoire du surréalisme* (Paris: Editions du Seuil, 1964), p. 310.

19. S. Dali, *The Conquest of the Irrational*, trans. D. Gascoyne (New York: Julien Levy, 1935), pp. 13–15.

20. Ibid., p. 13.

21. Ibid., pp. 13–18.

22. Ibid., p. 19.

23. Ibid., pp. 19–23.

24. Ibid., p. 24.

25. Dali, "The Stinking Ass," p. 53.

26. W. Worringer, *Abstraction and Empathy: A Contribution to the Psychology of Style*, trans. M. Bullock (London: Routledge & Kegan Paul, 1953), pp. 15–16.

27. Ibid., p. 18.

28. Ibid., p. 17.

29. W. Worringer, *"Zer Entwicklungsgeschichte der modernen Malerei,"* *Der Sturm* 2, no. 75 (August 1911): 598.

30. Worringer, *Abstraction and Empathy*, p. 15.

31. For additional discussions of the transcendental-occult-abstraction relationship, see *The Spiritual in Art: Abstract Painting 1890–1985*, ed. E. Weisberger (New York: Abbeville Press, 1986), esp. the essays by Long and Kuspit. Also see M. A. Cheatham, *The Rhetoric of Purity: Essentialist Theory and the Advent of Abstract Painting* (Cambridge: Cambridge University Press, 1991).

32. A. Balakian, *Andre Breton: Magus of Surrealism* (New York: Oxford University Press, 1971), p. 17.

33. Ibid., p. 105.

34. A. Breton, *Mad Love*, trans. M. A. Caws (Lincoln: University of Nebraska Press, 1987), p. 19.

35. Ibid., p. 114.

36. A. Breton, *Communicating Vessels*, trans. M. A. Caws and G. T. Harris (Lincoln: University of Nebraska Press, 1990), p. 87.

37. A. Jarry, "The Passion Considered As an Uphill Bicycle Race," in *Selected Works of Alfred Jarry*, ed. R. Shattuck and S. W. Taylor (New York: Grove Press, 1965), pp. 122–24.

38. G. Bataille, "The Jesuve," in *Visions of Excess, Selected Writings, 1927–1939*, trans. A. Stoekl (Minneapolis: University of Minnesota Press, 1985), pp. 73–78; also see Stoekl's commentary on "jesuve" on p. 259.

39. Balakian, *Andre Breton*, pp. 106–7; Breton, *Mad Love*, p. 15.

40. H. N. Finkelstein, *Surrealism and the Crisis of the Object* (Ann Arbor: UMI Research Press, 1979), p. 11.

152 NOTES

41. M. Foucault, *The Order of Things: An Archaeology of the Human Sciences* (New York: Vintage Books, 1970), p. xviii.

42. A. Balakian, *Surrealism: The Road to the Absolute* (New York: Dutton), p. 46.

43. Balakian, *Andre Breton*, pp. 151–52.

44. C. Rojas, *Salvador Dali, Or the Art of Spitting on Your Mother's Portrait*, trans. Alma Amell (University Park: Pennsylvania State University Press, 1993).

45. F. Nietzsche, *The Birth of Tragedy and the Case of Wagner*, trans. W. Kaufmann (New York: Vintage, 1967), p. 34.

46. G. de Chirico, *Hebdomeros*, trans. M. Crosland (New York: PAJ Publications, 1988); see preface by J. Ashbery, pp. iii–vi.

47. A. Breton, *Surrealism and Painting*, trans. S. W. Taylor (New York: Harper & Row, 1972), p. 1.

48. Breton, *Mad Love*, p. 8.

CHAPTER 1

1. R. Sokowlowski, "The Theory of Phenomenological Description," in *Descriptions*, ed. D. Ihde and H. J. Silverman (Albany: State University of New York Press, 1985), pp. 14–24.

2. H. Spiegelberg, *The Phenomenological Movement: A Historical Introduction* (The Hague: Martinus Nijhoff, 1984), p. 693.

3. E. Husserl, *Cartesian Meditations: An Introduction to Phenomenology*, trans. D. Cairns (The Hague: Martinus Nijhoff, 1977), p. 26.

4. E. Husserl, *Formal and Transcendental Logic*, trans. D. Cairns (The Hague: Martinus Nijhoff, 1969), p. 15.

5. E. Husserl, *The Crisis of European Sciences and Transcendental Phenomenology*, trans. D. Carr (Evanston: Northwestern University Press, 1970), p. 153.

6. Husserl, *Cartesian Meditations*, p. 33.

7. Husserl, *The Crisis of European Sciences*, p. 151–52.

8. Husserl, *Cartesian Meditations*, p. 34; Husserl, *Ideas: General Introduction to Pure Phenomenology*, trans. W. R. Boyce Gibson (New York: Collier Books, 1962), pp. 96–103.

9. Husserl, *Ideas*, p. 193.

10. Husserl, *The Crisis of European Sciences*, p. 152.

11. Husserl, *Cartesian Meditations*, p. 72.

12. E. Levinas, "Intuition of Essences," in *Phenomenology: The Philosophy of Edmund Husserl and Its Interpretation*, ed. J. J. Kockelmans (Garden City, N.Y.: Doubleday, 1967), p. 96.

13. J. J. Kockelmans, "Essences and Eidetic Reduction, Introduction," in *Phenomenology*, ed. Kockelmans, p. 80.

14. Husserl, *Ideas*, pp. 50–51.

15. Husserl, *Ideas*, pp. 182–84 (emphasis mine).

16. R. Sokolowski, "The Theory of Phenomenological Description," p. 23 (emphasis mine).

17. Husserl, *Ideas*, p. 183 (emphasis mine).

18. Levinas, "Intuition of Essences," p. 95.

19. Sokolowski, "The Theory of Phenomenological Description," p. 24.

20. E. Husserl, *Logical Investigations*, vol. 2, trans. J. N. Findlay (London: Routledge & Kegan Paul, 1970), p. 443.

21. Levinas, "Intuition of Essences," p. 85.

22. Husserl, *Ideas*, p. 40.

23. Ibid., p. 51.

24. Ibid., p. 183.

25. Ibid., p. 21.

26. Ibid., p. 47.

27. Husserl, *Cartesian Meditations*, p. 139.

28. Ibid., p. 140.

29. Breton, *Communicating Vessels*, p. 87.

30. Husserl, *Ideas*, pp. 177–78; *Formal and Transcendental Logic*, p. 287.

31. Husserl, *Ideas*, pp. 180–81.

32. M. Heidegger, *The Piety of Thinking*, trans. J. G. Hart and J. C. Maraldo (Bloomington: Indiana University Press, 1976), p. 79.

33. Levinas, "Intuition of Essences," p. 103.

34. Husserl, *Ideas*, pp. 190–91.

35. Ibid., p. 191.

36. Ibid., p. 190 (emphasis Husserl).

37. The first European exhibit was in Munich in 1913, and the first American exhibit was in New York in 1914.

38. From Russell's personal notebook, August 1912, quoted in G. Levin, *Synchromism and American Color Abstraction 1910–1925* (New York: George Braziller, 1978), p. 17.

39. See the general and individual introductions written by Russell and Macdonald-Wright for the second Synchromist exhibition in Paris, 1913, reproduced in Levin, *Synchromism*, pp. 129–31. This particular statement is from Russell's introduction, p. 130.

40. Ibid., p. 18.

41. Ibid., p. 17.

42. Ibid., p. 130.

43. Ibid., p. 18.

44. Ibid., p. 130.

45. Ibid., p. 18.

46. Ibid.

47. Ibid., p. 130.

48. Ibid., p. 25; also see M. S. Kushner, *Morgan Russell* (New York: Hudson Hills Press, 1990), p. 83.

49. Levin, *Synchromism*, p. 30.

50. Ibid.

51. Ibid.

52. Ibid., p. 131.

53. R.-C. W. Long, "Kandinsky's Vision," in *The Life of Vasilii Kandinsky in Russian Art: A Study of* On the Spiritual in Art, ed. J. E. Bowlt and R.-C. W. Long (Newtonville, Mass.: Oriental Research Partners, 1980), p. 44.

54. W. Kandinsky, *Concerning the Spiritual in Art*, trans. F. Golffing, M. Harrison, and F. Ostertag (New York: George Wittenborn, 1947), p. 29.

55. Ibid., p. 32.

56. P. Volboudt, "Wassily Kandinsky's Philosophy," in *Homage to Wassily Kandinsky: A Special Issue of the XX siècle Review*, ed. G. di San Lazzaro (New York: Leon Amiel, 1975), p. 74.

57. W. Kandinsky, *Ruckblicke* (Berlin, 1913; English edition, H. von Rebay, 1945) cited in A. Bovi, *Kandinsky* (London: Hamlyn, 1971), p. 18.

58. W. Kandinsky, *Concerning the Spiritual in Art*, p. 50; esp. see pp. 45–77.

59. R. Soupault-Niemeyer, "From the Horse to the Circle," in *Homage to Wassily Kandinsky*, p. 41.

60. Ibid., pp. 44–45.

61. Kandinsky, *Concerning the Spiritual in Art*, p. 47.

62. For a discussion of the translation of Kandinsky's use of the Russian term *dukhovnyi*, see R.-C. W. Long, *Kandinsky: The Development of an Abstract Style* (Oxford: Clarendon Press, 1980), p. 156 n.3.

63. Bovi, *Kandinsky*, p. 92 (emphasis mine).

64. J. E. Bowlt, "Vasilii Kandinsky: The Russian Connection," in Bowlt and Long, *The Life of Vasilii Kandinsky in Russian Art*, p. 26.

65. Volboudt, "Wassily Kandinsky's Philosophy," p. 79.

66. Ibid., p. 77.

67. For an excellent summary, offered by Kandinsky's nephew, Alexandre Kojeve, with Kandinsky's assistance, see "Why Concrete?" in *Homage to Wasilly Kandinsky*, pp. 123–24. Also see

W. Kandinsky, "Concrete Art [1938]," in *Theories of Modern Art: A Source Book by Artists and Critics*, ed. H. B. Chipp (Berkeley: University of California Press, 1968), pp. 346–49.

68. Volboudt, "Wassily Kandinsky's Philosophy," p. 75 (emphasis mine).

69. Kandinsky, *Concerning the Spiritual in Art*, p. 74.

70. Kandinsky, *Point and Line to Plane*, pp. 36–37, quoted in Bovi, *Kandinsky*, pp. 11–12. For a comparison of Kandinsky's "point" and Breton's "point," see M. A. Caws, *The Art of Interference: Stressed Readings in Verbal and Visual Texts* (Princeton: Princeton University Press, 1989), chap. 11, esp. pp. 148–49.

71. Kandinsky, *Concerning the Spiritual in Art*, p. 73.

72. Volboudt, "Wassily Kandinsky's Philosophy," p. 79.

73. I arbitrarily use 1916 as a pivotal point, for this is when he "names" the "unknown." However, his work was very much abstract prior to that date. For a discussion of the issue of his "first" abstract painting, see Long, *Kandinsky*, pp. 2–4.

74. Kandinsky, *Concerning the Spiritual in Art*, p. 10. Compare this with Husserl's insight that essences have an experiential priority and fulfillable immediacy whose concreteness becomes more dense as empirical reality accrues.

75. Kandinsky, *Concerning the Spiritual in Art*; see "Part B: Painting" for a detailed discussion of techniques involved. Also see Bowlt, "Vasilii Kandinsky: The Russian Connection," in *The Life of Vasilii Kandinsky in Russian Art*, pp. 48–51; Long, *Kandinsky*, pp. 65–74.

76. Kandinsky, *Concerning the Spiritual in Art*, p. 49.

77. Ibid., p. 77.

78. Ibid., p. 73.

79. For a discussion of translations bearing on "objectless" versus "nonobjective," see Long, *Kandinsky*, p. 156 n.11.

80. Kandinsky, *Concerning the Spiritual in Art*, p. 77.

81. Ibid., p. 3.

82. A. Breton, *Conversations: The Autobiography of Surrealism*, trans. M. Polizzotti (New York: Paragon House, 1993), p. 3.

83. See note 62, this chapter.

84. In 1913 German critics labeled Kandinsky, who had lived in Germany since 1896, a representative of a "new idealism." For instance, see Wilhelm Hausenstein, "Für Kandinsky," *Der Sturm* 3, nos. 150/151 (March 1913): 277. Kandinsky rejected this interpretation of his work, as did Husserl vis-à-vis similar interpretations of his.

85. S. Dali, *The Conquest of the Irrational*, trans. D. Gascoyne (New York: Julien Levy, 1935), p. 19.

86. See M. A. Cheatham, *The Rhetoric of Purity: Essentialist Theory and the Advent of Abstract Painting* (Cambridge: Cambridge University Press, 1991), esp. chap. 4, "Purity as Aesthetic Ideology."

87. Dali, *The Conquest of the Irratioinal*, p. 11.

88. Without unity, "supposedly," is important for it underscores that Breton and the Surrealists did not accept a Hegelian rational synthesis of disparate realities. That they did acknowledge a dialectical synthesis of opposites and a binary form of logic is the subject of the next chapter.

89. A. Breton, "What is Surrealism" (1934), in *What Is Surrealism: Selected Writings*, ed. F. Rosemont (New York: Monad and Pathfinder Presses, 1978), p. 138.

90. J. Derrida, *The Truth in Painting*, trans. G. Bennington and I. McLeod (Chicago: University of Chicago Press, 1987), p. 119.

91. See Dali, *The Conquest of the Irrational*, pp. 7–11; also see P. Roumeguère, "Cannaibalism and Aesthetic," in *Dali . . . Dali . . . Dali* (New York: Harry N. Abrams, 1974), pp. 1–5.

92. D. M. Levin, *Reason and Evidence in Husserl's Phenomenology* (Evanston, Ill.: Northwestern University Press, 1970).

93. S. Dali, "The Stinking Ass," in *This Quarter: Surrealist Number*, ed. A. Breton (New York: Arno, 1969), p. 51.

94. Ibid., p. 53.

95. G. Bataille, *L'Erotism* (Paris: Minuit, 1957), translated as *Death and Sensuality*, ed. R. Kastenbaum (New York: Arno, 1977), p. 17.

96. L. Kolakowski, *Husserl and the Search for Certitude* (New Haven: Yale University Press, 1975), p. 81.

CHAPTER 2

1. For this term I am grateful to Barbara Lekatsas, Curator, Weingrow Collection of Avant-Garde Art and Literature, Hofstra University. Portions of this chapter were written during an NEH Summer Seminar on Dada and Surrealism, conducted by Anna Balakian and assisted by Lekatsas, and it was then that she suggested the term *dalilectics*.

2. H. Finkelstein, "Dali's Paranoia-Criticism or the Exercise of Freedom," *Twentieth Century Literature* 21 (February 1975): 68.

3. D. Hollier, *Against Architecture: The Writings of Georges Bataille*, trans. B. Wing (Cambridge: MIT Press, 1989), see pp. 3–56, esp. pp. 10–13.

4. E. Levinas, *Totality and Infinity: An Essay on Exteriority*, trans. A. Lingis (Pittsburgh: Duquesne University Press, 1969), p. 33.

5. Dali, "The Stinking Ass," pp. 49–53.

6. See Rojas, *Salvador Dali*, for a psychoanalytic, psychocultural interpretation of Dali's masturbatory acts as a "spitting" on this mother's grave.

7. Dali, "The Stinking Ass," p. 53.

8. Ibid., p. 54.

9. Breton, *Communicating Vessels*, p. 139.

10. Breton, *Mad Love*, p. 8; Breton, *Point du jour*, p. 250.

11. Breton, *Communicating Vessels*, p. 139.

12. Breton, *Conversations*, p. 118. Also see M. Carrouges, *André Breton and the Basic Concepts of Surrealism*, trans. M. Prendergast (Tuscaloosa: University of Alabama Press, 1974), and F. Alquié, *The Philosophy of Surrealism*, trans. B. Waldrop (Ann Arbor: University of Michigan Press, 1965).

13. W. Chadwick, *Myth in Surrealist Painting, 1929–1939* (Ann Arbor: UMI Research Press, 1980), p. xiii.

14. S. Dali, "*Interpretation Paranoiaque-critique de l'image obsedante L'Angelus de Millet*," *Minotaure* no. 1 (1933): 65.

15. S. Dali, "The Object as Revealed in Surrealist Experiment," in *This Quarter: Surrealist Number*, ed. A. Breton (New York: Arno Press, 1969), p. 202 (emphasis mine).

16. Dali, "The Stinking Ass," p. 54.

17. Dali, "The Object as Revealed in Surrealist Experiment," p. 202.

18. See Dali's poem "Dandled Brochure," cited in Breton, "Surrealist Situation of the Object," pp. 270–71.

19. Comte de Lautréamont, cited by A. Breton, "Surrealism: Yesterday, To-Day and To-Morrow," in Breton, *This Quarter: Surrealist Number*, p. 7.

20. Ibid., p. 44.

21. Dali, "The Object as Revealed in Surrealist Experiment," pp. 201–2.

22. See A. Breton, "The Dali 'Case,'" in *Surrealism and Painting*, trans. S. W. Taylor (New York: Harper & Row, 1972), pp. 130–35.

23. Chadwick, *Myth in Surrealist Painting, 1929–1939*, pp. 1–18.

24. Ibid., p. 61.

25. M. Jean, *The History of Surrealist Painting*, trans. S. W. Taylor (New York: Grove Press, 1960), p. 199.

26. G. Bataille, *Visions of Excess*, p. 238.

27. For a relevant discussion of time, see S. Shaviro, *Passion and Excess: Blanchot, Bataille, and Literary Theory* (Tallahassee: Florida State University, 1990), p. 106.

28. G. Bataille, *Inner Experience*, trans. L. A. Boldt (Albany: State University of New York Press, 1988), pp. 73–74.

29. Carrouges, *Andre Breton and the Basic Concepts of Surrealism*, p. 229.

30. Chadwick, *Myth in Surrealist Painting, 1929–1939*, p. 105.

31. M. Foucault, "Preface," in *Anti-Oedipus: Capitalism and Schizophrenia*, ed. G. Deleuze and F. Guattari (New York: Viking Press, 1977), pp. xiii–xiv.

32. S. Dali, *The Conquest of the Irrational*, p. 17.

33. In Husserl's phenomenology, the noetic and the noematic are not considered to be discrete, and their occurrence together would suggest that they are consubstantial. In Dali's radical phenomenology, however, the noetic and the noematic are already multiply *con-fused* via other noetic and noematic incursions such that the noetic/noematic duet is the promise of delirium rather than coherence.

34. Dali, *The Conquest of the Irrational*, p. 15.

35. Ibid., pp. 12, 15–16.

36. Ibid., p. 16.

37. Ibid., p. 17.

38. Ibid., p. 16.

39. Ibid., p. 14.

40. Ibid., p. 12.

41. Ibid., p. 8.

42. Ibid., p. 13 (emphasis mine).

43. Ibid., p. 15.

44. Ibid.

45. Ibid.

46. Ibid., p. 13.

47. Ibid., p. 14.

48. Ibid., p. 9.

49. Ibid., p. 12.

50. Ibid., p. 11.

51. Alquié, *The Philosophy of Surrealism*, pp. 34–41, 133–34.

52. Dali, "The Stinking Ass," p. 52.

53. Finkelstein, "Dali's Paranoia-Criticism," pp. 66–68.

54. Ibid., p. 70.

55. M. Berman, *All That Is Solid Melts into Air: The Experience of Modernity* (New York: Simon & Schuster, 1982).

56. On the relation of irony and dialectical movement in Hegel's reaction to Schlegel, see G. F. W. Hegel, *The Philosophy of Fine Art*, vol. 1,trans. F. Osmaston (London: G. Bell, 1920), pp. 91–92; also see Hegel, *Philosophy of Right*, trans. T. Knox (London: Oxford University Press, 1942), 101n.

57. For examples of such interpretations, which are numerous, see Finkelstein, "Dali's Paranoia-Criticism"; Chadwick, *Myth in Surrealist Painting, 1929–1939*, p. 63; Rojas, *Salvador Dali.*

58. T. Pynchon, *Gravity's Rainbow* (New York: Viking Press, 1973), p. 506.

59. L. Bunuel, *Un Perro Andaluz* (La Edad de Oro: Mexico Ediciones Era, 1971), p. 7.

60. G. Bataille, "The Sorcerer's Apprentice," in *Visions of Excess*, p. 229.

61. G. Bataille, *Oeuvres complètes. Vol. 6: La Somme athe-ologique II, Sur Nietzsche*, ed. H. Ronse and J.-M. Rey (Paris: Gallimard, 1973), p. 429.

62. J. Gracq, *The Castle of Argol*, trans. L. Varese (Norfolk, Conn.: New Direction Books, 1938), p. 5.

CHAPTER 3

1. For an interpretation focusing on the specter of Lorca in *Endless Enigma*, see Rojas, *Salvador Dali*, pp. 166–68.

2. The basis of this term, of course, is Derrida's *economimesis* (J. Derrida, *The Truth in Painting*, trans. G. Bennington and I. McLeod [Chicago: University of Chicago Press, 1987], p. 119).

3. J. Derrida, "Living On: Border Lines," in *Deconstruction and Criticism*, ed. H. Bloom et al. (New York: Seabury Press, 1979), p. 176.

4. Levinas, *Totality and Infinity*, section 1, pp. 33–105.

5. Dali, *The Conquest of the Irrational*, pp. 12–13.

6. J. Baudrillard, *The Ecstasy of Communication*, trans. B. Schutze and C. Schutze (New York: Semiotext(e), 1988), p. 55.

7. Ibid., pp. 51–53.

8. Ibid., p. 55.

9. Ibid., p. 51.

10. For discussions of "the fatal," see Baudrillard, *The Ecstasy of Communication*, esp. pp. 57–95. Also see "The Power of Reversibility That Exists in the Fatal," in *Baudrillard Live: Selected Interviews*, ed., M. Gane (New York: Routledge, 1993), pp. 43–49.

11. Baudrillard, *The Ecstasy of Communication*, p. 55.

12. Ibid., p. 55.

13. Dali, "The Object as Revealed in Surrealist Experiment," p. 202.

14. G. Deleuze and F. Guattari, *Anti-Oedipus: Capitalism and Schizophrenia*, trans. R. Hurley, M. Seem, and H. R. Lane (New York: Viking Press, 1977).

15. Ibid., p. 76 (emphasis mine).

16. P. Virilio, *War and Cinema: The Logistics of Perception*, trans. P. Camiller (New York: Verso, 1989), p. 4.

17. Ibid.

18. P. Virilio, *The Aesthetics of Disappearance*, trans. P. Beitchman (New York: Semiotext(e), 1991), pp. 108–9.

19. Contrast the reading offered here with Sellin's more dialectically oriented rendering of "simultaneity" in E. Sellin, *Reflections on the Aesthetics of Futurism, Dadaism, and Surrealism: A Prosody beyond Words* (Lewiston, N.Y.: Edwin Mellin Press, 1993), esp. pp. 41–56 ("Simultaneity: The Driving Force of the Surrealist Aesthetic").

20. G. Deleuze and F. Guattari, *On the Line*, trans. J. Johnston (New York: Semiotext(e), 1983), p. 57.

CHAPTER 4

1. Rojas, *Salvador Dali*, pp. 166–68.

2. I. Kant, *Critique of Judgment* (Oxford: Oxford University Press, 1952), p. 68.

3. J. Derrida, *The Truth in Painting*, trans. G. Bennington and I. MacLeod (Chicago: University of Chicago Press, 1987), pp. 24–26.

4. Breton, *Surrealism and Painting*, p. 73.

5. Breton, *Manifestoes of Surrealism*, pp. 19, 29.

6. Ibid., p. 21.

7. Breton, *Communicating Vessels*, p. 52.

8. Breton, *What Is Surrealism?*, p. 45.

9. Ibid. Note that for Breton the sky is "up," requiring elevation and ascension. For another view of the "limpid" and "pellucid" sky in Dali's paintings, see N. J. Capasso, "Salvador Dali and the Barren Plain: A Phenomenological Analysis of a Surrealist Landscape Environment," *Arts Magazine* 60, no. 10 (summer 1986): 72–83.

10. Breton, *Mad Love*, p. 19.

11. Breton, *Communicating Vessels*, pp. 52–53.

12. Ibid., p. 53.

13. In "Objets surrealistes," *Le Surréalisme au service de la révolution* 3 (December 1931), Dali credited Giacometti for inspiring

his "symbolically functioning objects." It is interesting to note that Breton's "phantom object," Giacometti's "mobile and mute objects," and Dali's symbolically functioning objects appeared together in this issue.

14. Breton, *Communicating Vessels*, p. 54.

15. Ibid., p. 55.

16. Breton, *What Is Surrealism?* p. 45.

17. Breton, *Surrealism and Painting*, p. 1.

18. Breton, *What Is Surrealism?* p. 45.

19. A. Giacometti, "Objets mobiles and muets," *Le Surréalisme au service de la révolution* 3 (December 1931): 18–19.

20. J. Derrida, "From Restricted to General Economy: A Hegelianism without Reserve," in *Writing and Difference*, trans. A. Bass (Chicago: University of Chicago Press, 1978), pp. 251–77.

21. Levinas, *Totality and Infinity*, p. 256. Compare with Breton, "The secret of Surrealism lies in the fact that we are convinced that something is hidden behind them [the moral order and the physical world]" (*What Is Surrealism?* p. 45).

22. A. Lingis, *Libido: The French Existential Theories* (Bloomington: Indiana University Press, 1985), p. 64.

23. Levinas, *Totality and Infinity*, pp. 256–57.

24. M. Ernst, *Beyond Painting* (New York: Wittenborn, Schultz, 1948), pp. 19–20. In 1921 Breton used the idea of the "principle of identity" in his catalog commentary for Ernst's exhibit of collages in Paris.

25. Breton, in Ernst, *Beyond Painting*, p. 177.

26. Dali, *The Conquest of the Irrational*, p. 11.

27. D. Cottom, *Text and Culture: The Politics of Interpretation* (Minneapolis: University of Minnesota Press, 1989), p. 29.

28. Ibid., p. 19.

29. Ibid., pp. 21, 28, 69–71, 85, 112.

30. Ibid., p. 105.

31. Ibid.

32. Ibid., p. 112.

33. Ibid., pp. 118, 151.

34. Breton, *Communicating Vessels*, p. 86.

35. Cottom, *Text and Culture*, p. 144.

36. Ibid., p. 118.

37. Ibid., p. 113.

38. Ibid., pp. 125, 144.

39. R. Cardinal, "Surrealism and the Paradigm of the Creative Subject," in *Parallel Visions: Modern Artists and Outsider Art* (Princeton: Los Angeles County Museum of Art and Princeton University Press, 1992), p. 107.

40. Cottom, *Text and Culture*, p. 29.

41. Ibid.

42. For an interesting discussion of the politics of Surrealism, see D. Kuspit, "Dispensable Friends Indispensable Ideologies," pp. 56–63.

43. Contrast the reading offered here with that of Rojas (in his *Salvador Dali*), who offers his under the sign of a psychoanalytic hermeneutics.

44. J. Baudrillard, *The Mirror of Production*, trans. M. Poster (St. Louis: Telos Press, 1975), p. 48.

45. Ibid., pp. 47–51.

46. J. Baudrillard, *Simulations*, trans. P. Foss, P. Patton, and P. Beitchman (New York: Semiotext(e), 1983), p. 11.

47. For instance, see G. Bataille, *Visions of Excess*, esp. "The Solar Anus," "The "Old Mole," and the prefix *Sur* in the Words *Surhomme* (Superman) and *Surrealist*," "Rotten Sun," and "The Pineal Eye."

48. Breton, *What Is Surrealism?* p. 154.

49. Ibid., p. 188.

50. Breton, *Surrealism and Painting*, pp. 12, 16.

51. Ibid., p. 12.

52. Breton, *Communicating Vessels*, p. 87.

53. J. Chenieux-Gendron, *Surrealism*, trans. V. Folkenflik (New York: Columbia University Press, 1984), pp. 82–84.

54. A. Balakian, "The Surrealists in the Light of Recent Theoretical Criticism," *Symposium* 42, no. 3 (fall 1988): 175.

55. Breton, *Point du jour* (Paris: Gallimard, 1970), p. 171.

56. Chenieux-Gendron, *Surrealism*, p. 91.

57. Bataille, *Visions of Excess*, p. 15 (emphasis Bataille's).

58. Breton, *Point du jour* (Paris: Gallimard, 1970), p. 67, translation by and cited in Caws, *The Art of Interference*, p. 73.

59. Ibid., pp. 71–85.

60. See R. Descharnes, *Salvador Dali: The Work, The Man*, trans. E. R. Morse (New York: Harry N. Abrams, 1984), p. 239.

61. Ibid.

62. Reference here is to G. de Chirico's *Hebdomeros*, trans. M. Crosland (New York: PAJ Publications, 1988), and to L. Aragon's *The Adventures of Telemachus*, trans. R. R. Hubert and J. D. Hubert (Lincoln: University of Nebraska Press, 1988).

63. Aragon, *The Adventures of Telemachus*, pp. 35–36.

64. Ibid., pp. 32–36, 101.

65. Ibid., p. 101.

66. Ibid., p. 102.

67. P. Beitchman, *I Am a Process with No Subject* (Gainesville: University of Florida Press, 1988), pp. 262–63, n. 35.

68. Aragon, *The Adventures of Telemachus*, p. 59.

69. G. Bataille, *Inner Experience*, pp. 93–97.

70. See "The Sorcerer's Apprentice," in Bataille's *Visions of Excess*, pp. 223–34.

71. Bataille, *Oeuvres complètes*, vol. 6, p. 429.

72. Bataille, *Inner Experience*, pp. 37–41.

73. Bataille, *Oeuvres complètes*, vol. 6, p. 429.

74. Bataille, *Inner Experience*, p. 97; also see the "principle of insufficiency" in *Visions of Excess*, p. 172.

75. Bataille, *Inner Experience*, p. 16; *Visions of Excess*, p. 31.

76. Bataille, *Inner Experience*, pp. 39–40.

77. Ibid., p. 36.

78. Ibid., p. 52.

79. Bataille, *Visions of Excess*, p. 143.

80. Ibid., p. 7.

81. Bataille, *Inner Experience*, p. 94.

82. Ibid., p. 59.

83. Ibid., p. 95.

84. G. Bataille, *Death and Sensuality*, ed. R. Kestenbaum (New York: Arno, 1977), p. 36.

85. Ibid., p. 19.

86. Bataille, *Inner Experience*, p. 95.

87. Ibid., pp. 73–73.

88. Ibid., p. 37.

89. Aragon, *The Adventures of Telemachus*, p. 33.

90. Ibid.

91. Ibid., pp. 44–45 (emphasis Aragon's).

92. Bataille, *Inner Experience*, pp. 73–74.

93. Bataille, *Visions of Excess*, pp. 216, 220.

94. H. Cixous, *Souffles* (Paris: des femmes, 1975), pp. 21–22.

95. Bataille, *Inner Experience*, pp. 46–47.

96. Ibid., p. 181.

97. Bataille, *Death and Sensuality*, p. 17.

98. G. Bataille, *My Mother, Madame Edwarda, The Dead Man*, trans. A. Wainhouse (London: Marion Boyars, 1989), p. 222.

99. Bataille, *Inner Experience*, pp. 67–68.

100. Carrouges, *Andre Breton*, p. 43.

101. For a discussion of these ideas, see A. S. Weiss, *The Aesthetics of Excess* (Albany: State University of New York, 1989), esp. chaps. 2 and 3.

102. I. Kant, *Critique of Pure Reason* (New York: St. Martin's Press, 1965), p. 653.

103. L. Irigaray, "The Fecundity of the Caress," in *Face to Face with Levinas,* ed. R. A. Cohen (Albany: State University of New York Press, 1986), p. 253.

104. Deleuze and Guattari, *Anti-Oedipus,* p. 18.

105. G. Deleuze and F. Guattari, *Nomadology: The War Machine,* trans. B. Massumi (New York: Semiotext(e), 1986), p. 37.

106. Cixous, *Souffles,* pp. 79–80.

107. Ibid., p. 172.

108. S. Shaviro, *Passion and Excess,* pp. 101–2.

109. Ibid., p. 107.

110. Cixous, *Souffles,* pp. 9–10.

111. Bataille, *Visions of Excess,* pp. 199, 221–22.

112. Ibid., p. 199.

113. See G. Bataille, "Base Materialism and Gnosticism," in *Visions of Excess,* pp. 45–52. For a related discussion, see A. S. Weiss, "Impossible Sovereignty: Between the Will to Power and the Will to Chance," *October* no. 36 (spring 1986).

114. Bataille, *Death and Sensuality,* p. 11.

115. Bataille, *Inner Experience,* p. 153.

116. Ibid., p. 33.

CHAPTER 5

1. Breton, "Surrealist Situation of the Object," pp. 178–79.

2. Breton, "The Automatic Message," p. 147.

3. Breton, "Surrealist Situation of the Object," pp. 178–79.

4. Dali, *The Conquest of the Irrational,* pp. 13–14.

5. Levinas, *Otherwise than Being.*

6. Ibid., p. 38. Also see E. Levinas, "Meaning and Sense," in *Collected Philosophical Papers,* trans. A. Lingis (The Hague: Martinus Nijhoff, 1987), pp. 104–6.

7. Levinas, *Totality and Infinity,* p. 37.

8. Ibid., section 1, "The Same and the Other"; later, in *Otherwise than Being,* the phenomenology of the Same is refigured linguistically as the Said.

9. Levinas, *Otherwise than Being,* p. 25.

10. Breton, "The Automatic Message," p. 147.

11. Levinas, *Totality and Infinity,* p. 39. Contrast this view with that of Kandinsky (see chapter 1), who anticipated in *Concerning the*

Spiritual in Art that the final abstract expression of every art is number.

12. Levinas, *Otherwise than Being*, pp. 125, 111, 115, respectively.

13. Ibid., pp. 117–18, 127.

14. Ibid., pp. 121, 114, 138, respectively.

15. Rojas, *Salvador Dali*.

16. Derrida, *Positions*, pp. 42–43.

17. M. Blanchot, *The Writing of Disaster*, trans. A. Smock (Lincoln: University of Nebraska Press, 1986), p. 116.

18. S. Suleiman, "(Re)Writing the Body: The Politics and Poetics of Female Eroticism," in *The Female Body in Western Culture*, ed. S. Suleiman (Cambridge: Harvard University Press, 1986), p. 24.

19. J. Derrida and C. V. MacDonald, "Choreographies," *diacritics* 12, no. 2: 76.

20. Suleiman, "(Re)Writing the Body," p. 24.

21. See D. Harraway, "A Manifesto for Cyborgs: Science, Technology, and Socialist Feminism in the 1980s," in *The Female Body in Western Culture*, ed. Suleiman.

22. C. Smith-Rosenberg, *Disorderly Conduct* (Oxford: Oxford University Press, 1985), p. 291.

23. G. Deleuze and F. Guattari, *On the Line*, trans. J. Johnston (New York: Semiotext(e), 1983), p. 58.

24. For an alternative approach to such rhizomatic choreography, see S. Bordo, "Feminism, Postmodernism, and Gender-Scepticism," in *The Female Body in Western Culture*, ed. Suleiman, pp. 133–56.

25. G. Bataille, "The Sorcerer's Apprentice," in *The College of Sociology (1937–39)*, ed. D. Hollier (Minneapolis: University of Minnesota Press, 1988), p. 20

26. G. Apollinaire, "The New Spirit and the Poets," in *Selected Writings of Guillaume Apollinaire*, trans. R. Shattuck (New York: New Directions, 1950), p. 232.

27. See J.-F. Lyotard, *Discours, figure* (Paris: Klincksieck, 1971). The figural was first discussed in *Discours, figure*, but continually appears throughout Lyotard's works, including *The Postmodern Condition* and *The Differend*.

28. J.-F. Lyotard, "Rewriting Modernity," *SubStance* 54: 8–9.

29. A. Breton, *Nadja*, trans. R. Howard (New York: Grove Weidenfeld, 1960), p. 144.

30. J.-F. Lyotard, *The Postmodern Condition: A Report on Knowledge*, trans. G. Bennington and B. Massumi (Minneapolis: University of Minnesota Press, 1984), pp. 77–82.

31. Ibid., pp. 77–78.

32. J.-F. Lyotard, *The Differend: Phrases in Dispute*, trans. G. Van Den Abbeele (Minneapolis: University of Minnesota Press, 1988), p. 168.

33. Lyotard, *The Postmodern Condition*, p. 81.

34. Bataille, *Visions of Excess*, p. 129.

35. Breton, "Surrealist Situation of the Object," p. 179.

36. Ibid., p. 173.

37. Lyotard, *The Postmodern Condition*, pp. 78–79.

38. Ibid., p. 81.

39. Ibid.

40. Ibid. This very factor permits my analysis to avoid the concerns of Rojas and so many others with deciphering Dali's enormously complex and enigmatic iconography.

41. Ibid.

42. Ibid., p. 80.

43. Ibid., p. 77.

44. For mention of Beznos, see Breton, *Nadja*, p. 55. For Galluixka, see Rojas, *Salvador Dali*, pp. 135, 149. For "S," see J. Baudrillard, *Les Strategies Fatales* (Paris: Grasset, 1983), *Please Follow Me* (with Sophie Calle), *Suite Venitienne* (Paris: Editions de l'Etoile, 1983), and "Dawn of the Dead," *Emergency* 5:48–57.

45. See Stoekl, *Politics, Writing, Mutilation*.

46. Ibid., p. xii.

47. W. Benjamin, *Illuminations*, trans. H. Zohn (New York: Harcourt, Brace, & World, 1968), p. 194.

48. Bataille, *Visions of Excess*, p. 128.

49. S. Shaviro, *Passion and Excess*, p. 41.

50. Lyotard, *The Postmodern Condition*, p. 61.

51. Deleuze and Guattari, *Nomadology*, p. 32.

52. Blanchot, *The Writing of Disaster*, p. 60.

53. M. Blanchot, *L'Entretien infini* (Paris: Gallimard, 1969), p. 408.

54. M. Blanchot, *The Step Not Beyond*, trans. L. Nelson (Albany: State University of New York Press, 1992), p. 12.

55. Ibid., pp. 3–6.

56. Blanchot, *The Writing of Disaster*, p. 1.

57. Ibid.

58. Ibid., p. 100.

59. Ibid., p. 117.

60. Bataille, *Oeuvre complètes*, vol. 6, p. 429.

61. M. Blanchot, *L'attente l'oubli* (Paris: Gallimard, 1951, 1962). This translation is offered by Beitchman, *I Am a Process with No Subject*, p. 117.

62. Rojas, *Salvador Dali,* p. 142.

63. T. Tzara, *Oeuvres complètes,* vol. 5, ed. H. Behar (Paris: Flammarion, 1982), p. 130. See Beitchman, *I Am a Process with No Subject,* pp. 262–63, n. 35, for an interesting comparison of Blanchot and Tzara.

64. See F. Guattari, *Molecular Revolution: Psychiatry and Politics,* trans. R. Sheed (New York: Penguin Books, 1977).

65. C. O. Schrag, *The Resources of Rationality: A Response to the Postmodern Challenge* (Bloomington: Indiana University Press, 1992), pp. 142–79.

66. Blanchot, *The Step Not Beyond,* p. 50.

67. Breton, *Nadja,* p. 1.

68. Ibid., pp. 19–24.

69. Ibid., p. 155 (emphasis mine).

70. Breton, "The Automatic Message," p. 153.

71. Breton, *Nadja,* p. 20.

72. Ibid.

73. Ibid., p. 19.

74. Ibid., p. 17.

75. Ibid., p. 160.

76. Ibid., p. 19.

77. Ibid., p. 158.

78. Ibid., p. 23.

79. Ibid., p. 157.

80. R. Champigny, "The First Person in *Nadja,*" in *About French Poetry from Dada to 'Tel Quel',* ed. M. A. Caws (Detroit: Wayne State University Press, 1974), p. 246.

81. Breton, *Nadja,* p. 12.

82. R. Cardinal, *Breton: Nadja* (London: Grant & Cutler, 1986), p. 9.

83. See references to Baudrillard in note 44 this chapter. For a discussion of *eminence grise,* see M. Gane, *Baudrillard: Critical and Fatal Theory* (London: Routledge, 1991), pp. 167–77.

84. For a discussion and an example of these and related notions and their moral significance, see M. Foucault, *The History of Sexuality,* vols. 2 and 3, trans. R. Hurley (New York: Vintage Books, 1990, 1988). Also *Technologies of the Self: A Seminar with Michel Foucault,* ed. L. H. Martin, H. Gutman, and P. H. Hutton (Amherst: University of Massachusetts Press, 1988).

85. A. Breton and P. Eluard, *The Immaculate Conception,* trans. J. Graham (London: Atlas Press, 1990), p. 34.

86. Deleuze and Guattari, *Nomadology,* p. 38.

87. Peter Bürger (*Theory of the Avant-Garde,* trans. M. Shaw

[Minneapolis: University of Minnesota Press, 1984], p. 53) correctly noted Breton's concerns with radical individualism and the threat of solipsism, and thus his preference for collectives. Breton could not have imagined, however, that "collective" or "community" could ever be refigured in the fashion suggested here, where crisscrossing and accidental encounters are the sites where *eros* (though not necessarily the erotic couple of *Mad Love*) moves as interruption, evocation, and response-ibility.

88. See Levinas, *Totality and Infinity*, esp. sec. 4.B; also L. Irigaray, "The Fecundity of the Caress," in *Face to Face with Levinas*, ed. R. A. Cohen (Albany: State University of New York Press, 1986).

89. A. Lingis, *Libido: The French Existential Theories* (Bloomington: Indiana University Press, 1985), p. 64.

90. Breton, *Nadja*, p. 159.

91. Levinas, *Totality and Infinity*, p. 21.

92. Breton, *Nadja*, p. 159.

93. Dali, "The Stinking Ass," p. 54.

94. Ibid., pp. 51–53.

95. Bataille, "The Sorcerer's Apprentice," p. 429.

96. Blanchot, *The Step Not Beyond*, p. 137.

97. Foucault, *The History of Sexuality*, vol. 3, pp. 43–45.

INDEX

H

Harraway, D., 124
hasard objectif, 59, 63, 100–103
hatred of reality, 45
Hebdomeros, 105, 123
Hegel, G. W. F., 58, 68–70, 117, 139
heterology, xvi, 17, 21, 46, 107, 126
Heraclitus, 57
hero, 53, 62
Hollier, D., xiv
hope, 9, 14, 40, 47, 70, 80, 92, 105, 121, 139
hors-de-soi, 54
humor, black, 102–103
humor, objective, 102–103
Husserl, E., 4, 10, 20, 23–47, 58, 115
hypertextuality, xii, 64–65
hysteria, 54, 67–68, 74, 76–87, 99, 110

I

idealism, 11, 15, 27, 101, 103
identity, 2, 70–71, 76–87, 96–97, 107, 110, 134, 137, 141, 144
imagination, 25–26, 36, 42, 59, 69, 115, 131
Immaculate Conception, The, 82
impossibility, 26, 105, 107, 110, 114, 134, 138, 142–148
inner experience, 34–35, 107, 109
interiority, 6, 34, 42–43, 52–56, 76, 90, 92, 101, 107, 110, 114, 121
Irigaray, L., 137
irony, 68, 77, 79, 97, 126

J

Jarry, A., 15, 105, 124
joke, 97–100
jouissance, 15, 124, 138

K

Kandinsky, V., 10, 20, 33–39, 115
Kant, I., 11, 39, 90–91, 110
Klossowski, P., 110, 140
Kuspit, D., 4

L

la vie à perdre haliende, 3, 111, 114, 138, 147
Lacan, J., 60, 64
laughter, 89, 92, 96–100, 114
Lautréamont, Comte de, 13
Levinas, E., 5–6, 28, 56, 77, 95, 118–122, 131, 137, 139–140, 142, 145
Lingis, A., 95, 138n89
Lyotard, J-F., 21, 91, 105, 125–131

M

Macdonald-Wright, S., 29–32
Mad Love, 14, 93, 100, 121
magnetic field, xiii, 55, 57, 67, 71, 76, 78, 89, 116, 118, 140, 148
Magritte, R., 72
marvelous, 13, 46, 72, 75, 78, 83, 99, 110, 117, 130, 148
Masson, A., 113
metastasis, 17, 77, 80–81
mimesis, 41, 73, 75, 77, 83, 91, 102, 143
modernism, 2–4, 9, 13, 17, 28, 67, 73, 76, 85, 121, 128, 133, 147
morality, 5, 101, 121, 126–148
mythology, 61–63, 76, 121–122

N

Nadeau, M., 4
Nadja, 13, 57, 70, 119, 121–122, 139
Nietzsche, F., 3, 9, 19, 44, 60, 62, 68, 76–77, 103, 124